ULTIMATE FANTASTIC FOUR

SILVER SURFER

ULTIMATE FANTASTIC FOUR

SILVER SURFER

writer:

MIKE CAREY

art:

PASQUAL FERRY

colors:

JUSTIN PONSOR

letters:

VIRTUAL CALLIGRAPHY'S RUS WOOTON

editors:

JOHN BARBER & BILL ROSEMANN

senior editor:

RALPH MACCHIO

collection editor:

JENNIFER GRÜNWALD

assistant editors:

CORY LEVINE & JOHN DENNING

associate editor:

MARK D. BEAZLEY

senior editor, special projects:

JEFF YOUNGQUIST

senior vice president of sales:

DAVID GABRIEL

production:

**JERRON QUALITY COLOR
& JERRY KALINOWSKI**

vice president of creative:

TOM MARVELLI

editor in chief:

JOE QUESADA

publisher:

DAN BUCKLEY

Previously:

Reed Richards, handpicked to join the Baxter Building think tank of young geniuses, spent his youth developing a teleport system that transported solid matter into a parallel universe called the N-Zone. Its first full-scale test was witnessed by Reed, fellow think tank members Sue Storm and her brother Johnny, as well as Reed's childhood friend Ben Grimm.

There was an accident. The quartet's genetic structures were scrambled and recombined in a fantastically strange way. Reed's body stretches and flows like water. Ben looks like a thing carved from desert rock. Sue can become invisible. Johnny generates flame. Together, they are the Fantastic Four!

For weeks, Reed has been obsessing over plans for a powerful cosmic device — plans that were planted in his mind by an alien force — and seeks a power source for this strange cube. Reed's efforts are interrupted when the team is forced to rescue their kidnapped loved ones, including Johnny's girlfriend; Ben's mother; Sue and Johnny's father; and Reed's sister, Enid.

Everyone made it home safe — though Enid has gained energy-manipulating superpowers... and Reed's parents are not happy about this...

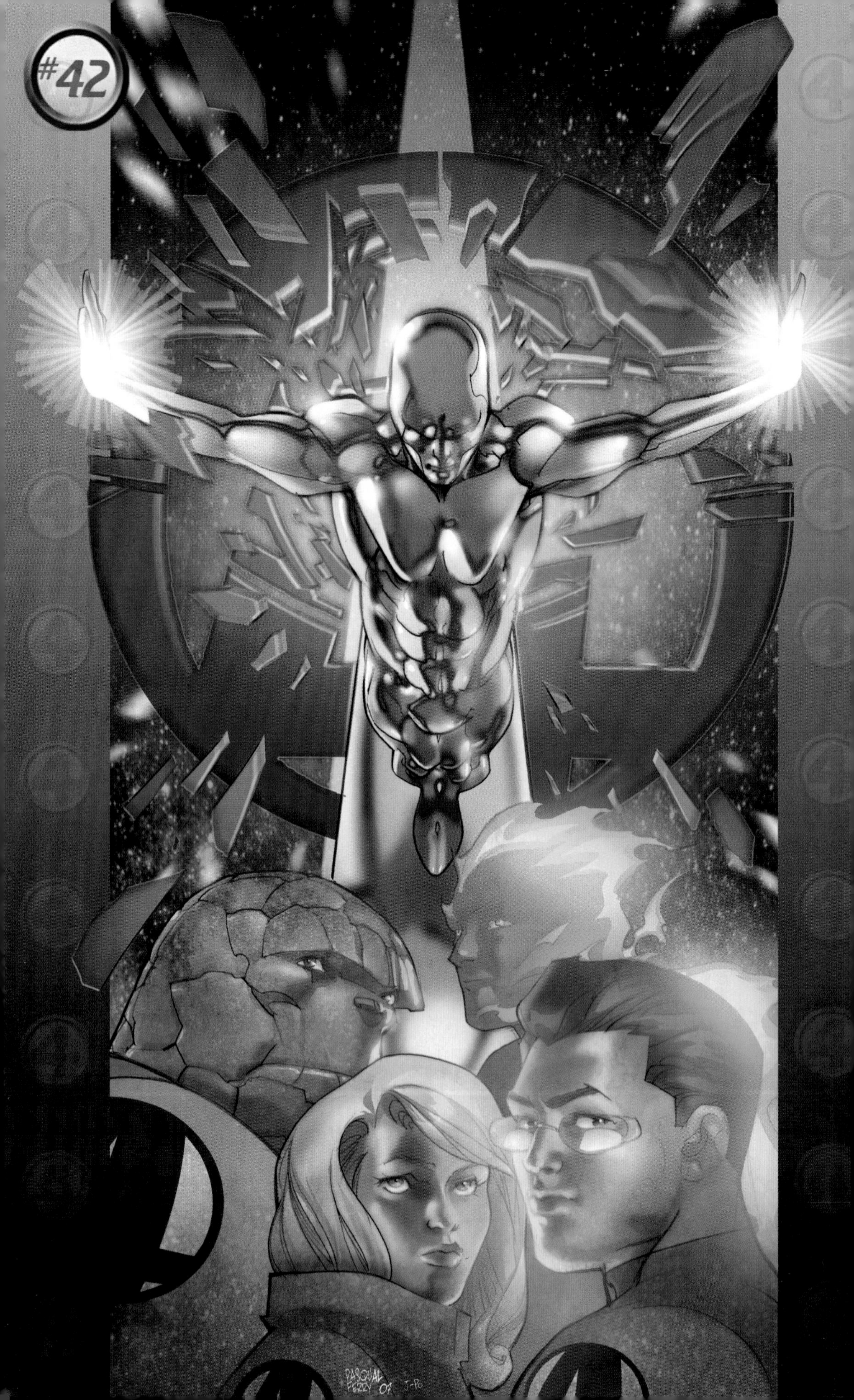
#42
PASQUAL FERRY 07
J-Po

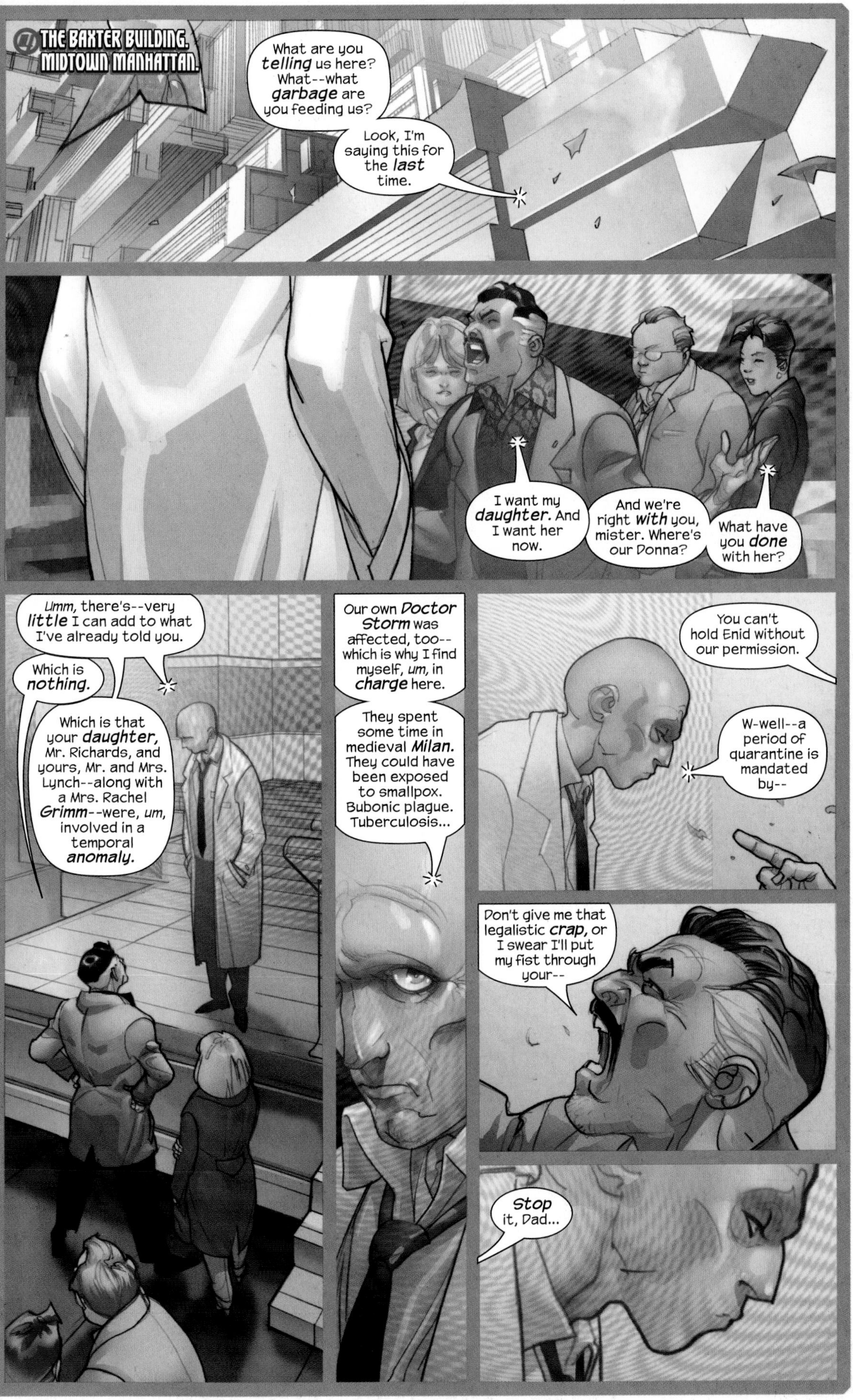
THE BAXTER BUILDING. MIDTOWN MANHATTAN.
What are you telling us here? What--what garbage are you feeding us?
Look, I'm saying this for the last time.
I want my daughter. And I want her now.
And we're right with you, mister. Where's our Donna?
What have you done with her?
Umm, there's--very little I can add to what I've already told you.
Which is nothing.
Which is that your daughter, Mr. Richards, and yours, Mr. and Mrs. Lynch--along with a Mrs. Rachel Grimm--were, um, involved in a temporal anomaly.
Our own Doctor Storm was affected, too--which is why I find myself, um, in charge here.
They spent some time in medieval Milan. They could have been exposed to smallpox. Bubonic plague. Tuberculosis...
You can't hold Enid without our permission.
W-well--a period of quarantine is mandated by--
Don't give me that legalistic crap, or I swear I'll put my fist through your--
Stop it, Dad...

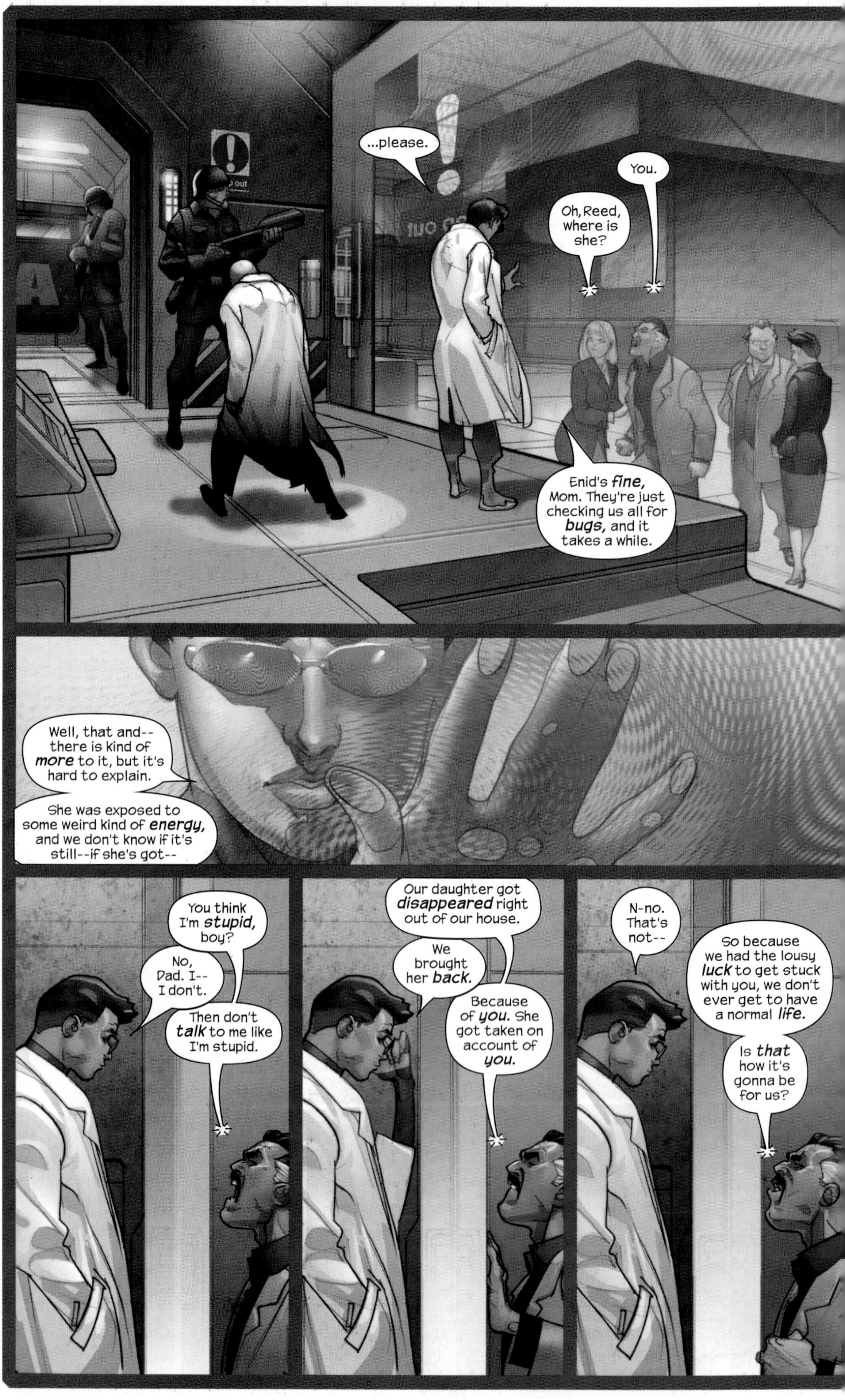
...please.
Oh, Reed, where is she?
You.
Enid's fine, Mom. They're just checking us all for bugs, and it takes a while.
Well, that and-- there is kind of more to it, but it's hard to explain.
She was exposed to some weird kind of energy, and we don't know if it's still--if she's got--
You think I'm stupid, boy?
No, Dad. I-- I don't.
Then don't talk to me like I'm stupid.
Our daughter got disappeared right out of our house.
We brought her back.
Because of you. She got taken on account of you.
N-no. That's not--
So because we had the lousy luck to get stuck with you, we don't ever get to have a normal life.
Is that how it's gonna be for us?

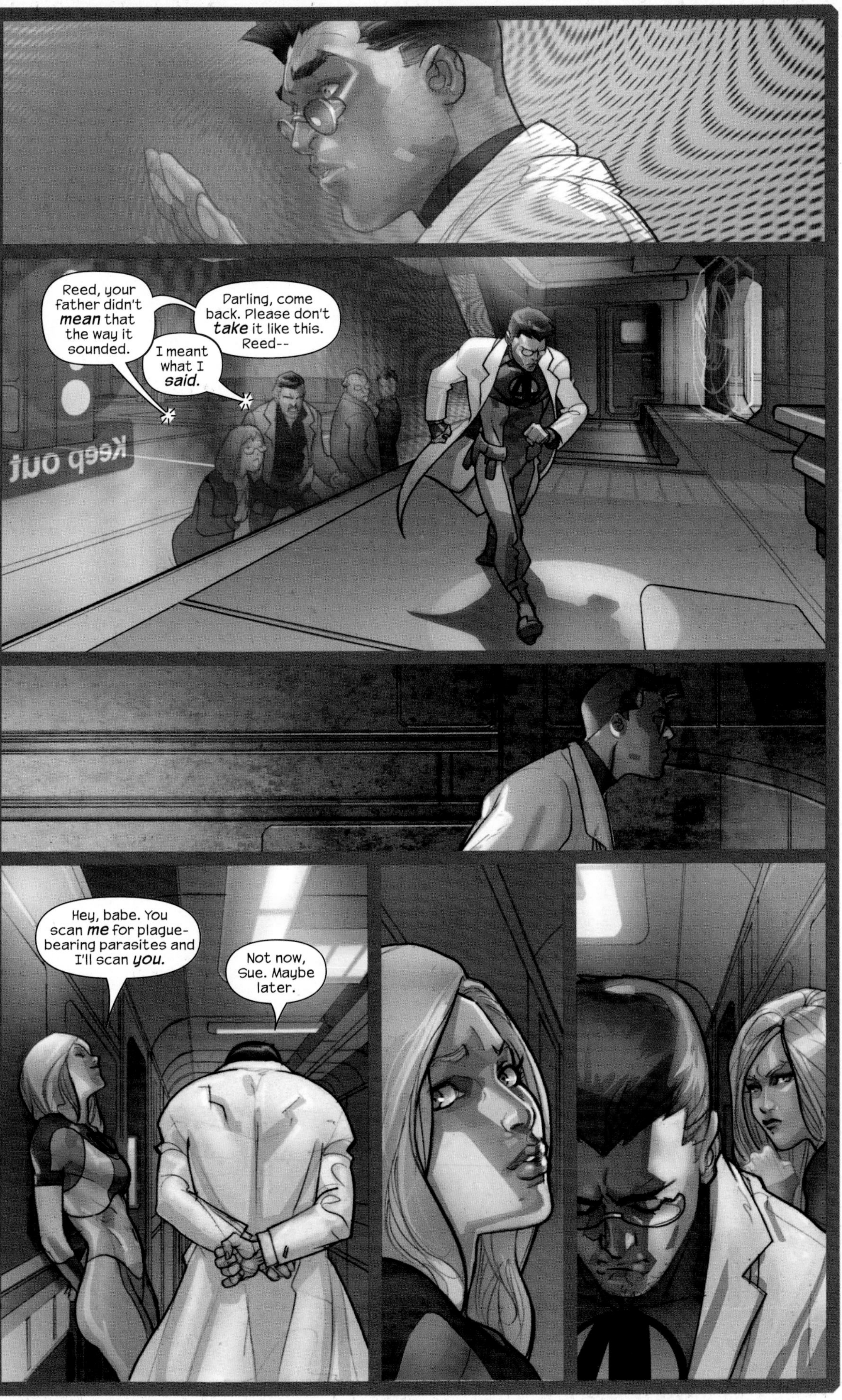
Reed, your father didn't *mean* that the way it sounded.
Darling, come back. Please don't *take* it like this. Reed--
I meant what I *said.*
Keep out
Hey, babe. You scan *me* for plague-bearing parasites and I'll scan *you.*
Not now, Sue. Maybe later.

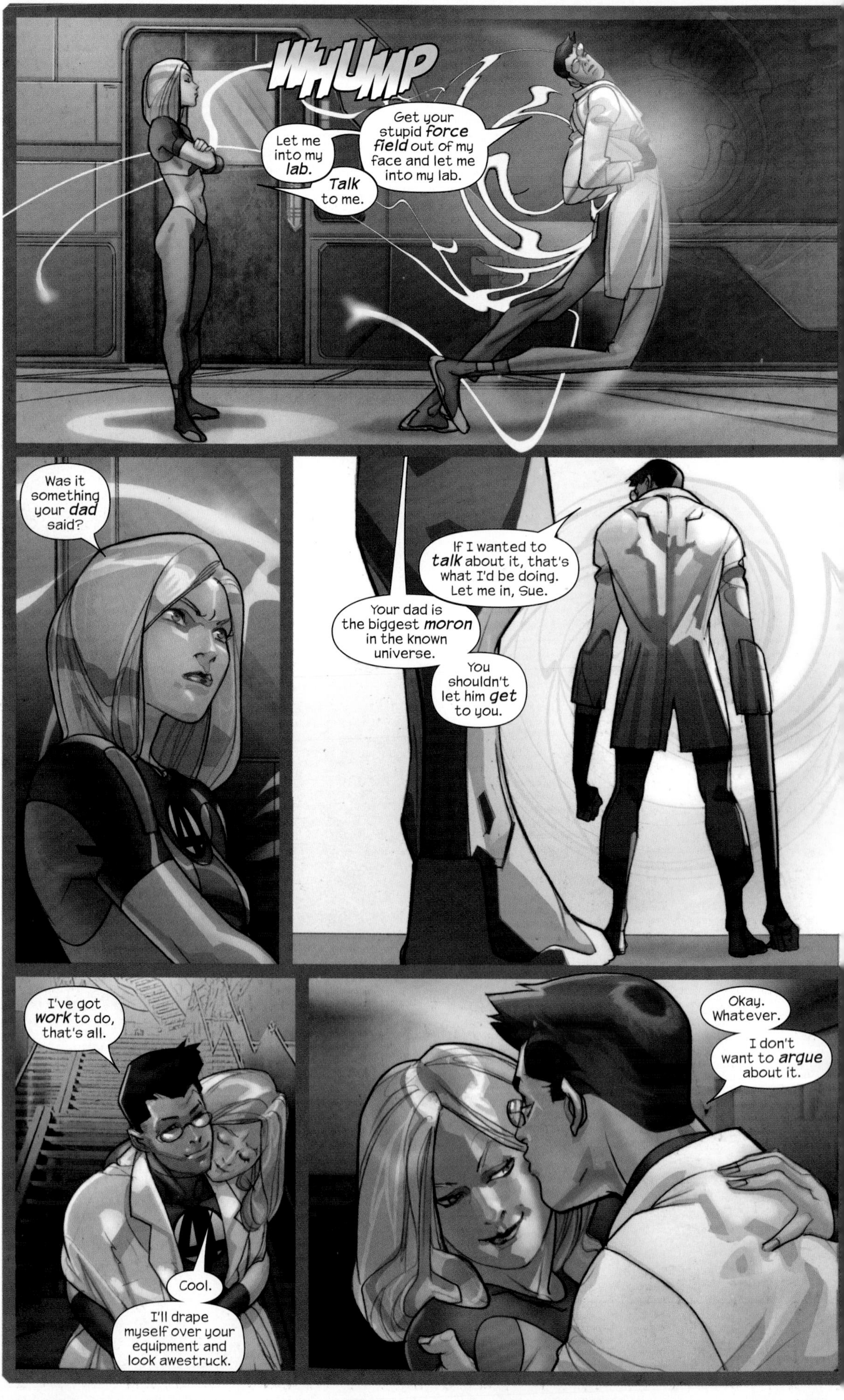
WHUMP
Get your stupid force field out of my face and let me into my lab.
Let me into my lab.
Talk to me.
Was it something your dad said?
If I wanted to talk about it, that's what I'd be doing. Let me in, Sue.
Your dad is the biggest moron in the known universe.
You shouldn't let him get to you.
I've got work to do, that's all.
Cool.
I'll drape myself over your equipment and look awestruck.
Okay. Whatever.
I don't want to argue about it.

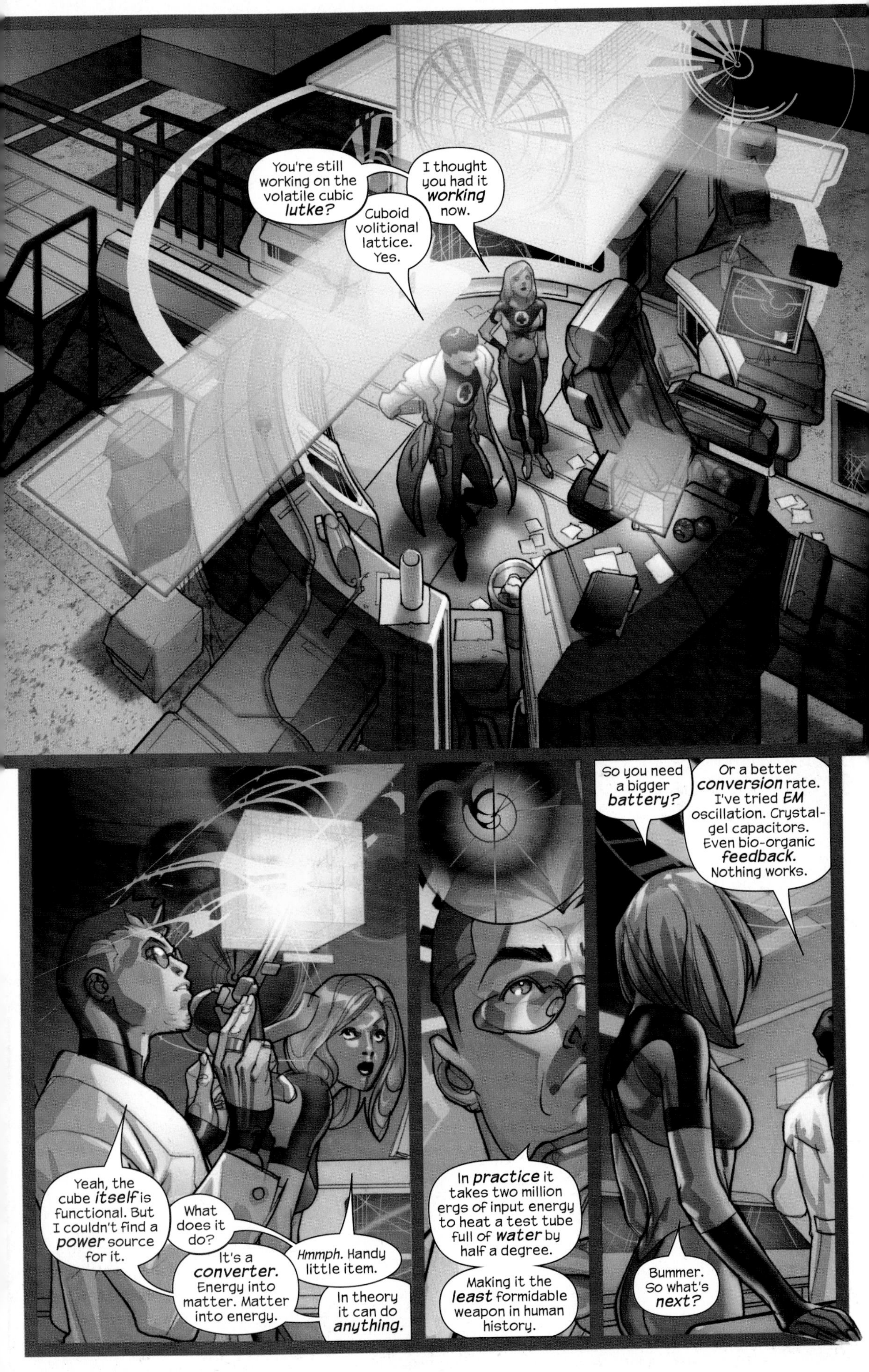
You're still working on the volatile cubic *lutke?*
I thought you had it *working* now.
Cuboid volitional lattice. Yes.
Yeah, the cube *itself* is functional. But I couldn't find a *power* source for it.
What does it do?
It's a *converter.* Energy into matter. Matter into energy.
Hmmph. Handy little item.
In theory it can do *anything.*
In *practice* it takes two million ergs of input energy to heat a test tube full of *water* by half a degree.
Making it the *least* formidable weapon in human history.
So you need a bigger *battery?*
Or a better *conversion* rate. I've tried *EM* oscillation. Crystal-gel capacitors. Even bio-organic *feedback.* Nothing works.
Bummer. So what's *next?*

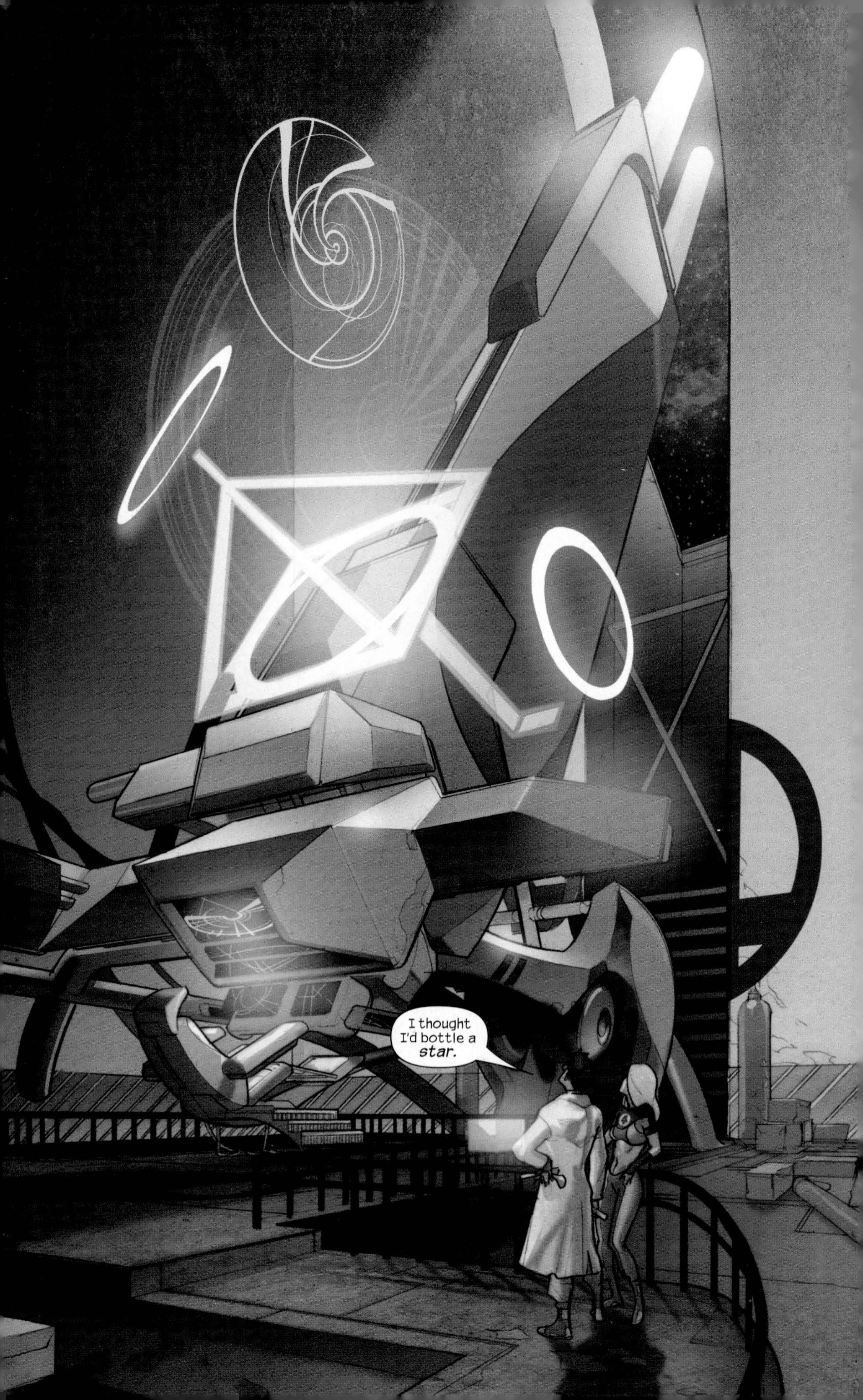
I thought I'd bottle a *star.*

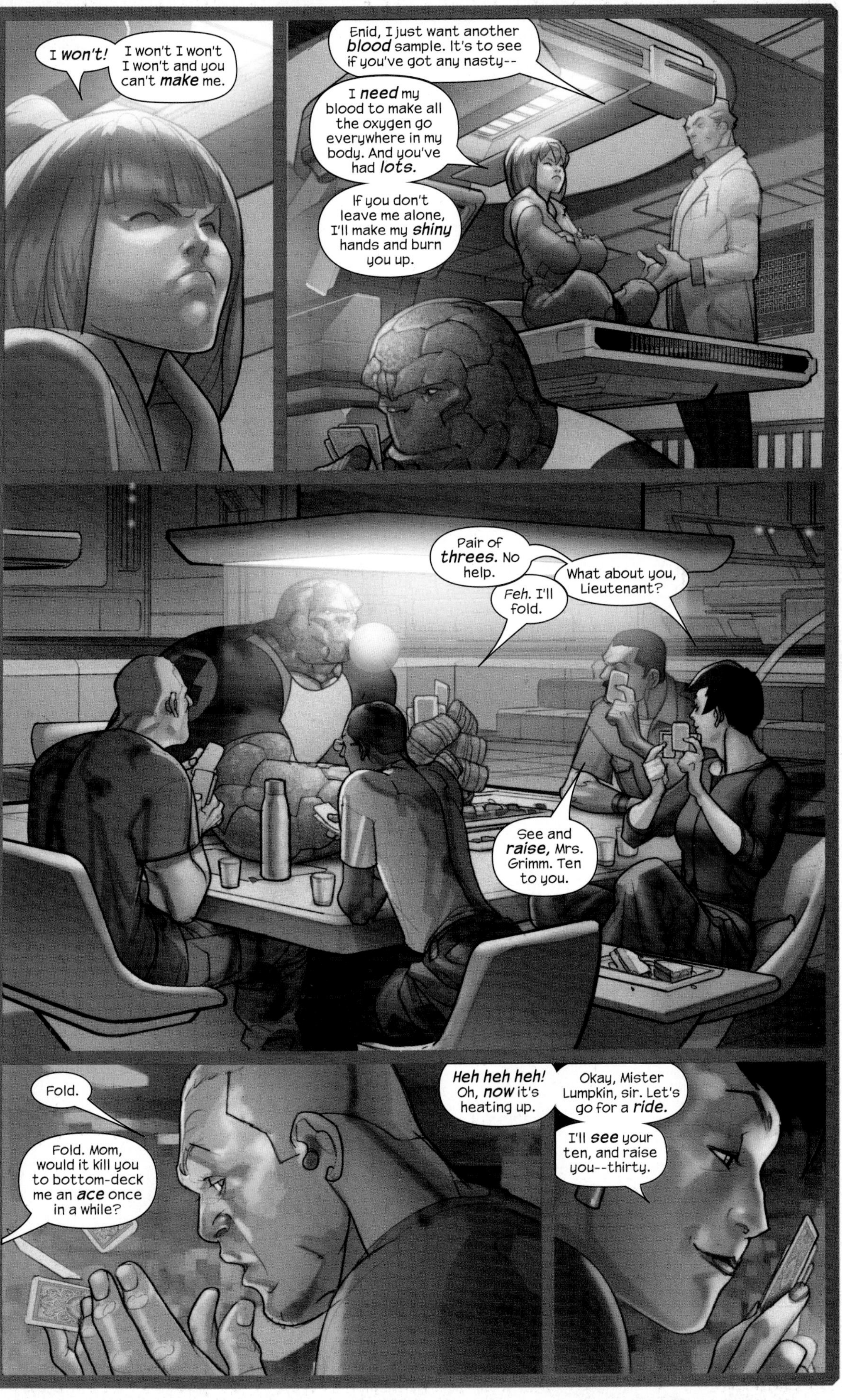
I won't!
I won't I won't I won't and you can't make me.
Enid, I just want another blood sample. It's to see if you've got any nasty--
I need my blood to make all the oxygen go everywhere in my body. And you've had lots.
If you don't leave me alone, I'll make my shiny hands and burn you up.
Pair of threes. No help.
Feh. I'll fold.
What about you, Lieutenant?
See and raise, Mrs. Grimm. Ten to you.
Fold.
Fold. Mom, would it kill you to bottom-deck me an ace once in a while?
Heh heh heh! Oh, now it's heating up.
Okay, Mister Lumpkin, sir. Let's go for a ride.
I'll see your ten, and raise you--thirty.

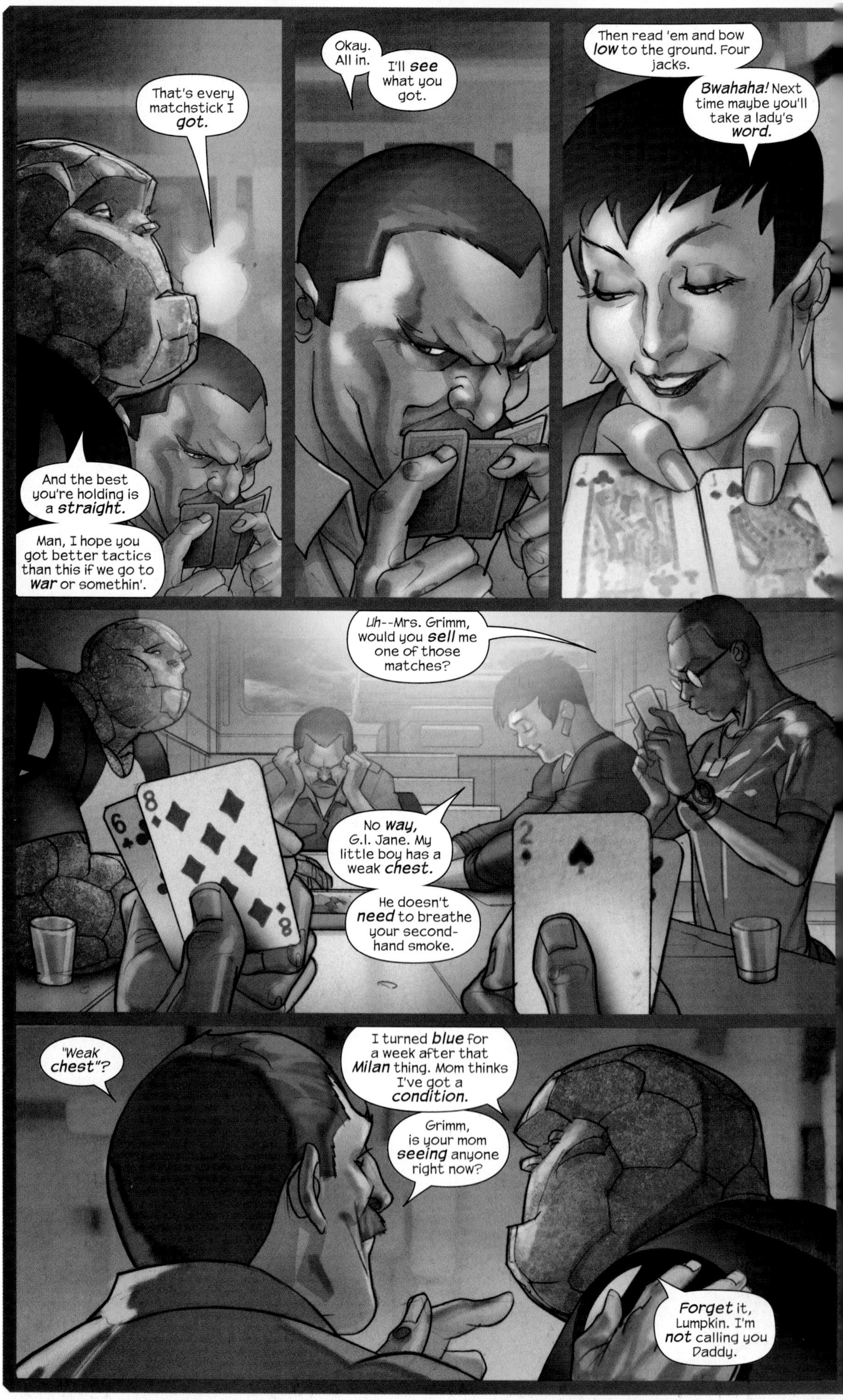
That's every matchstick I got.
And the best you're holding is a straight.
Man, I hope you got better tactics than this if we go to war or somethin'.
Okay. All in.
I'll see what you got.
Then read 'em and bow low to the ground. Four jacks.
Bwahaha! Next time maybe you'll take a lady's word.
Uh--Mrs. Grimm, would you sell me one of those matches?
No way, G.I. Jane. My little boy has a weak chest.
He doesn't need to breathe your second-hand smoke.
"Weak chest"?
I turned blue for a week after that Milan thing. Mom thinks I've got a condition.
Grimm, is your mom seeing anyone right now?
Forget it, Lumpkin. I'm not calling you Daddy.

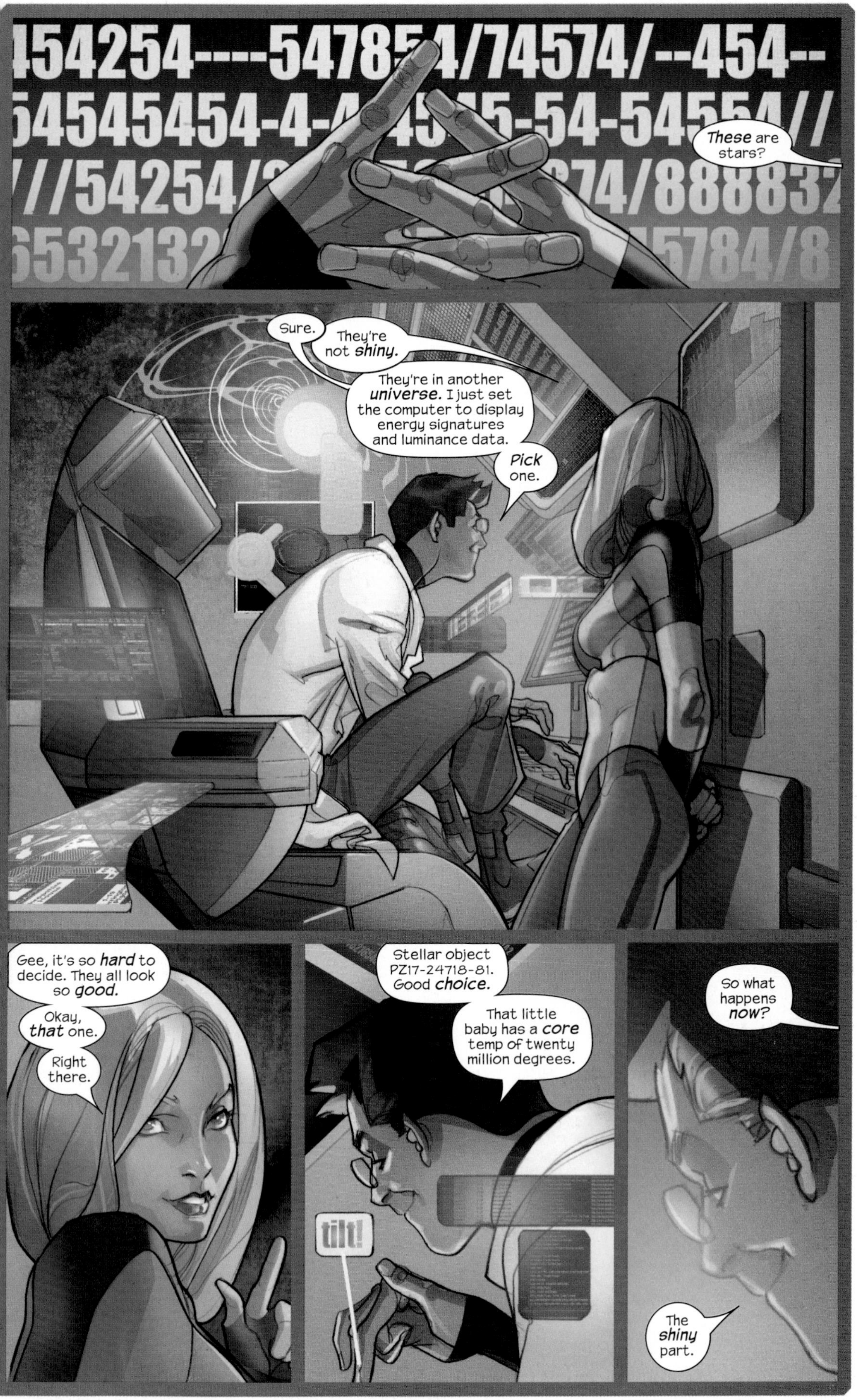
454254----547854/74574/--454--
54545454-4-4-4545-54-54554//
//54254/
874/888832
6532132
5784/8
These are stars?
Sure.
They're not shiny.
They're in another universe. I just set the computer to display energy signatures and luminance data.
Pick one.
Gee, it's so hard to decide. They all look so good.
Okay, that one.
Right there.
Stellar object PZ17-24718-81. Good choice.
That little baby has a core temp of twenty million degrees.
tilt!
So what happens now?
The shiny part.

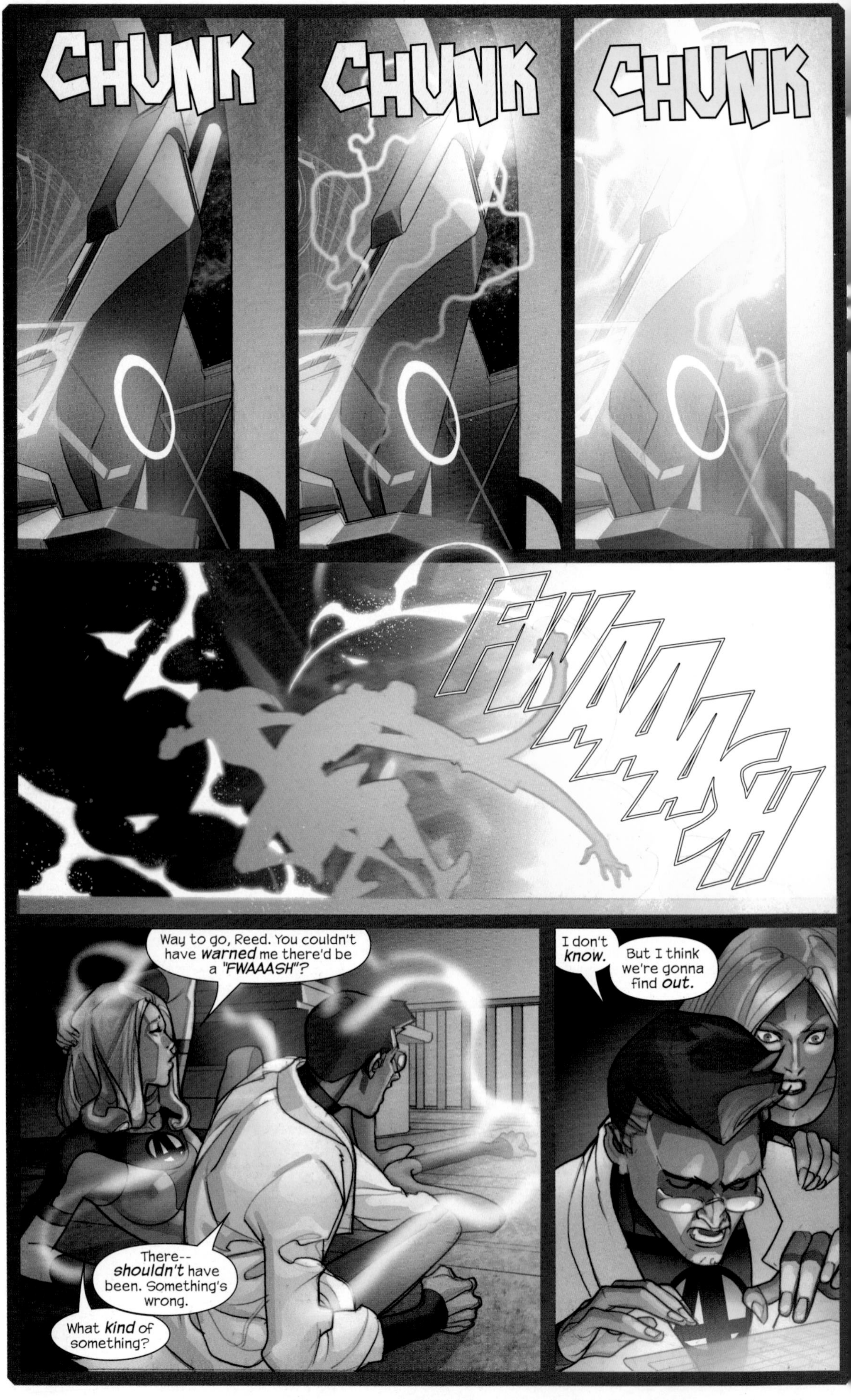
CHUNK
CHUNK
CHUNK
FWAAASH
Way to go, Reed. You couldn't have warned me there'd be a "FWAAASH"?
There-- shouldn't have been. Something's wrong.
What kind of something?
I don't know.
But I think we're gonna find out.

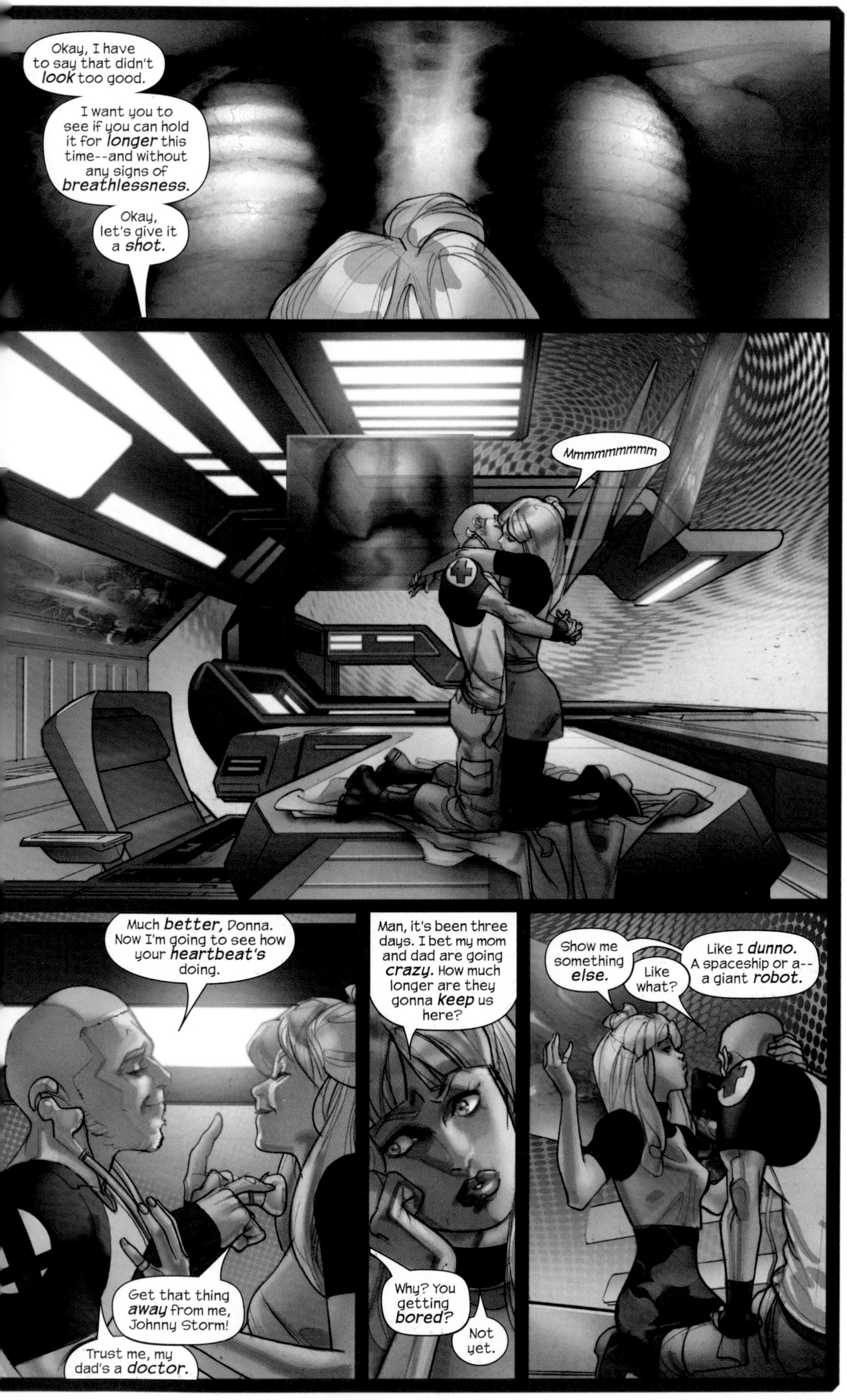
Okay, I have to say that didn't *look* too good.
I want you to see if you can hold it for *longer* this time--and without any signs of *breathlessness.*
Okay, let's give it a *shot.*
Mmmmmmmmm
Much *better,* Donna. Now I'm going to see how your *heartbeat's* doing.
Get that thing *away* from me, Johnny Storm!
Trust me, my dad's a *doctor.*
Man, it's been three days. I bet my mom and dad are going *crazy.* How much longer are they gonna *keep* us here?
Why? You getting *bored?*
Not yet.
Show me something *else.*
Like what?
Like I *dunno.* A spaceship or a-- a giant *robot.*

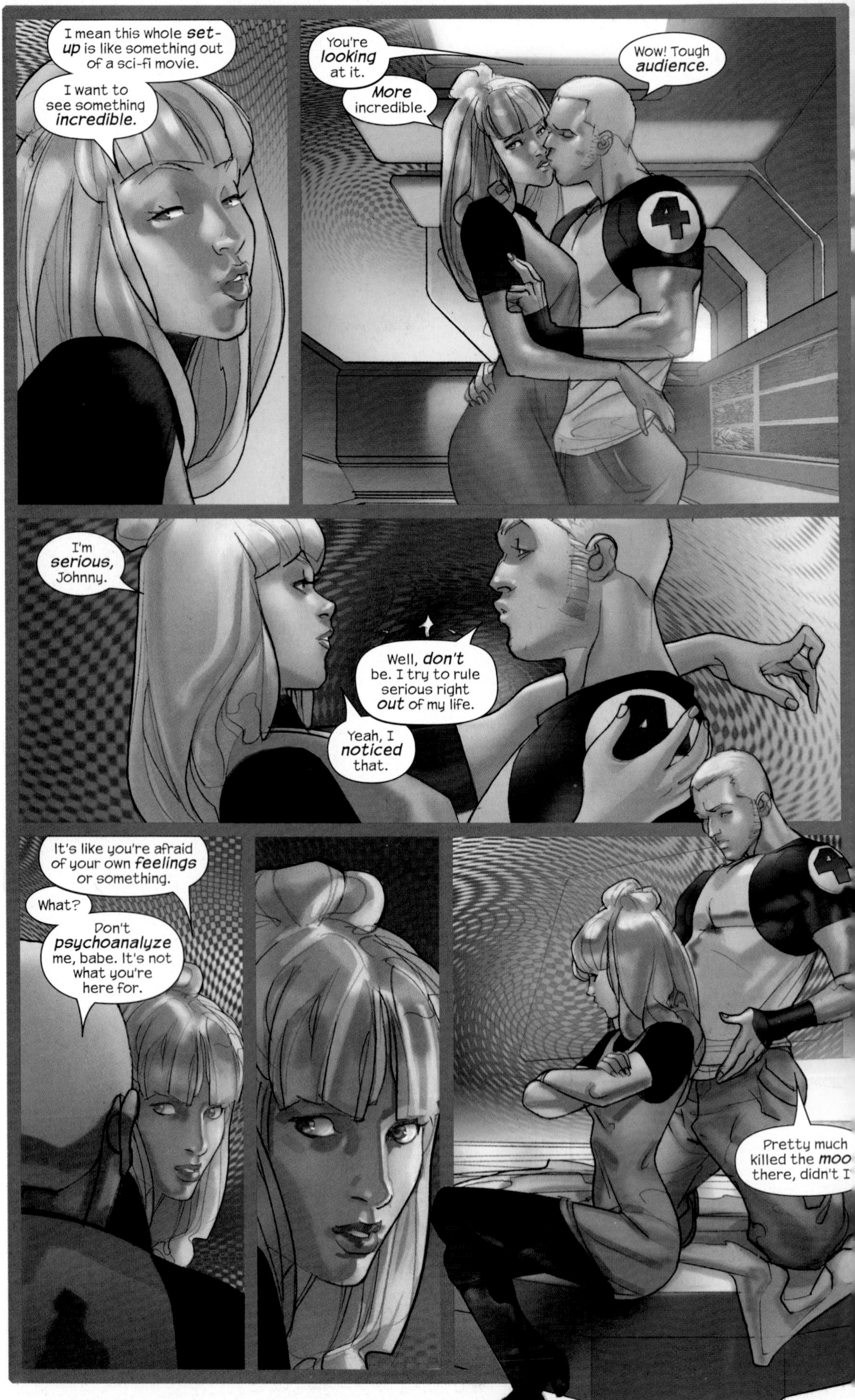
I mean this whole set-up is like something out of a sci-fi movie.
I want to see something incredible.
You're looking at it.
More incredible.
Wow! Tough audience.
I'm serious, Johnny.
Well, don't be. I try to rule serious right out of my life.
Yeah, I noticed that.
It's like you're afraid of your own feelings or something.
What?
Don't psychoanalyze me, babe. It's not what you're here for.
Pretty much killed the moo there, didn't I

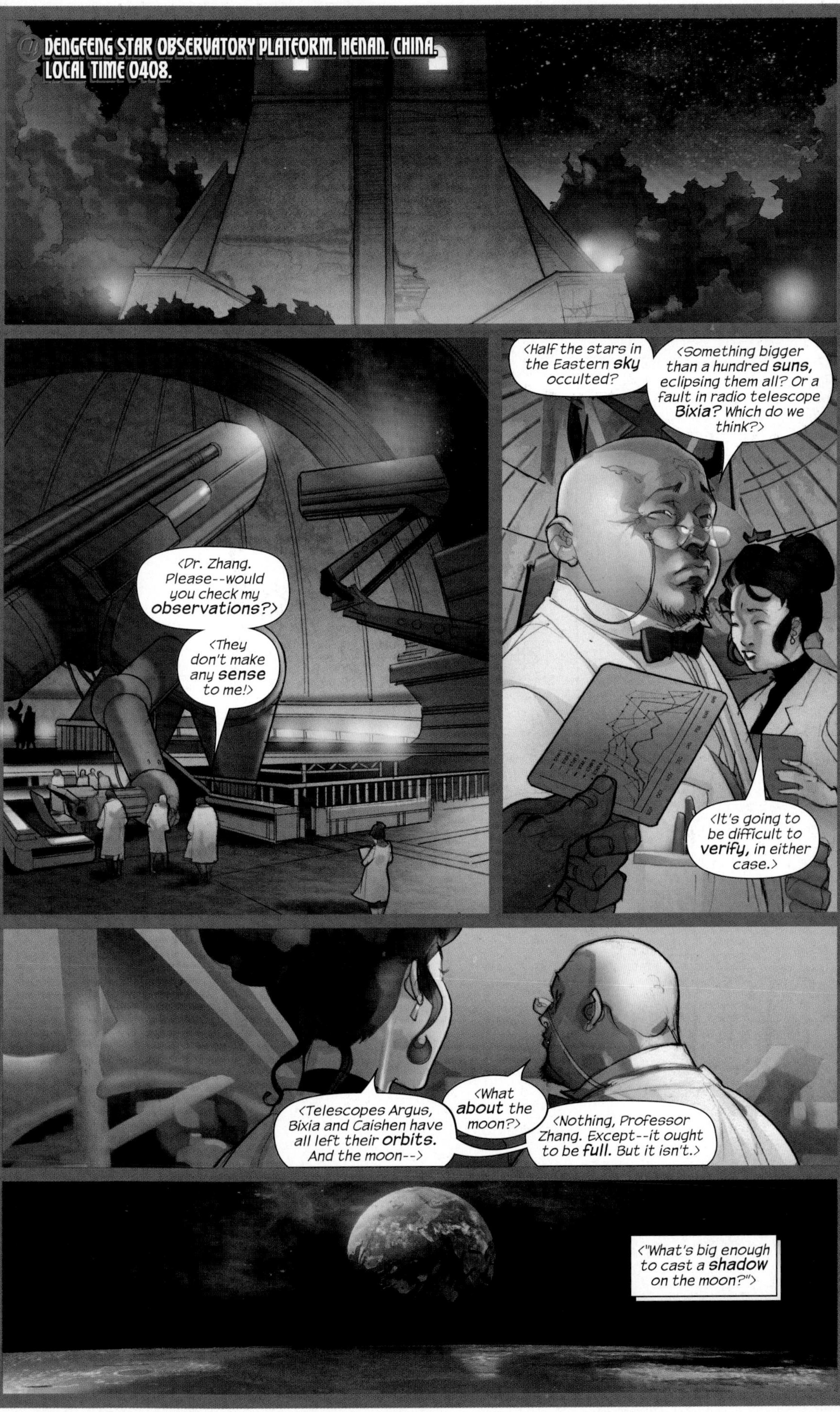
DENGFENG STAR OBSERVATORY PLATFORM. HENAN. CHINA. LOCAL TIME 0408.
<Dr. Zhang. Please--would you check my observations?>
<They don't make any sense to me!>
<Half the stars in the Eastern sky occulted?
<Something bigger than a hundred suns, eclipsing them all? Or a fault in radio telescope Bixia? Which do we think?>
<It's going to be difficult to verify, in either case.>
<Telescopes Argus, Bixia and Caishen have all left their orbits. And the moon-->
<What about the moon?>
<Nothing, Professor Zhang. Except--it ought to be full. But it isn't.>
<"What's big enough to cast a shadow on the moon?">

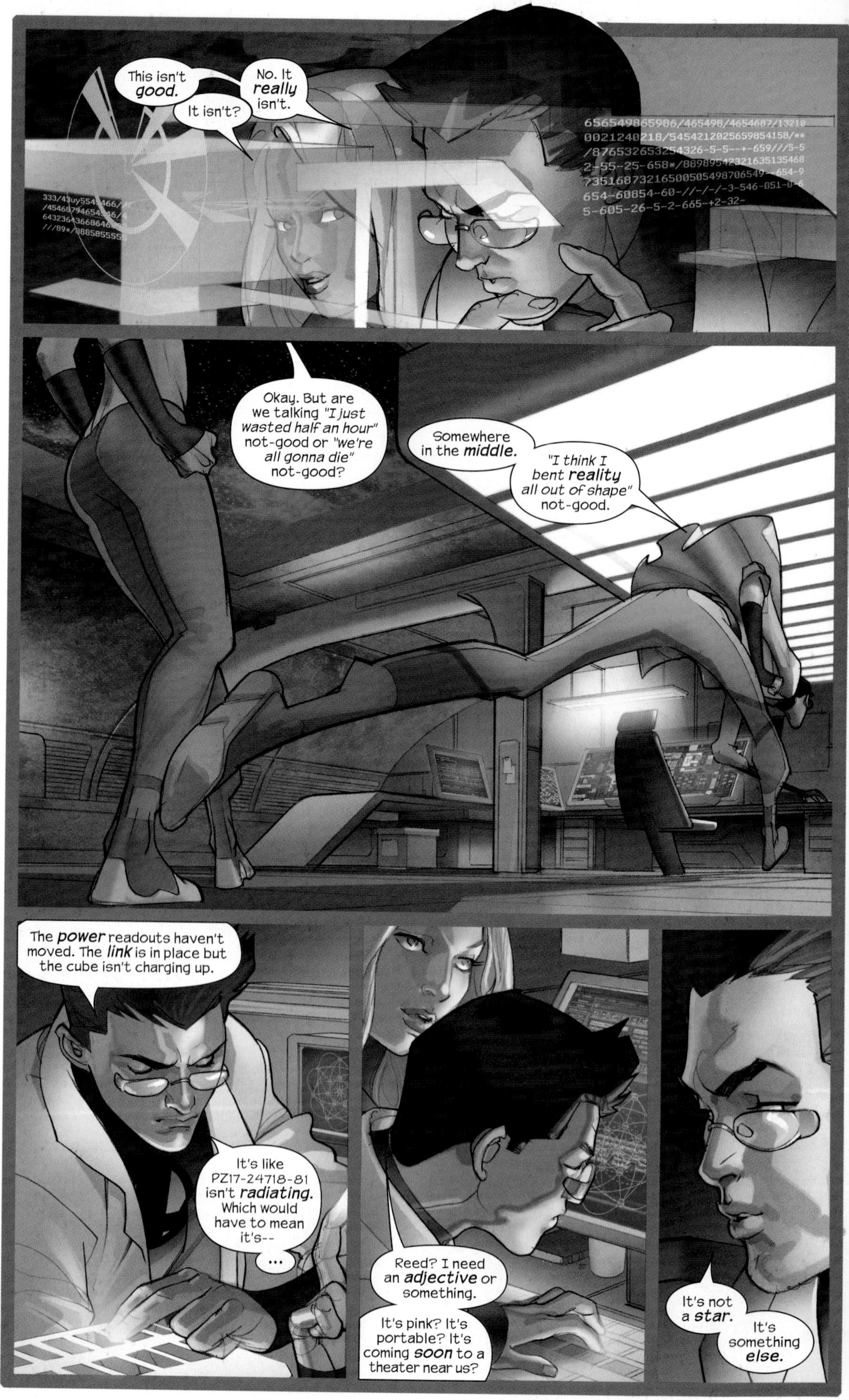
This isn't good.
It isn't?
No. It really isn't.
Okay. But are we talking "I just wasted half an hour" not-good or "we're all gonna die" not-good?
Somewhere in the middle.
"I think I bent reality all out of shape" not-good.
The power readouts haven't moved. The link is in place but the cube isn't charging up.
It's like PZ17-24718-81 isn't radiating. Which would have to mean it's--
...
Reed? I need an adjective or something.
It's pink? It's portable? It's coming soon to a theater near us?
It's not a star.
It's something else.

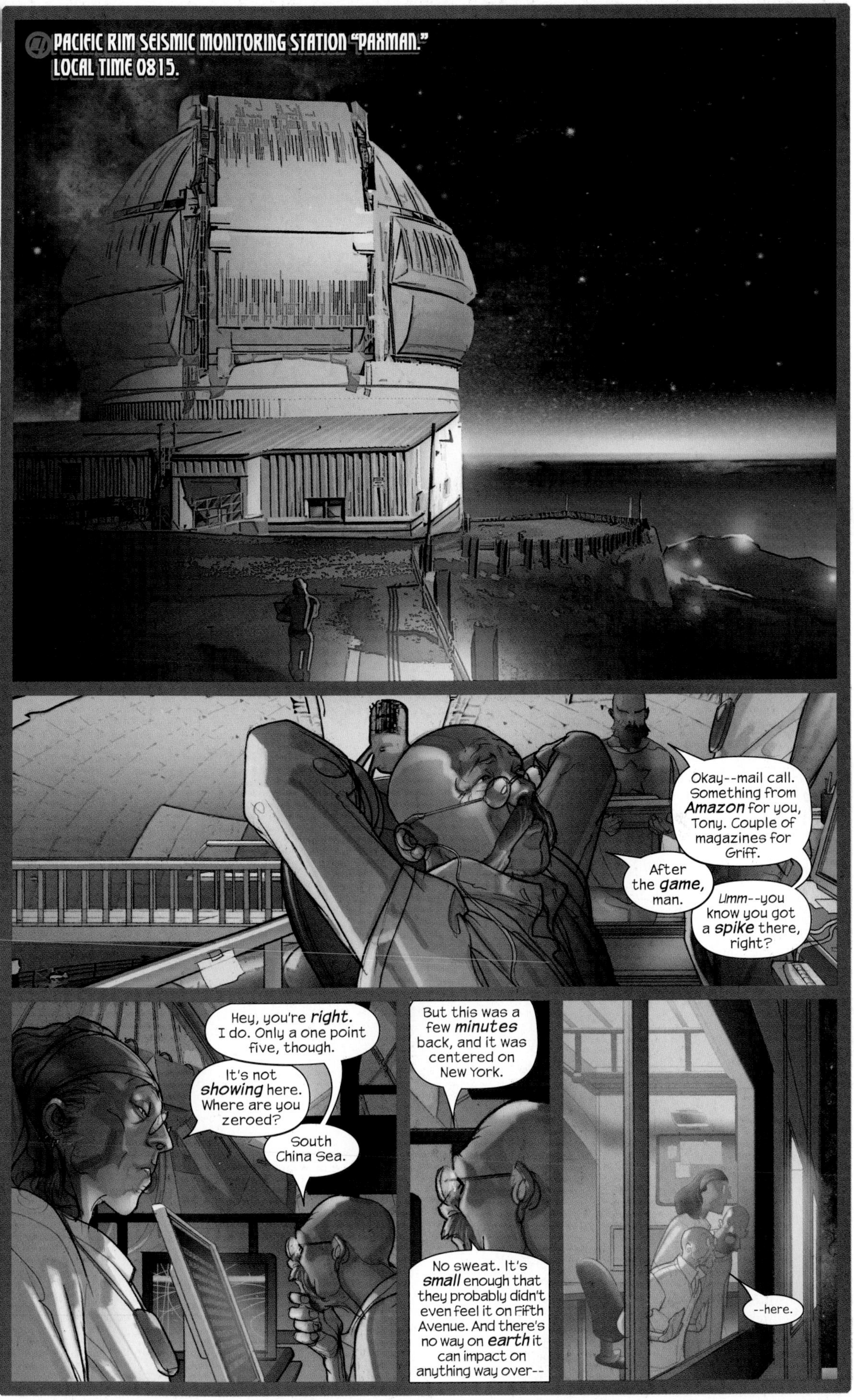

PACIFIC RIM SEISMIC MONITORING STATION "PAXMAN."
LOCAL TIME 0815.
Okay--mail call. Something from Amazon for you, Tony. Couple of magazines for Griff.
After the game, man.
Umm--you know you got a spike there, right?
Hey, you're right. I do. Only a one point five, though.
It's not showing here. Where are you zeroed?
South China Sea.
But this was a few minutes back, and it was centered on New York.
No sweat. It's small enough that they probably didn't even feel it on Fifth Avenue. And there's no way on earth it can impact on anything way over--
--here.

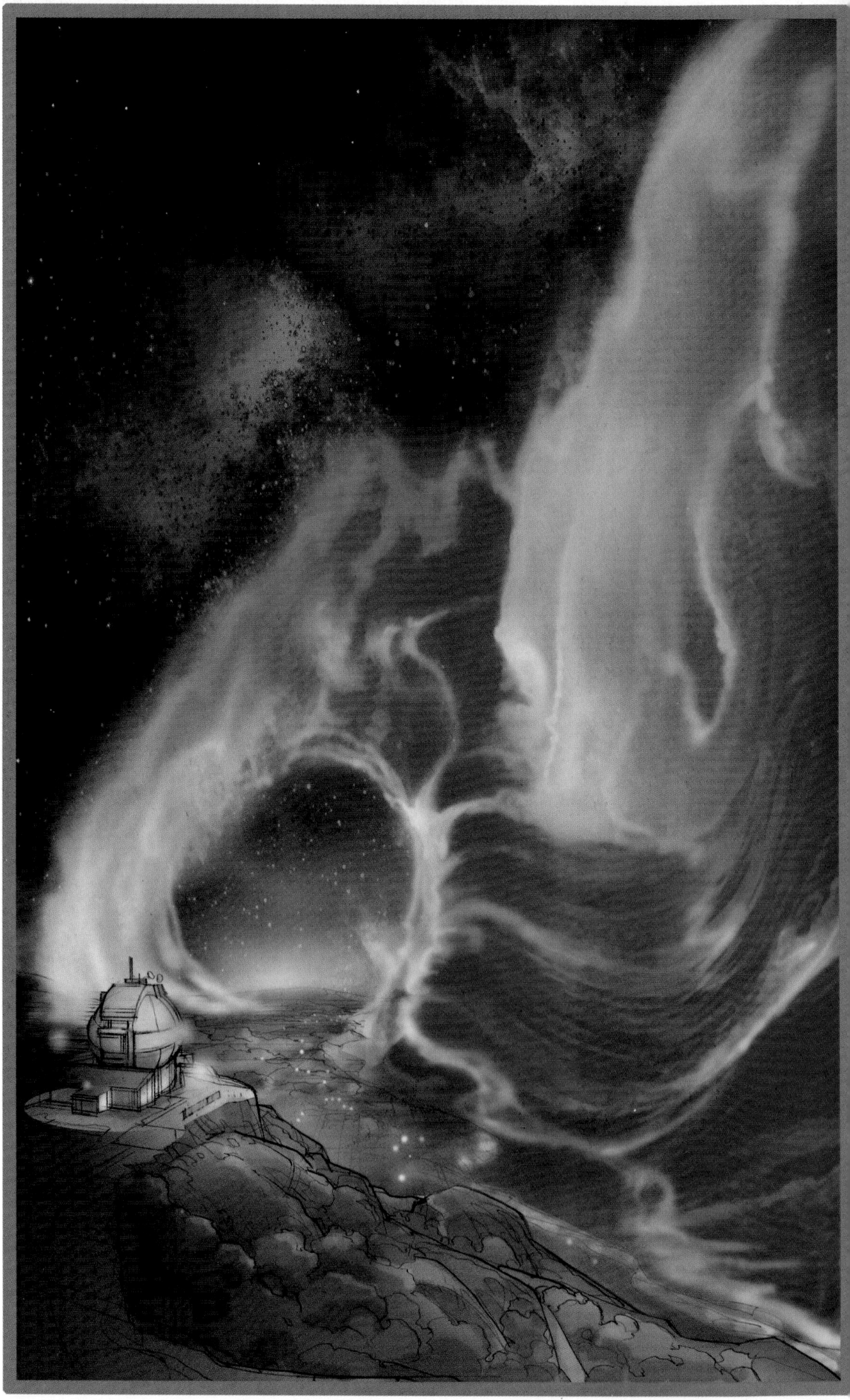

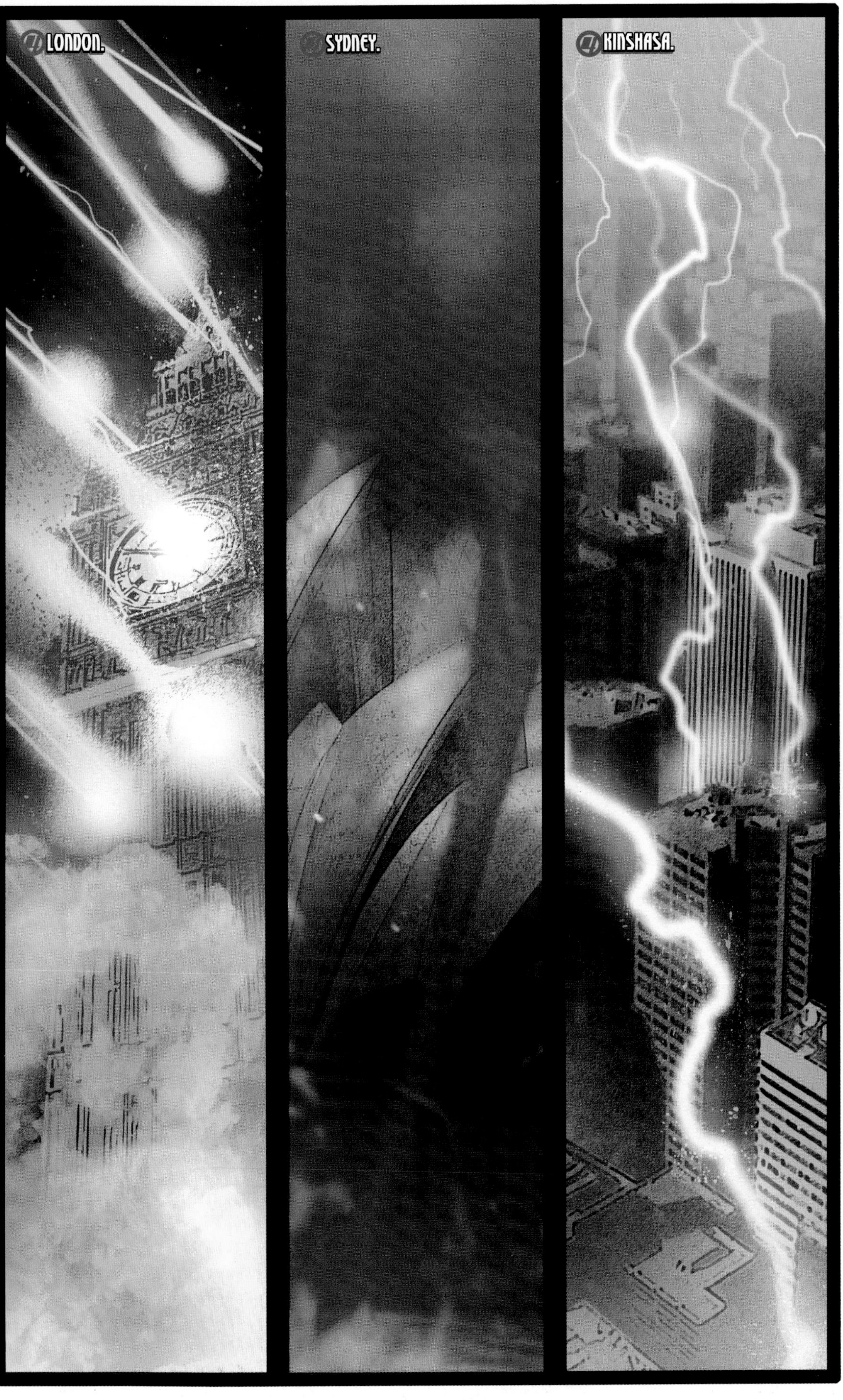
LONDON.
SYDNEY.
KINSHASA.

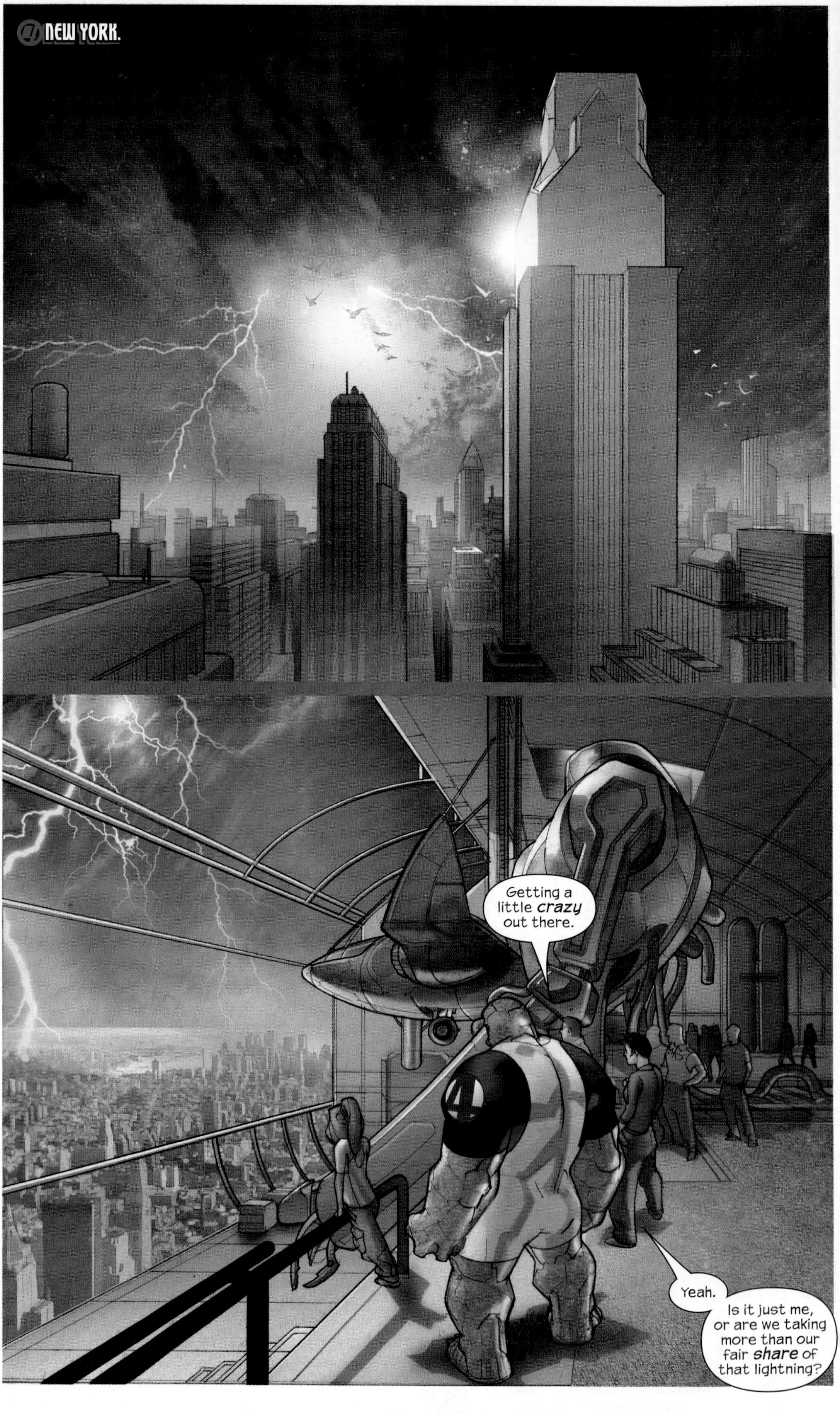
NEW YORK.
Getting a little *crazy* out there.
Yeah.
Is it just me, or are we taking more than our fair *share* of that lightning?

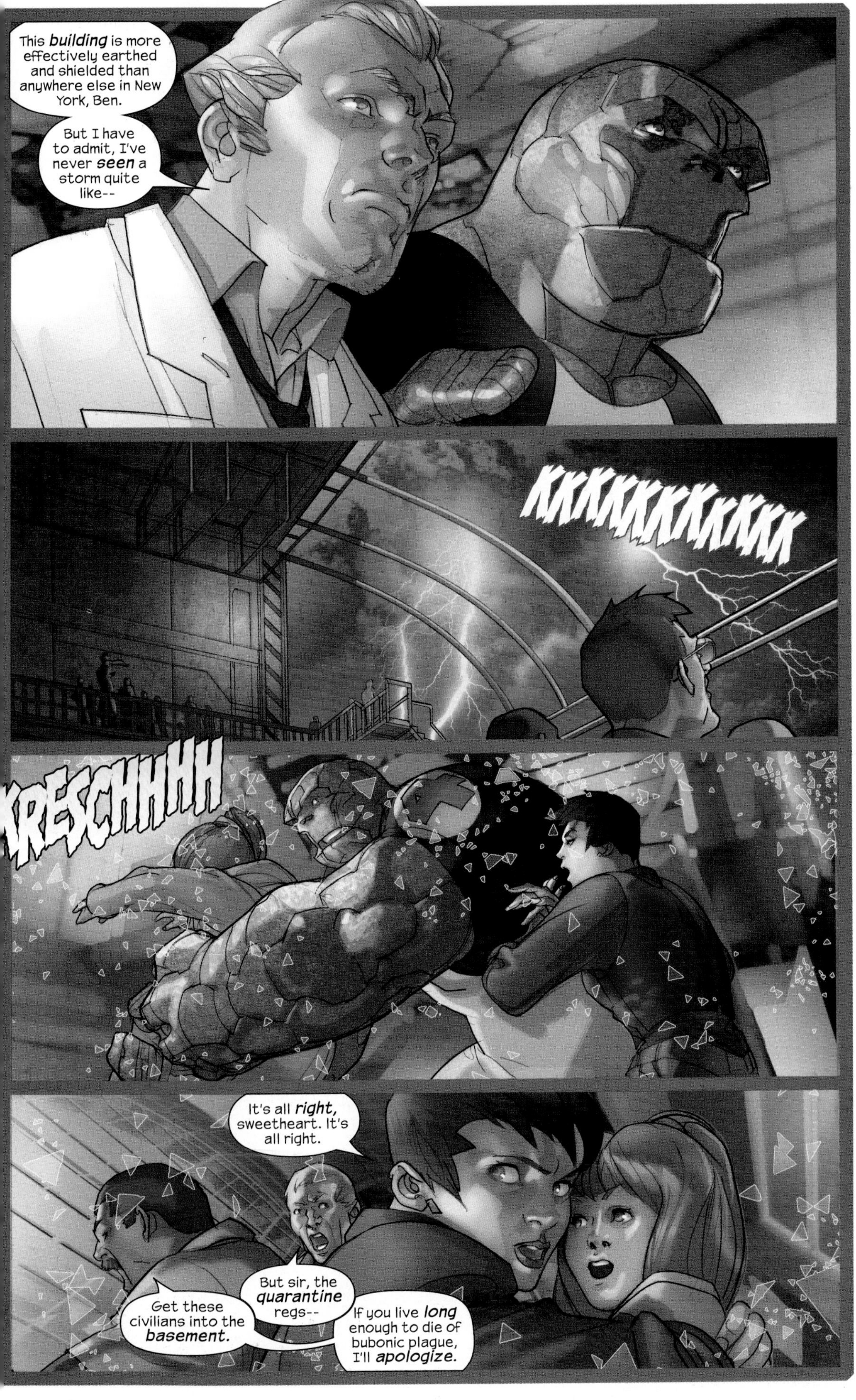
This building is more effectively earthed and shielded than anywhere else in New York, Ben.
But I have to admit, I've never seen a storm quite like--
KKKKKKKKKKKK
KRESCHHHH
It's all right, sweetheart. It's all right.
Get these civilians into the basement.
But sir, the quarantine regs--
If you live long enough to die of bubonic plague, I'll apologize.

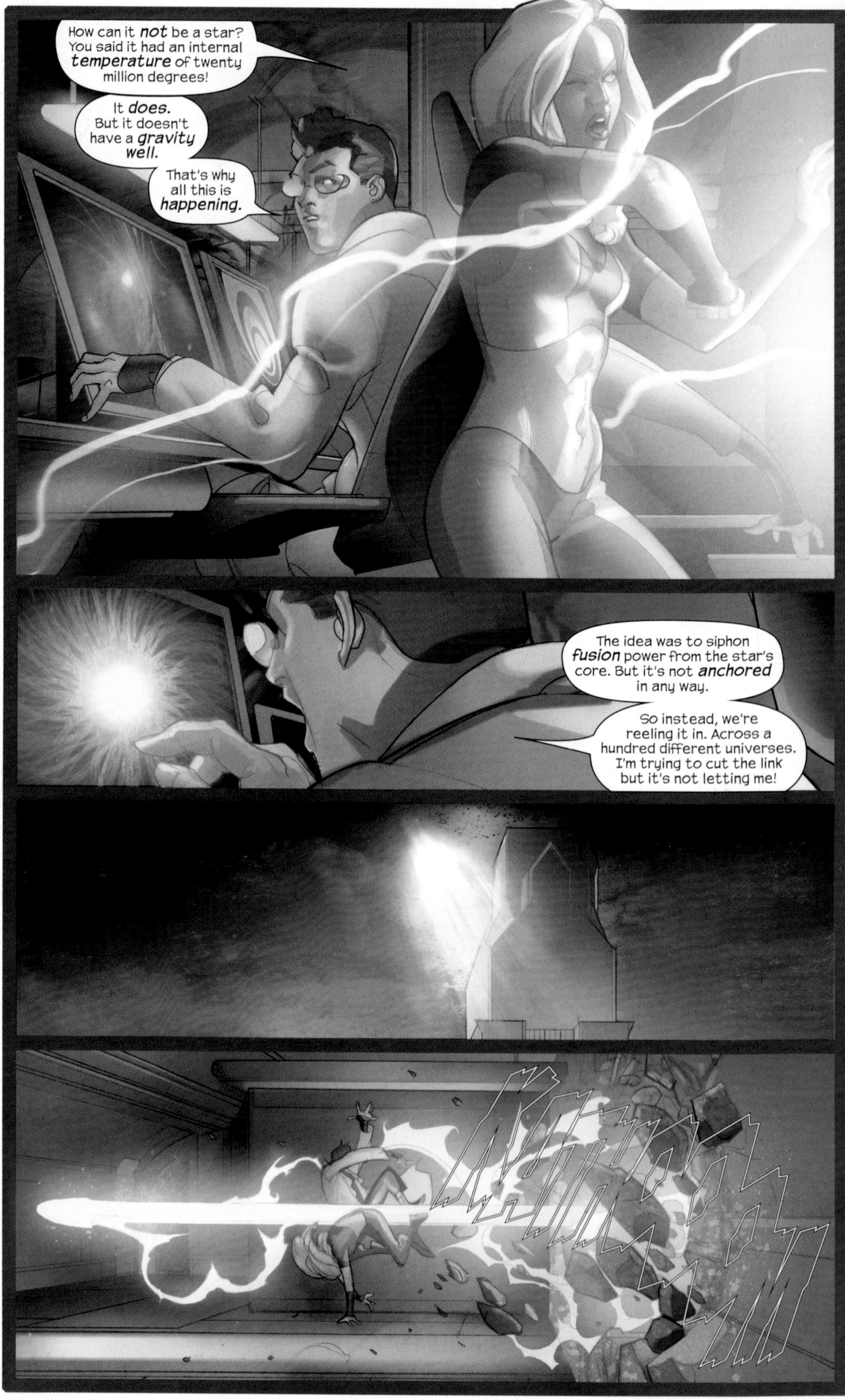
How can it not be a star? You said it had an internal temperature of twenty million degrees!
It does. But it doesn't have a gravity well.
That's why all this is happening.
The idea was to siphon fusion power from the star's core. But it's not anchored in any way.
So instead, we're reeling it in. Across a hundred different universes. I'm trying to cut the link but it's not letting me!

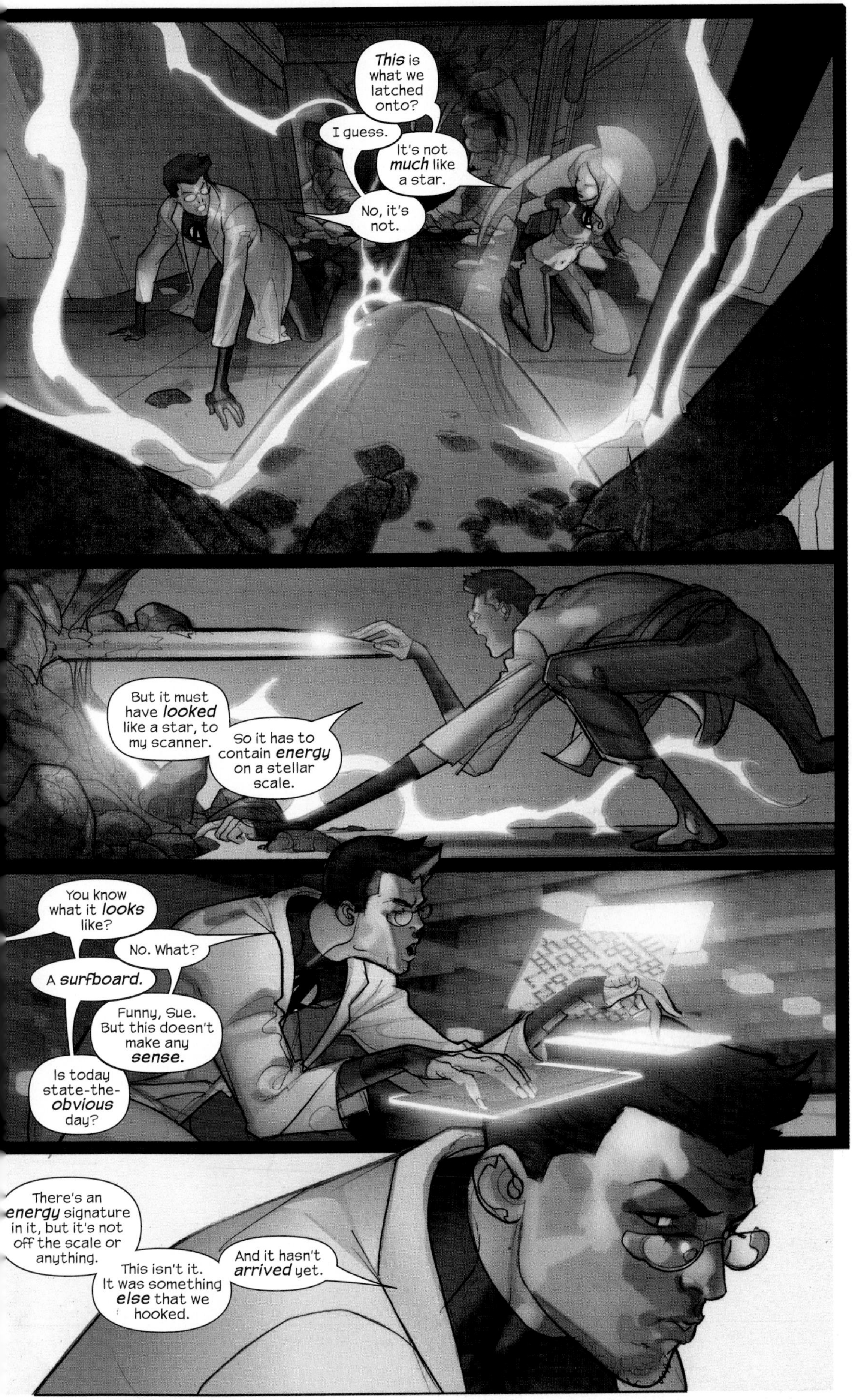
This is what we latched onto?
I guess.
It's not much like a star.
No, it's not.
But it must have looked like a star, to my scanner.
So it has to contain energy on a stellar scale.
You know what it looks like?
No. What?
A surfboard.
Funny, Sue. But this doesn't make any sense.
Is today state-the-obvious day?
There's an energy signature in it, but it's not off the scale or anything.
This isn't it. It was something else that we hooked.
And it hasn't arrived yet.

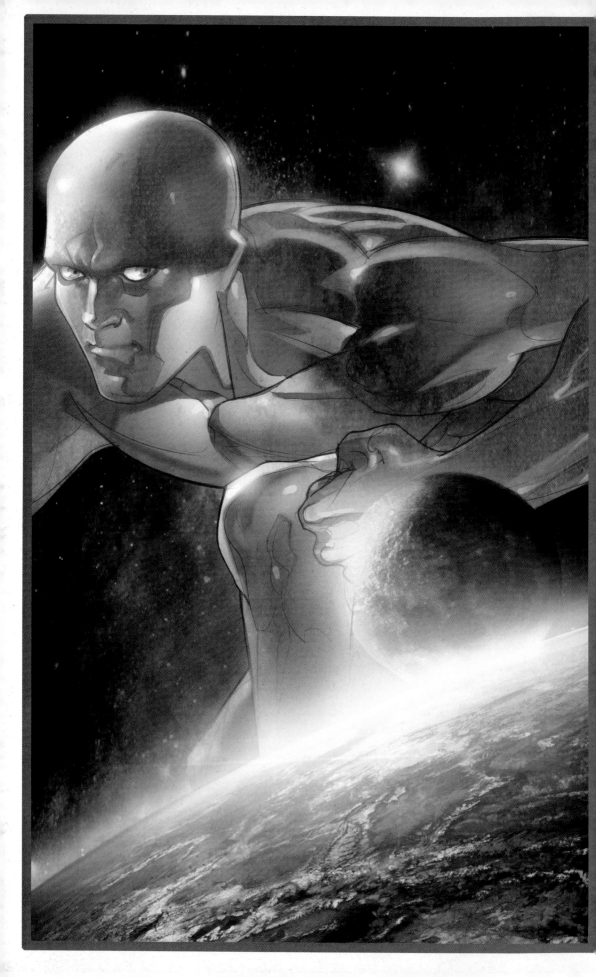

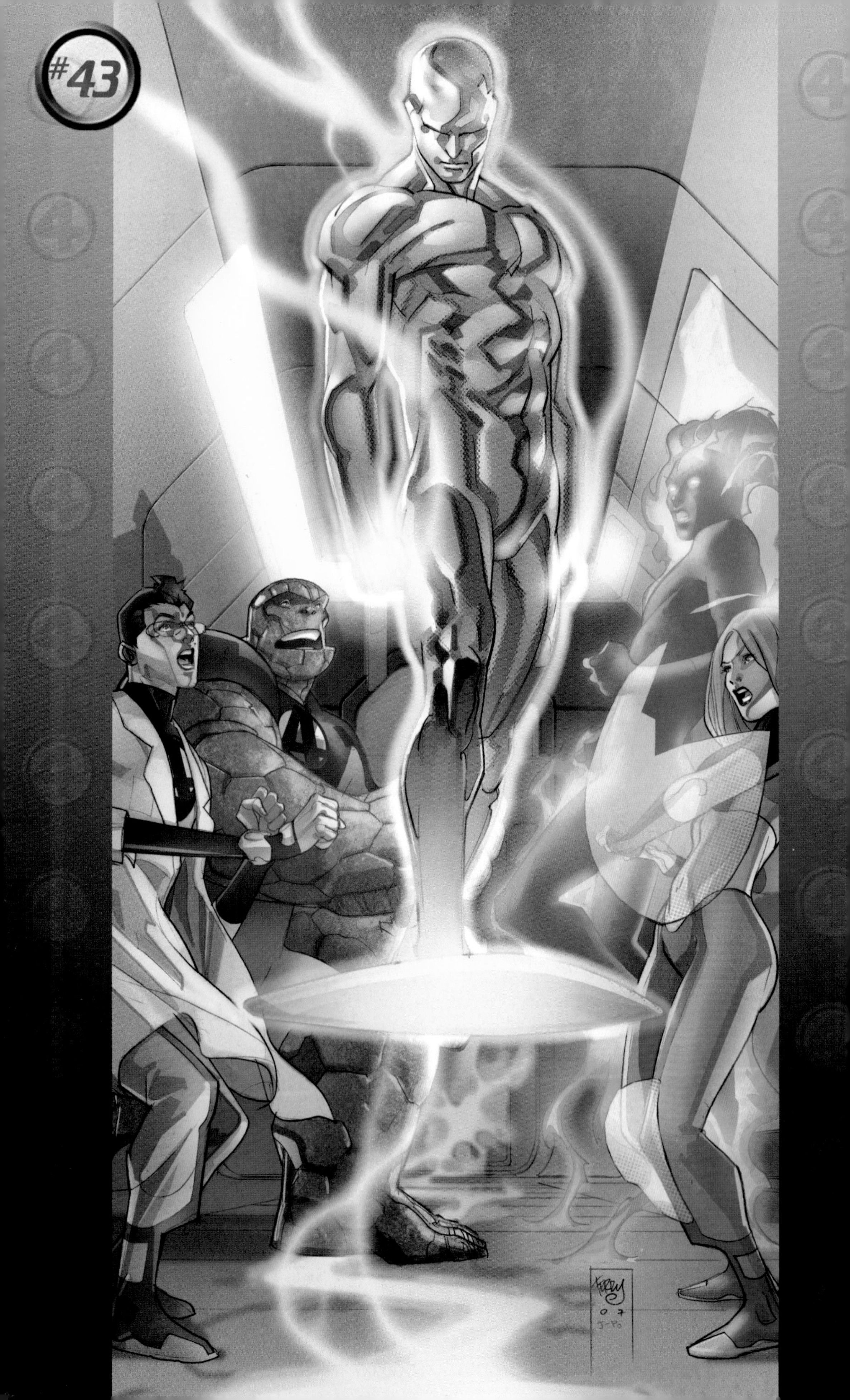
#43

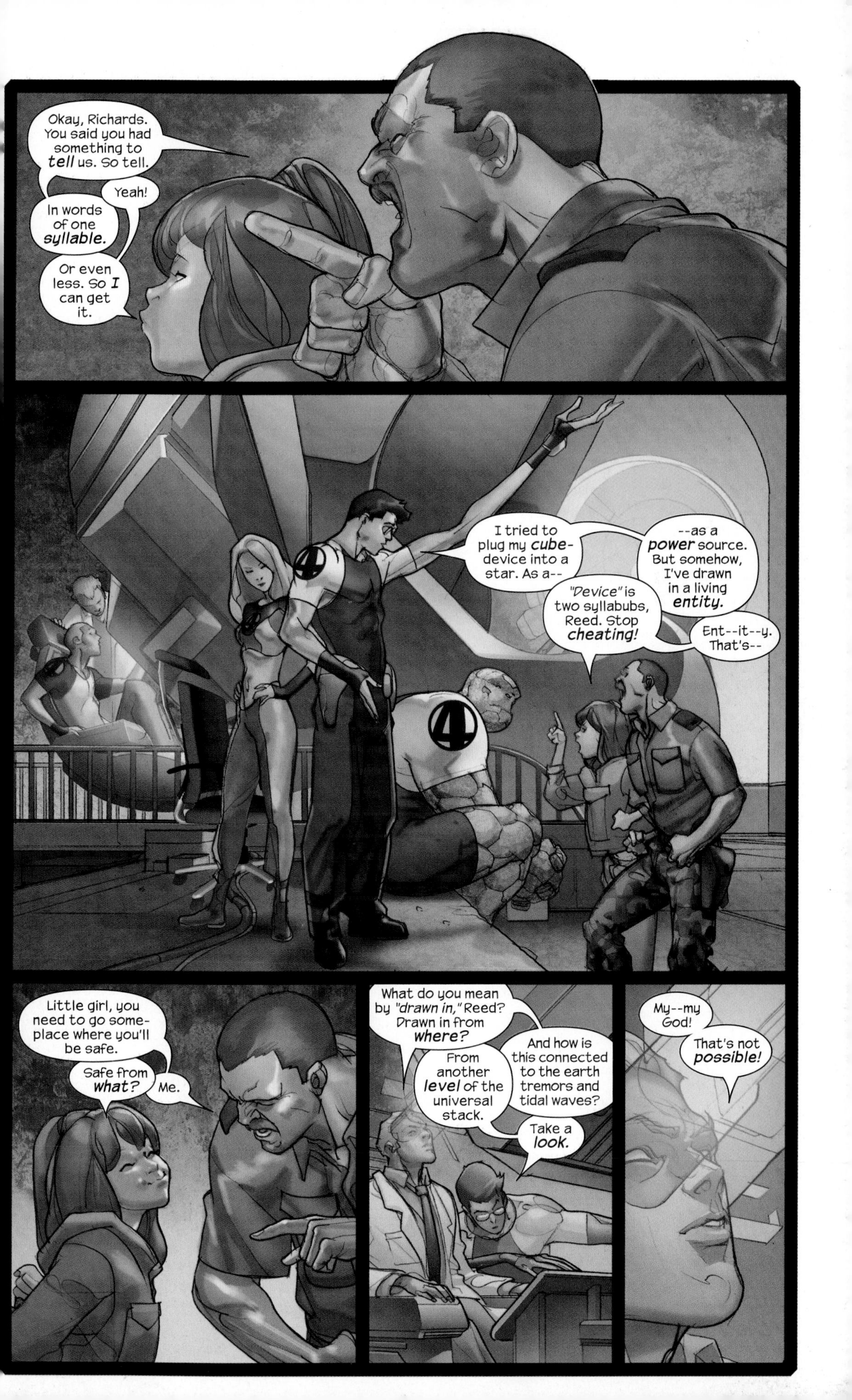

Okay, Richards. You said you had something to tell us. So tell.
Yeah!
In words of one syllable.
Or even less. So I can get it.
I tried to plug my cube-device into a star. As a--
--as a power source. But somehow, I've drawn in a living entity.
"Device" is two syllabubs, Reed. Stop cheating!
Ent--it--y. That's--
Little girl, you need to go someplace where you'll be safe.
Safe from what?
Me.
What do you mean by "drawn in," Reed? Drawn in from where?
From another level of the universal stack.
And how is this connected to the earth tremors and tidal waves?
Take a look.
My--my God!
That's not possible!

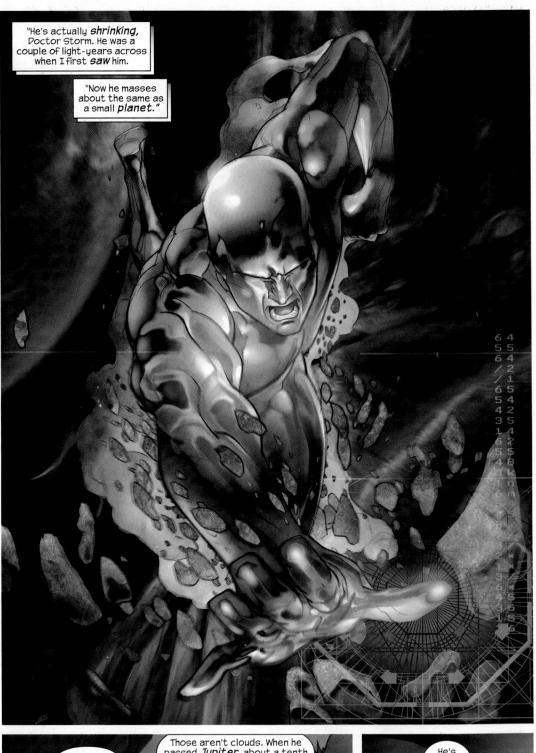

"He's actually *shrinking*, Doctor Storm. He was a couple of light-years across when I first *saw* him."

"Now he masses about the same as a small *planet.*"

Where did the *clouds* come from?

Those aren't clouds. When he passed *Jupiter*, about a tenth of its mass was sucked into his gravity field.

He punched straight through the *asteroid belt*, too--so now he's got an entourage. But the thing is--

He's coming *here.*

He's *homing in* on my signal.

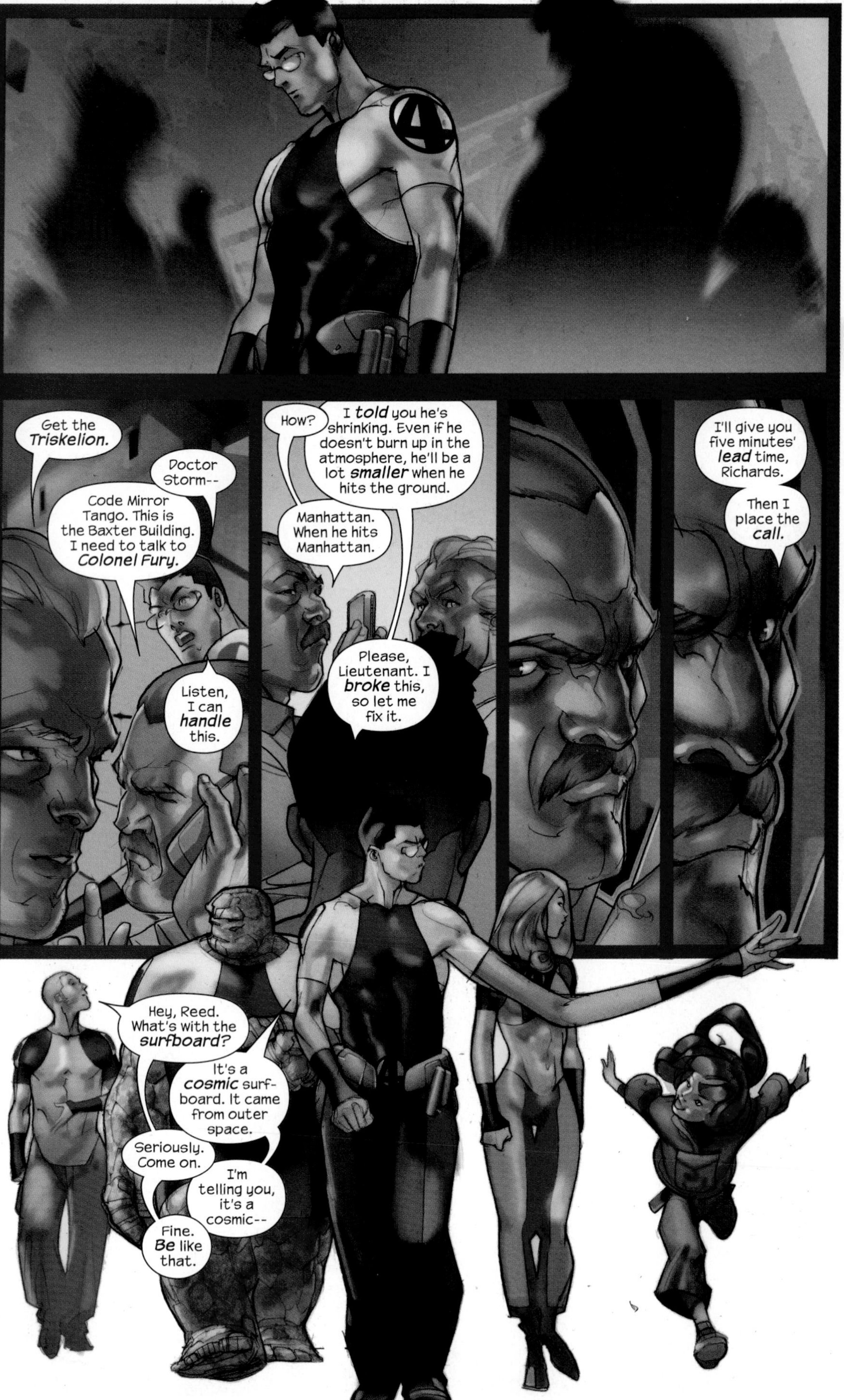
Get the Triskelion.
Doctor Storm--
Code Mirror Tango. This is the Baxter Building. I need to talk to Colonel Fury.
Listen, I can handle this.
How?
I told you he's shrinking. Even if he doesn't burn up in the atmosphere, he'll be a lot smaller when he hits the ground.
Manhattan. When he hits Manhattan.
Please, Lieutenant. I broke this, so let me fix it.
I'll give you five minutes' lead time, Richards.
Then I place the call.
Hey, Reed. What's with the surfboard?
It's a cosmic surfboard. It came from outer space.
Seriously. Come on.
I'm telling you, it's a cosmic--
Fine. Be like that.

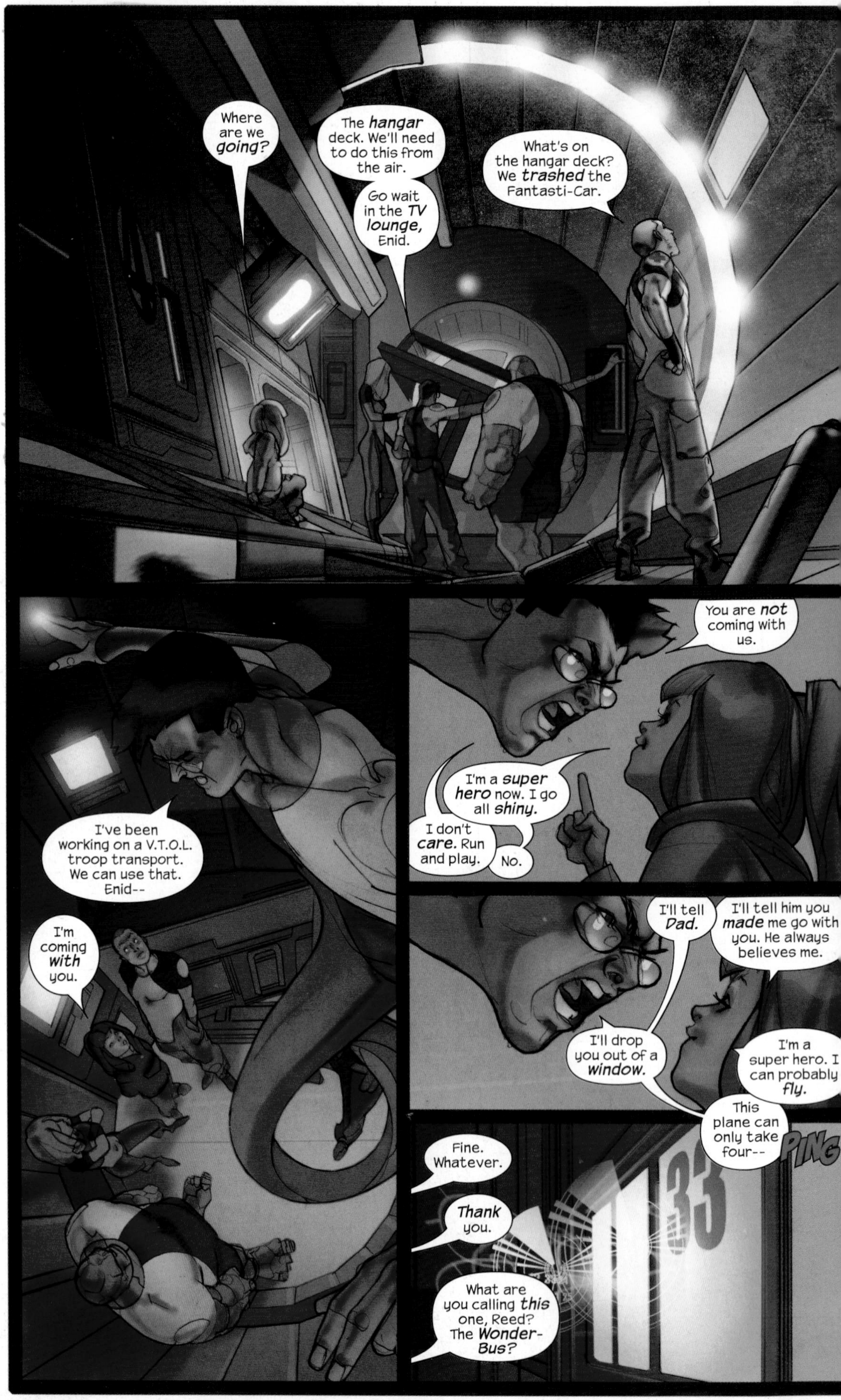
Where are we going?
The hangar deck. We'll need to do this from the air.
Go wait in the TV lounge, Enid.
What's on the hangar deck? We trashed the Fantasti-Car.
I've been working on a V.T.O.L. troop transport. We can use that. Enid--
I'm coming with you.
You are not coming with us.
I'm a super hero now. I go all shiny.
I don't care. Run and play.
No.
I'll tell Dad.
I'll tell him you made me go with you. He always believes me.
I'll drop you out of a window.
I'm a super hero. I can probably fly.
This plane can only take four--
PING
Fine. Whatever.
Thank you.
What are you calling this one, Reed? The Wonder-Bus?
133

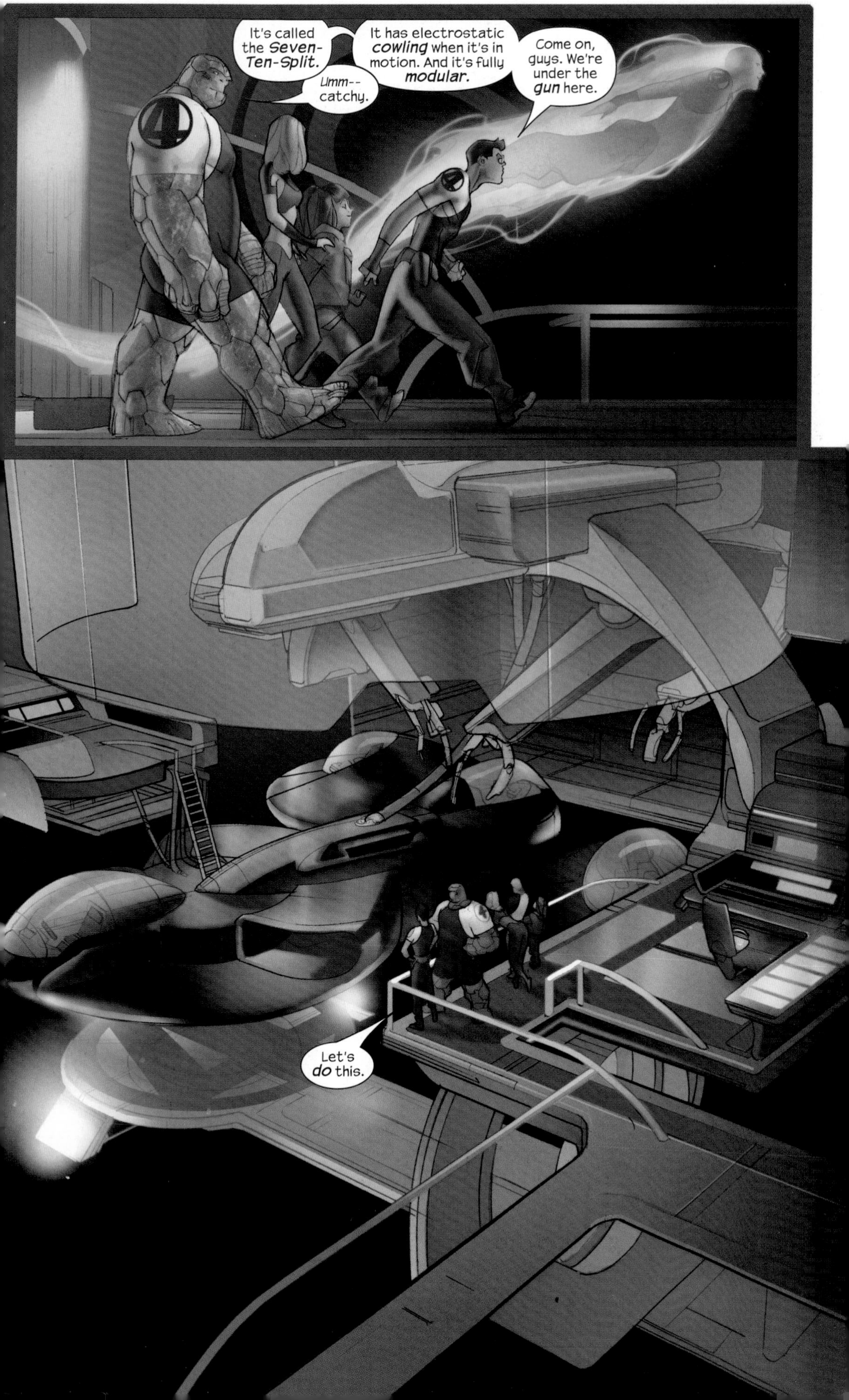

It's called the Seven-Ten-Split.
Umm-- catchy.
It has electrostatic cowling when it's in motion. And it's fully modular.
Come on, guys. We're under the gun here.
Let's do this.

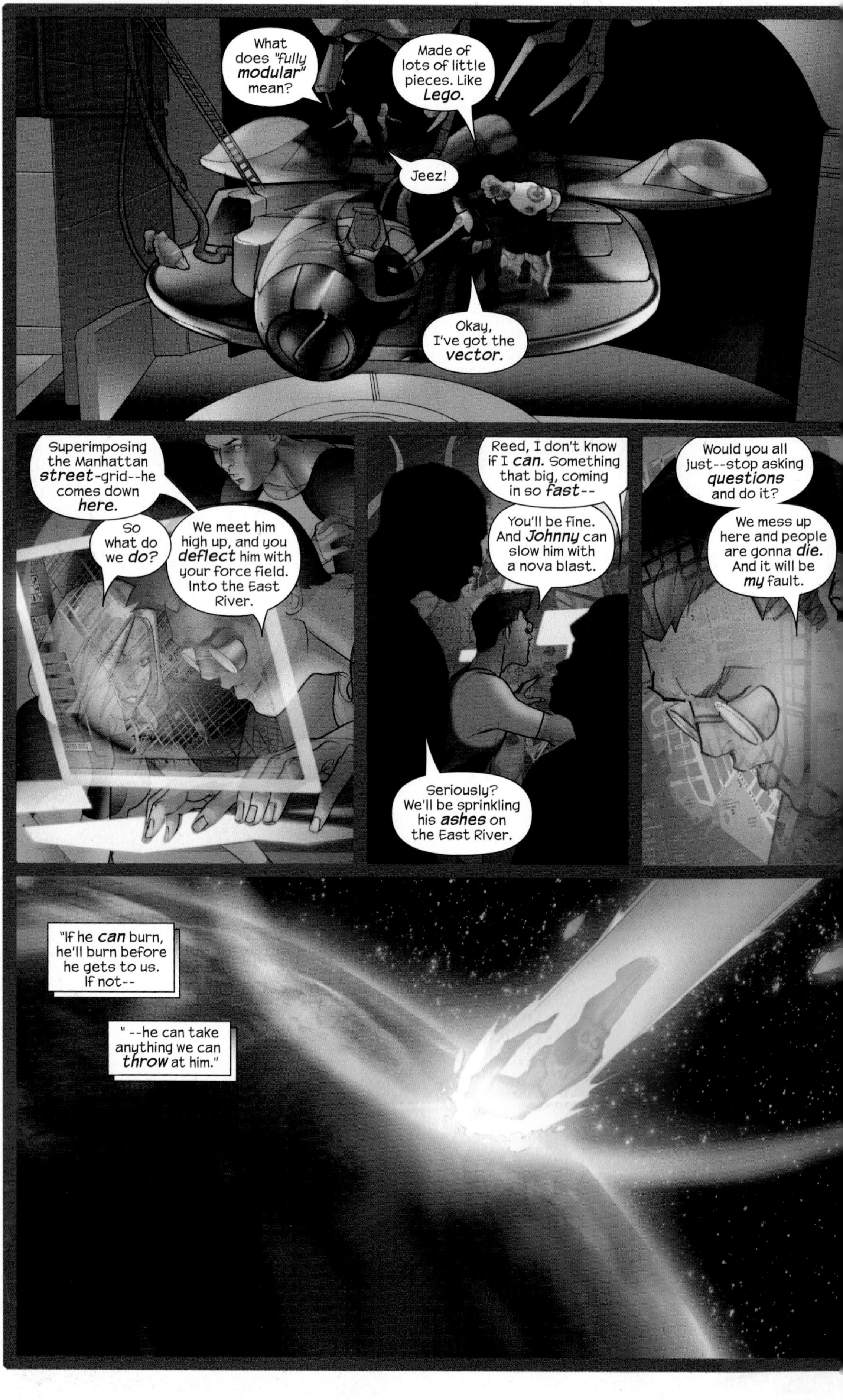

What does "fully modular" mean?
Made of lots of little pieces. Like Lego.
Jeez!
Okay, I've got the vector.
Superimposing the Manhattan street-grid--he comes down here.
So what do we do?
We meet him high up, and you deflect him with your force field. Into the East River.
Reed, I don't know if I can. Something that big, coming in so fast--
You'll be fine. And Johnny can slow him with a nova blast.
Seriously? We'll be sprinkling his ashes on the East River.
Would you all just--stop asking questions and do it?
We mess up here and people are gonna die. And it will be my fault.
"If he can burn, he'll burn before he gets to us. If not--
" --he can take anything we can throw at him."

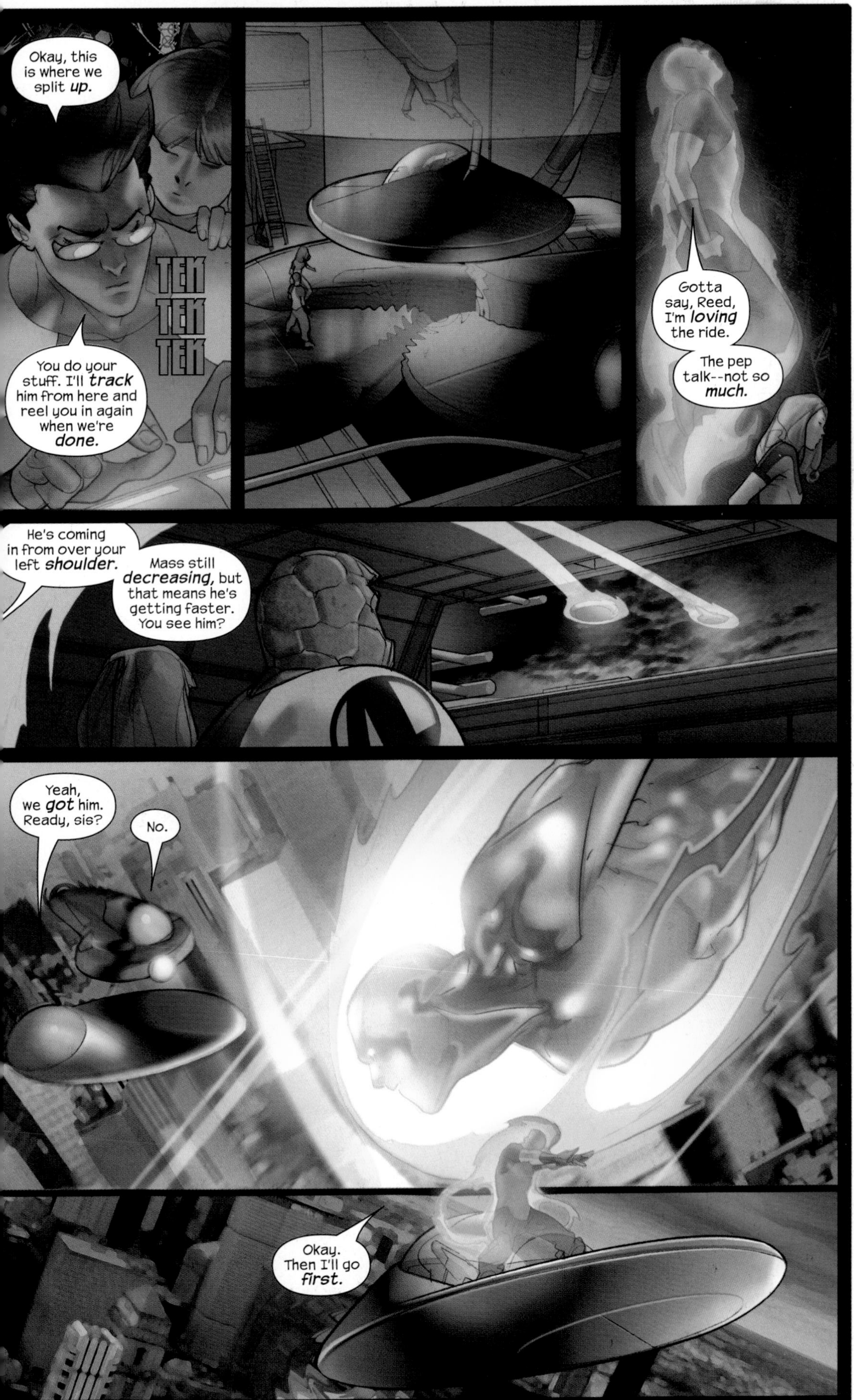
Okay, this is where we split up.
You do your stuff. I'll track him from here and reel you in again when we're done.
TEK TEK TEK
Gotta say, Reed, I'm loving the ride.
The pep talk--not so much.
He's coming in from over your left shoulder.
Mass still decreasing, but that means he's getting faster. You see him?
Yeah, we got him. Ready, sis?
No.
Okay. Then I'll go first.

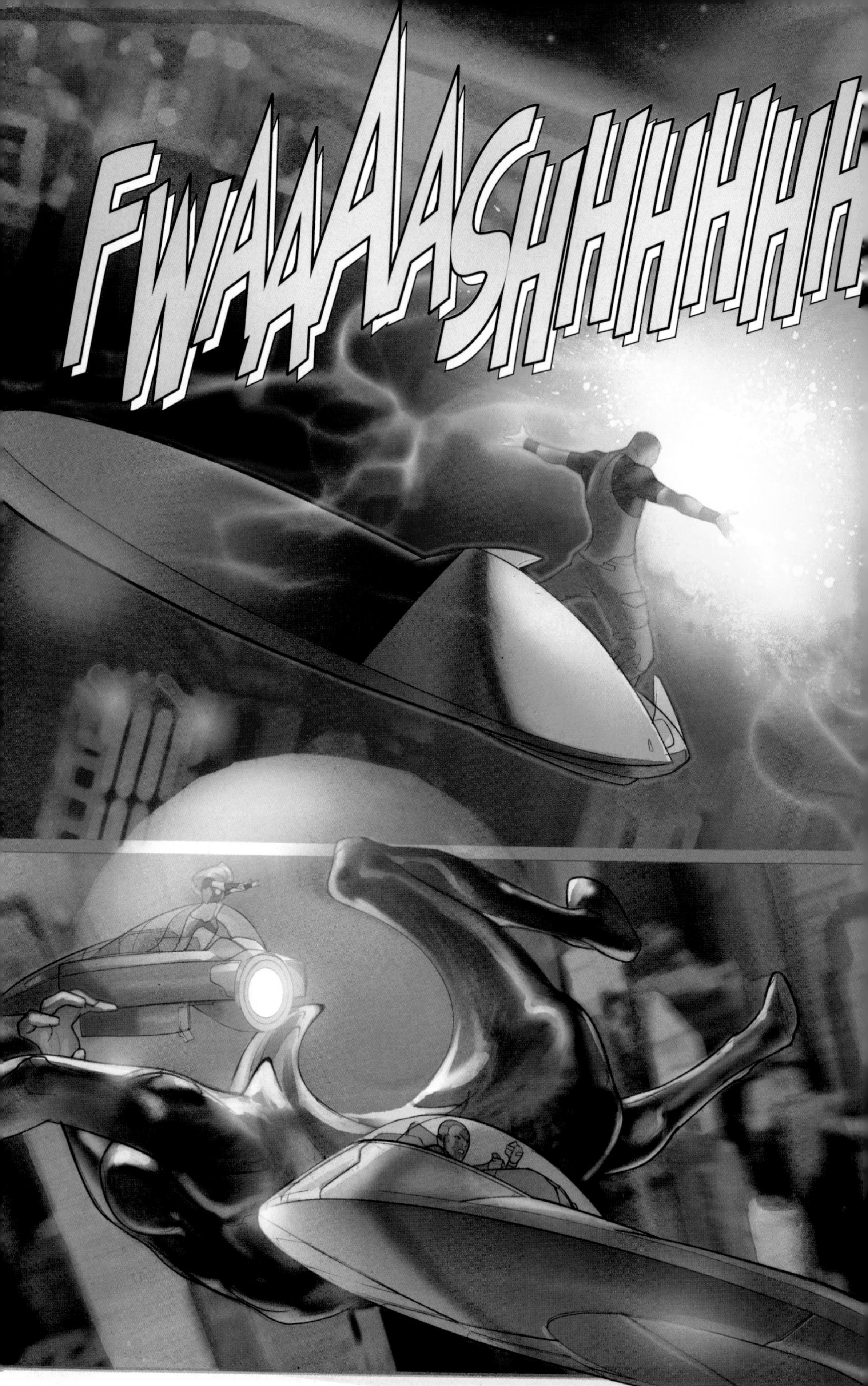
FWAAAASHHHHHH

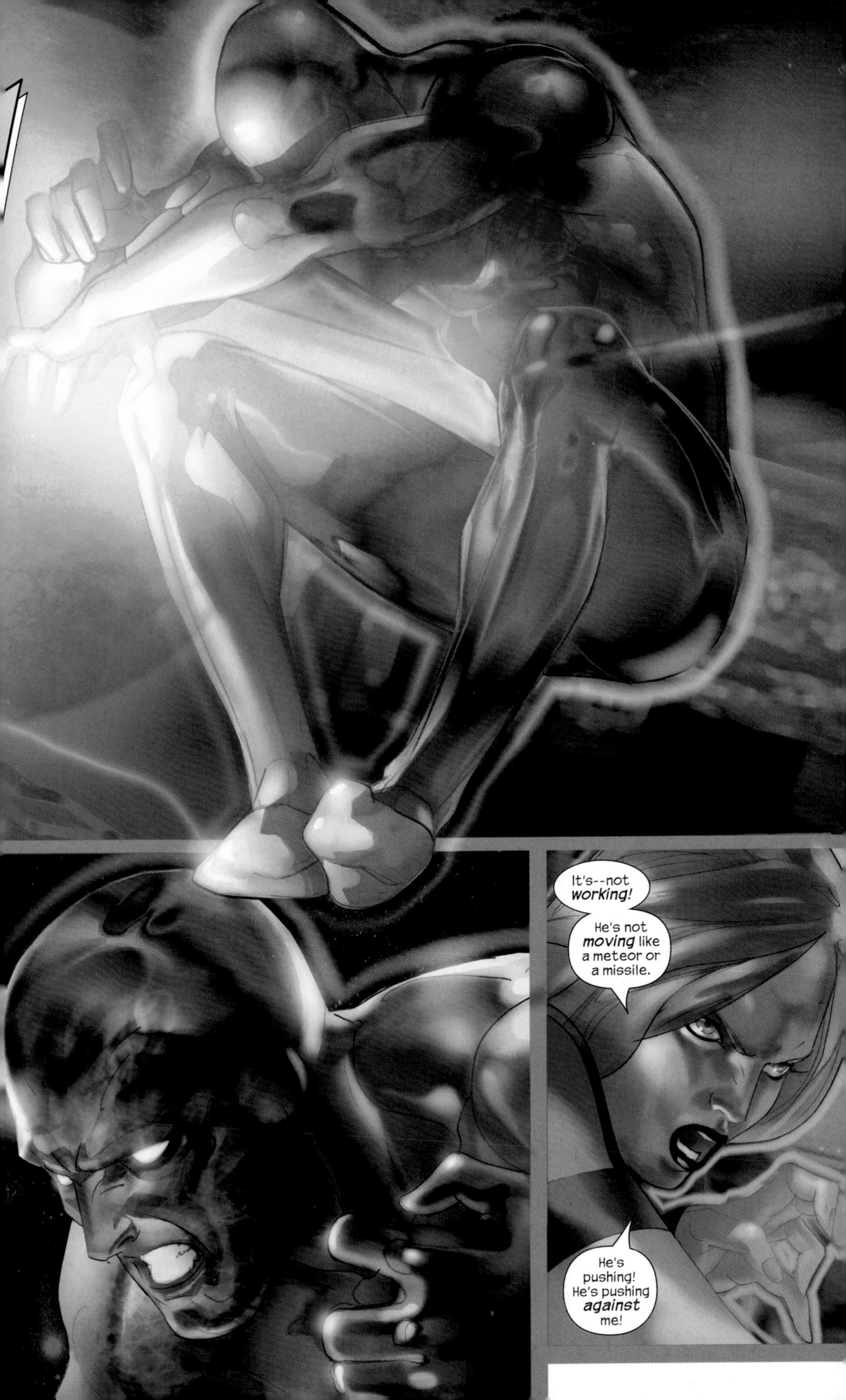
It's--not *working!*
He's not *moving* like a meteor or a missile.
He's pushing! He's pushing *against* me!

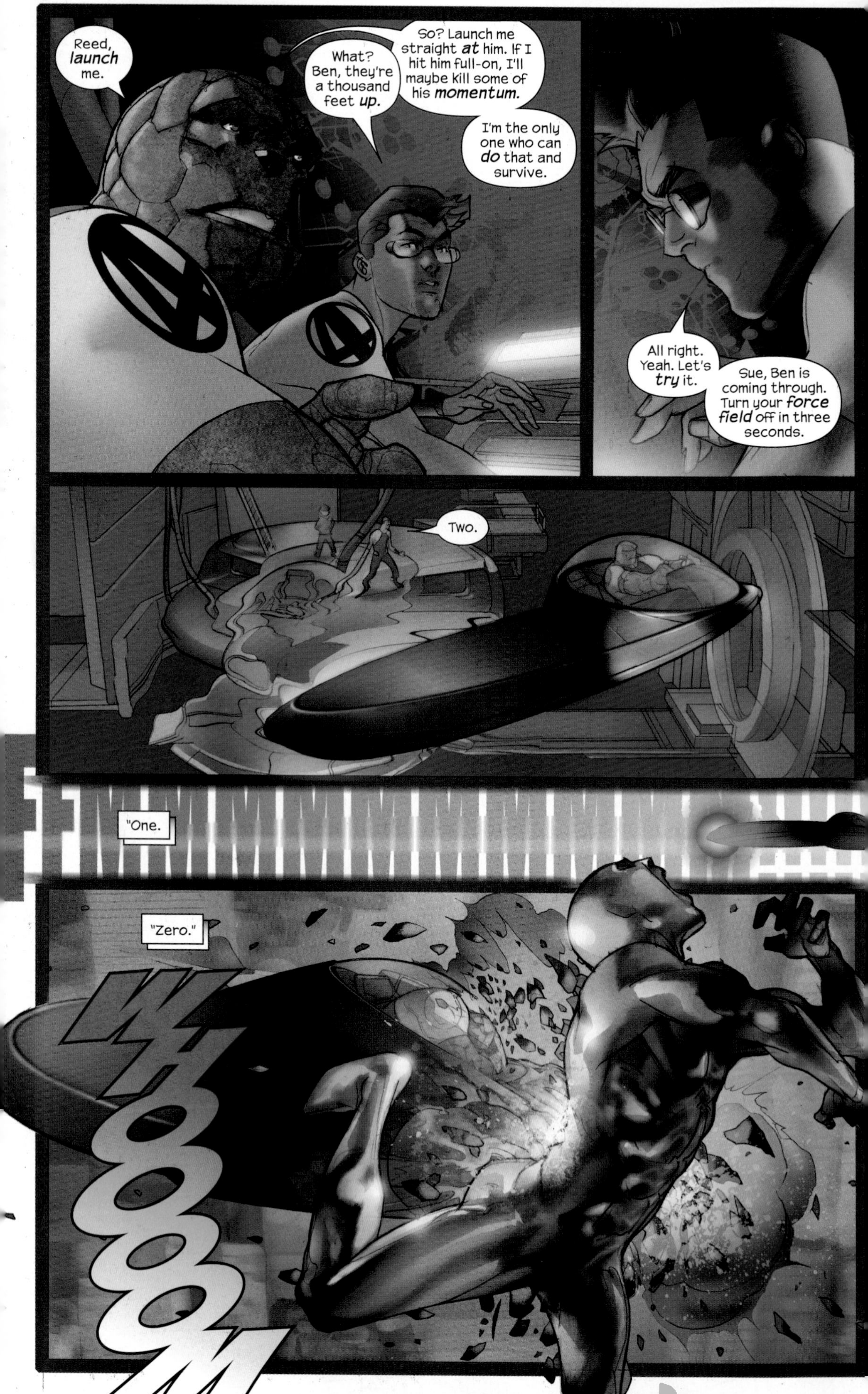

Reed, launch me.
What? Ben, they're a thousand feet up.
So? Launch me straight at him. If I hit him full-on, I'll maybe kill some of his momentum.
I'm the only one who can do that and survive.
All right. Yeah. Let's try it.
Sue, Ben is coming through. Turn your force field off in three seconds.
Two.
"One.
"Zero."
WHOOOOM

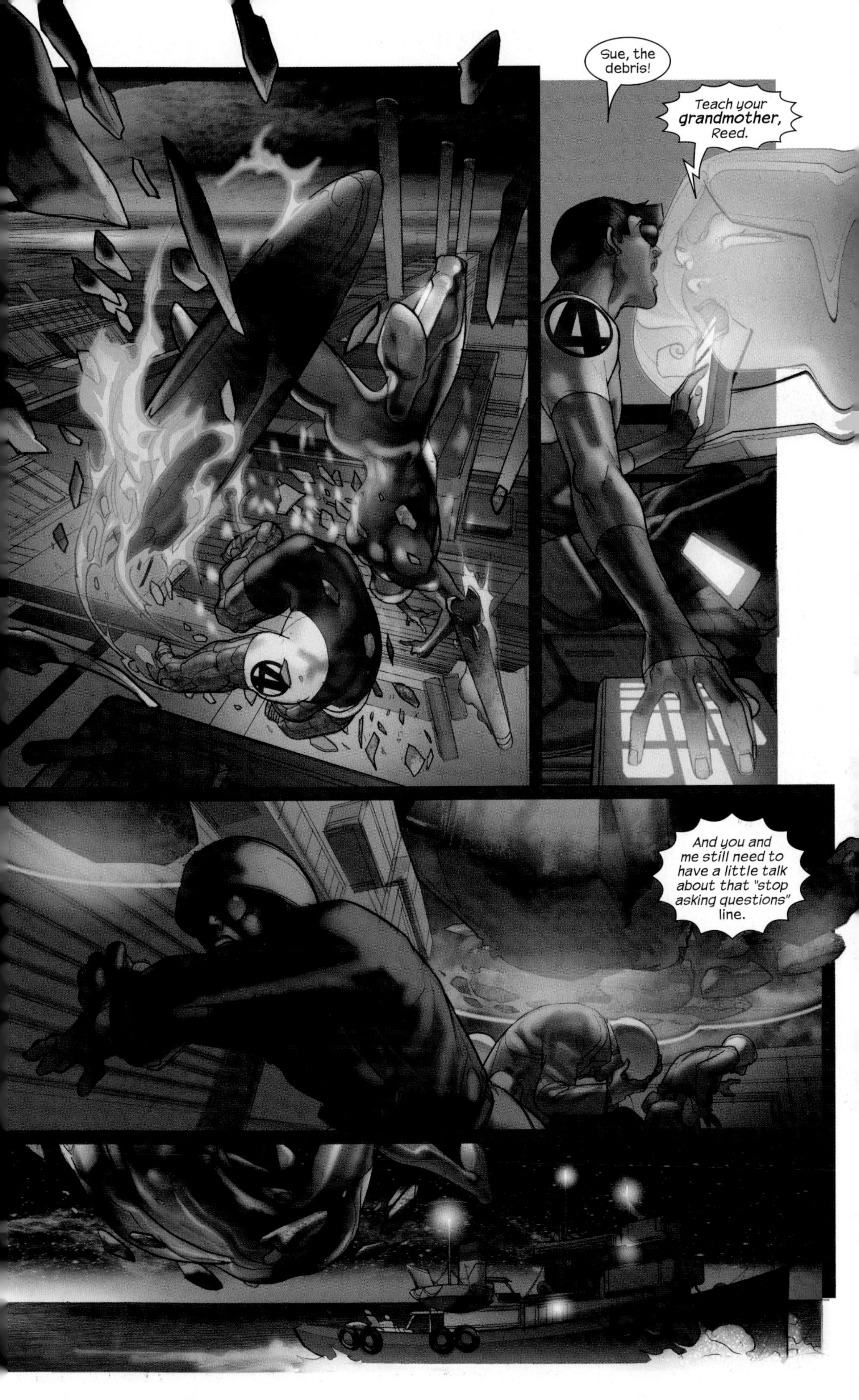
Sue, the debris!
Teach your **grandmother,** Reed.
And you and me still need to have a little talk about that "stop asking questions" line.

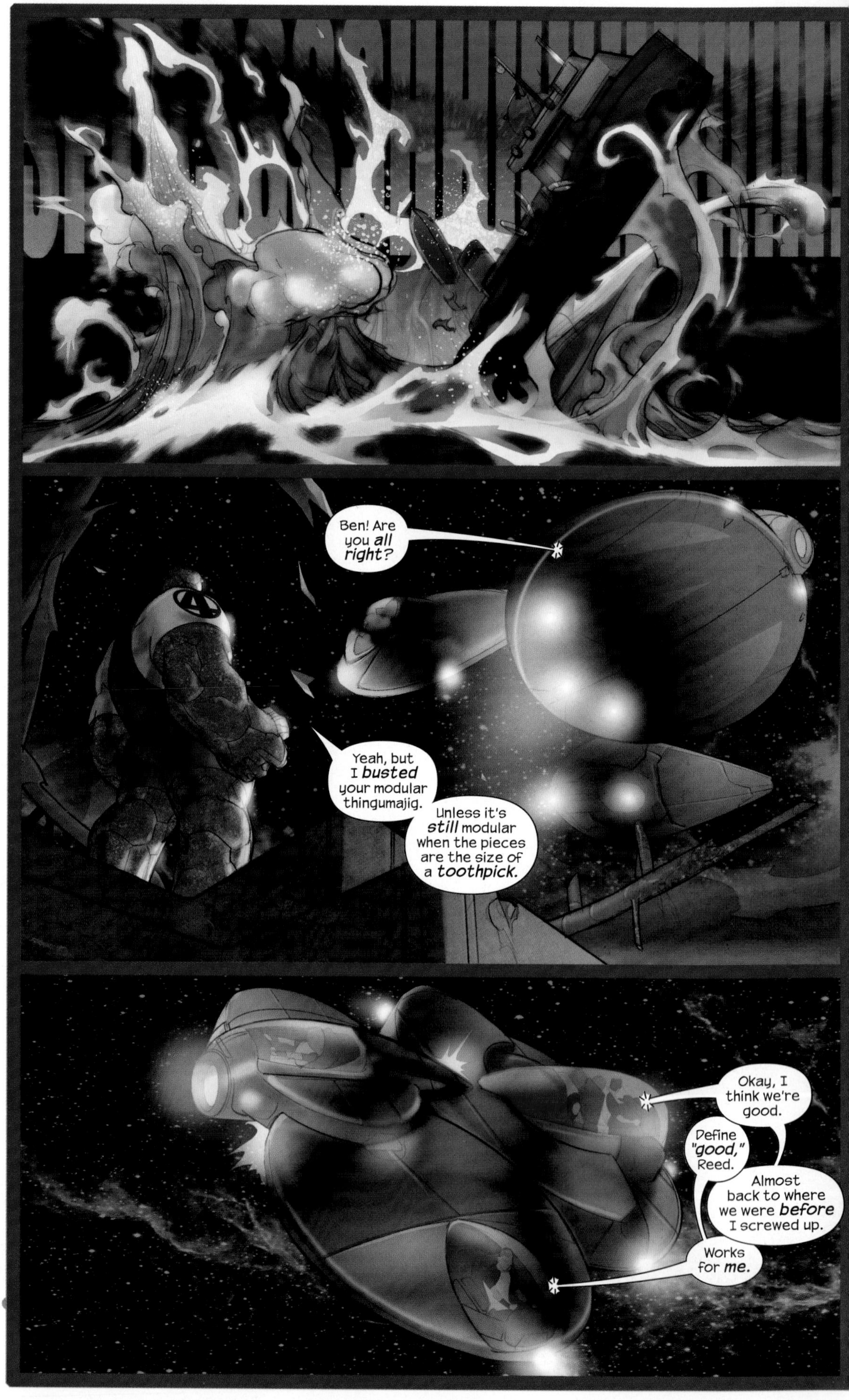
Ben! Are you all right?
Yeah, but I busted your modular thingumajig.
Unless it's still modular when the pieces are the size of a toothpick.
Okay, I think we're good.
Define "good," Reed.
Almost back to where we were before I screwed up.
Works for me.

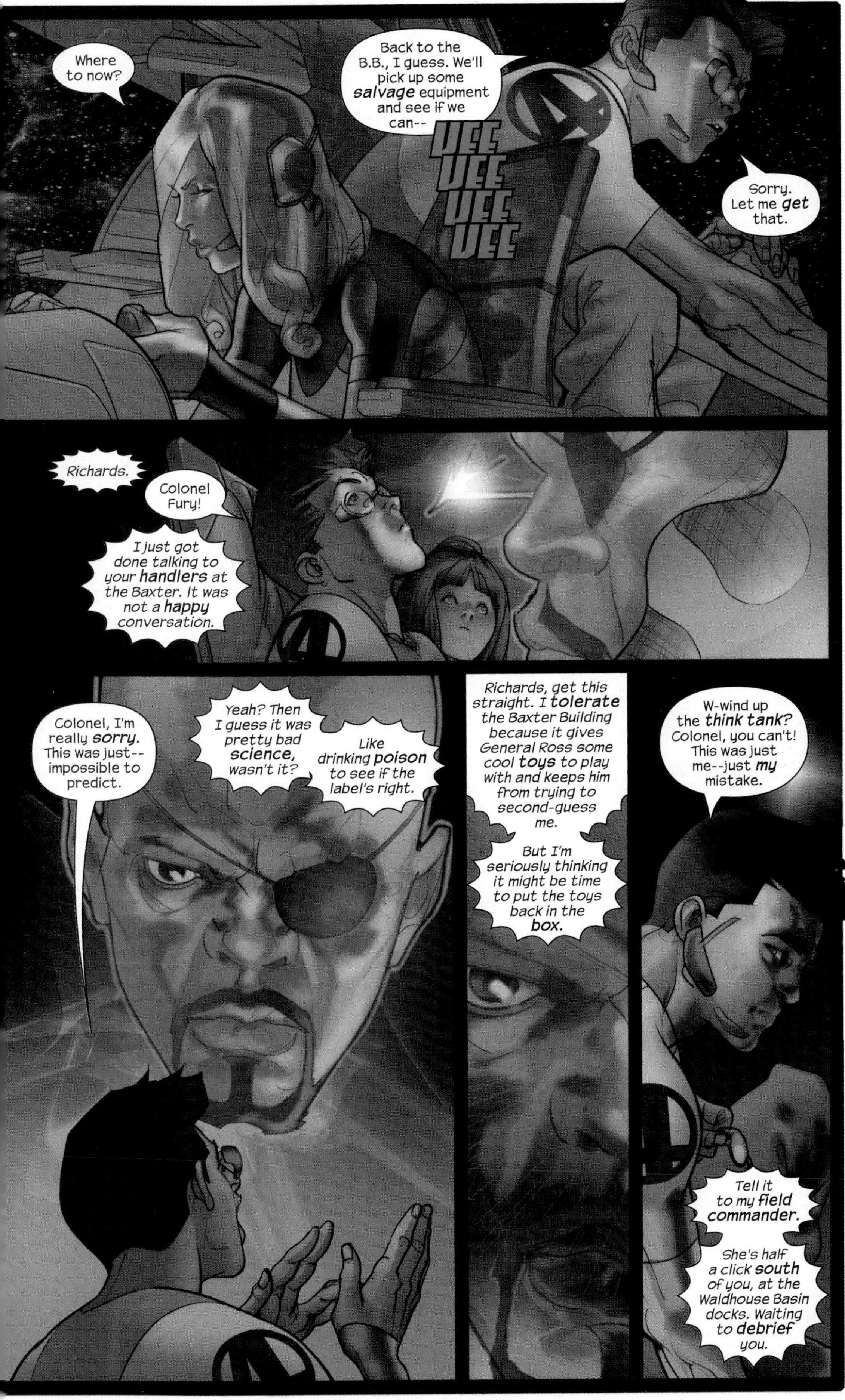
Where to now?
Back to the B.B., I guess. We'll pick up some salvage equipment and see if we can--
VEE VEE VEE VEE
Sorry. Let me get that.
Richards.
Colonel Fury!
I just got done talking to your handlers at the Baxter. It was not a happy conversation.
Colonel, I'm really sorry. This was just--impossible to predict.
Yeah? Then I guess it was pretty bad science, wasn't it?
Like drinking poison to see if the label's right.
Richards, get this straight. I tolerate the Baxter Building because it gives General Ross some cool toys to play with and keeps him from trying to second-guess me.
But I'm seriously thinking it might be time to put the toys back in the box.
W-wind up the think tank? Colonel, you can't! This was just me--just my mistake.
Tell it to my field commander.
She's half a click south of you, at the Waldhouse Basin docks. Waiting to debrief you.

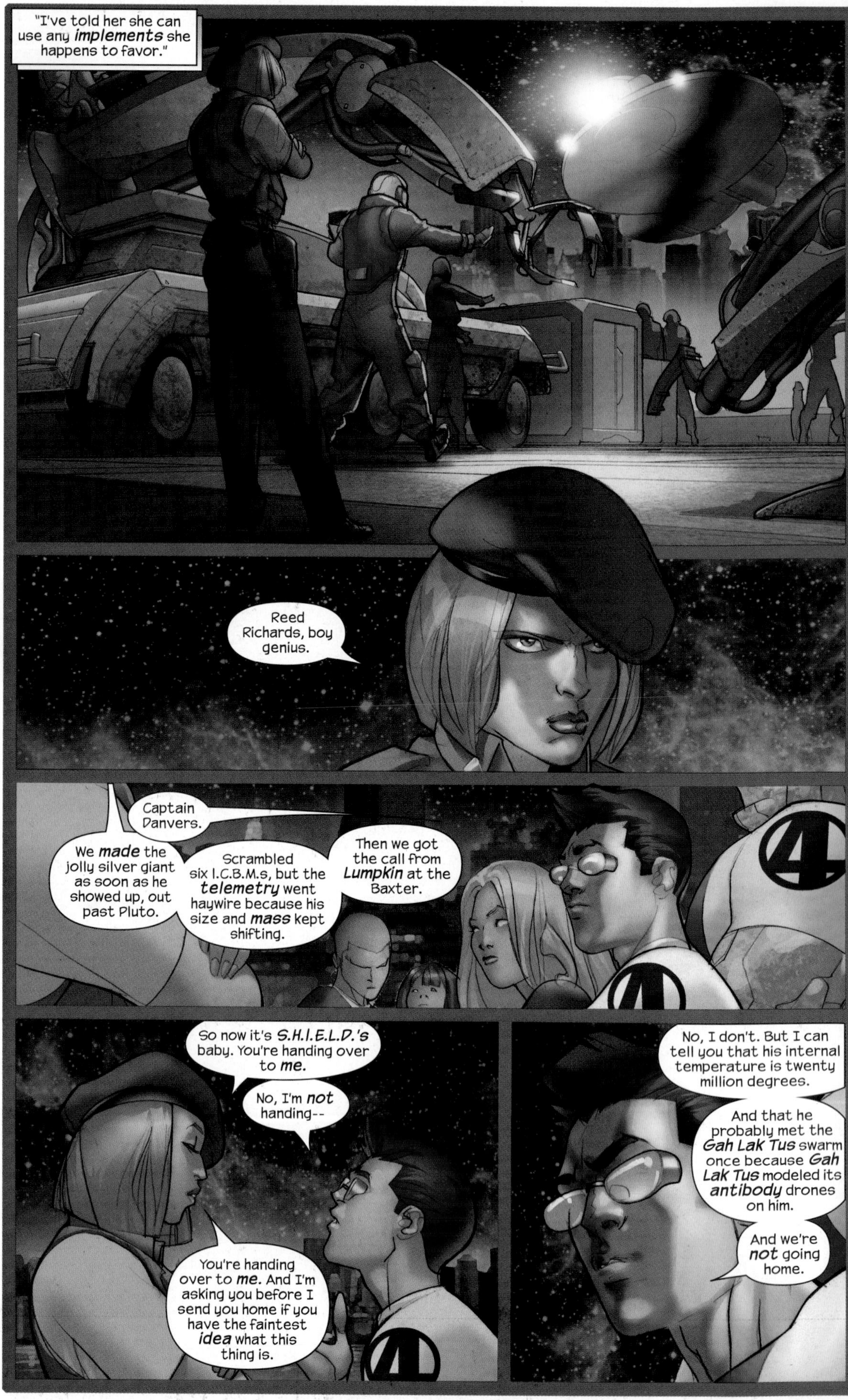
"I've told her she can use any *implements* she happens to favor."
Reed Richards, boy genius.
Captain Danvers.
We *made* the jolly silver giant as soon as he showed up, out past Pluto.
Scrambled six I.C.B.M.s, but the *telemetry* went haywire because his size and *mass* kept shifting.
Then we got the call from *Lumpkin* at the Baxter.
So now it's *S.H.I.E.L.D.'s* baby. You're handing over to *me.*
No, I'm *not* handing--
You're handing over to *me.* And I'm asking you before I send you home if you have the faintest *idea* what this thing is.
No, I don't. But I can tell you that his internal temperature is twenty million degrees.
And that he probably met the *Gah Lak Tus* swarm once because *Gah Lak Tus* modeled its *antibody* drones on him.
And we're *not* going home.

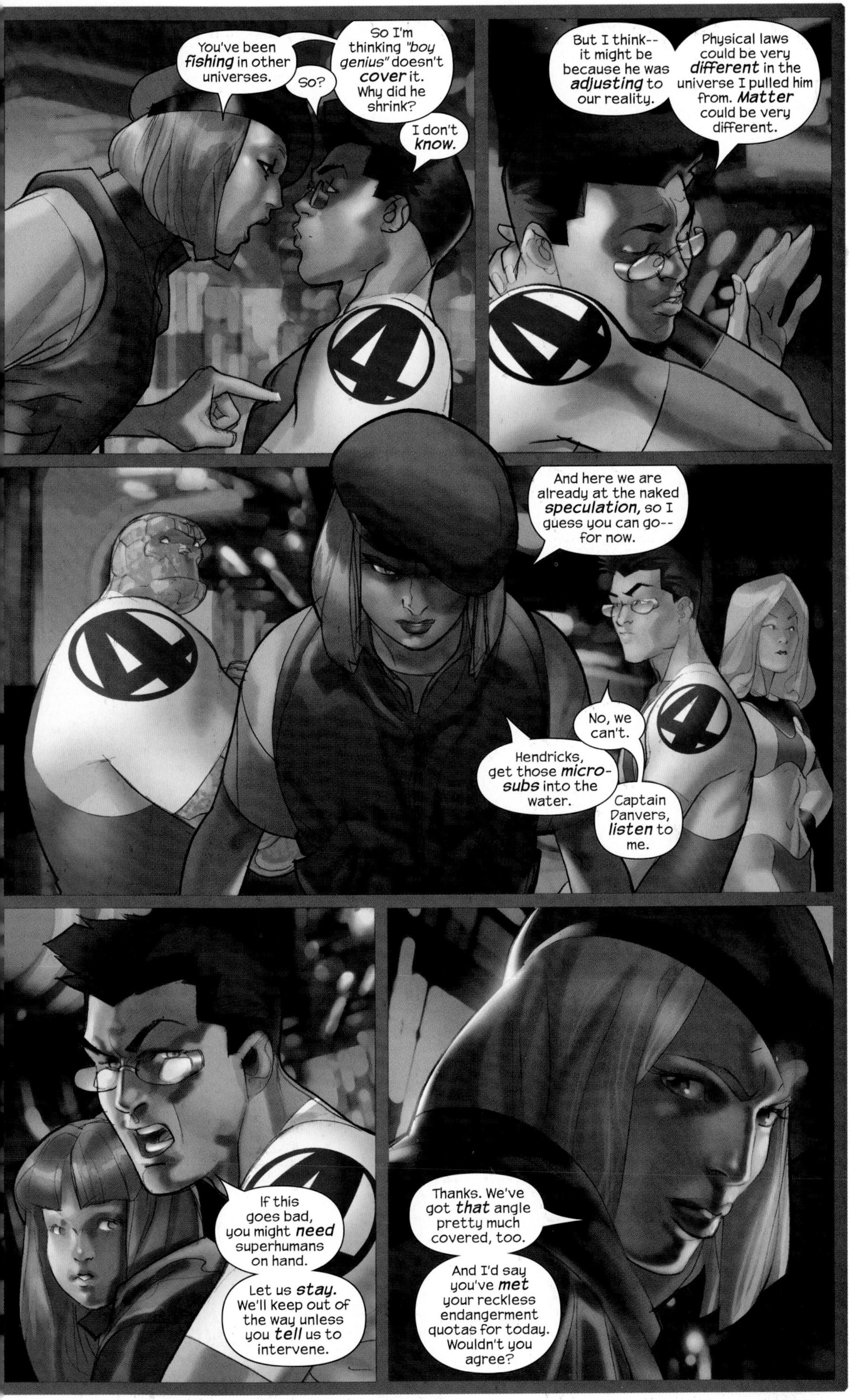
You've been *fishing* in other universes.
So?
So I'm thinking *"boy genius"* doesn't *cover* it. Why did he shrink?
I don't *know.*
But I think--it might be because he was *adjusting* to our reality.
Physical laws could be very *different* in the universe I pulled him from. *Matter* could be very different.
And here we are already at the naked *speculation,* so I guess you can go--for now.
No, we can't.
Hendricks, get those *micro-subs* into the water.
Captain Danvers, *listen* to me.
If this goes bad, you might *need* superhumans on hand.
Let us *stay.* We'll keep out of the way unless you *tell* us to intervene.
Thanks. We've got *that* angle pretty much covered, too.
And I'd say you've *met* your reckless endangerment quotas for today. Wouldn't you agree?

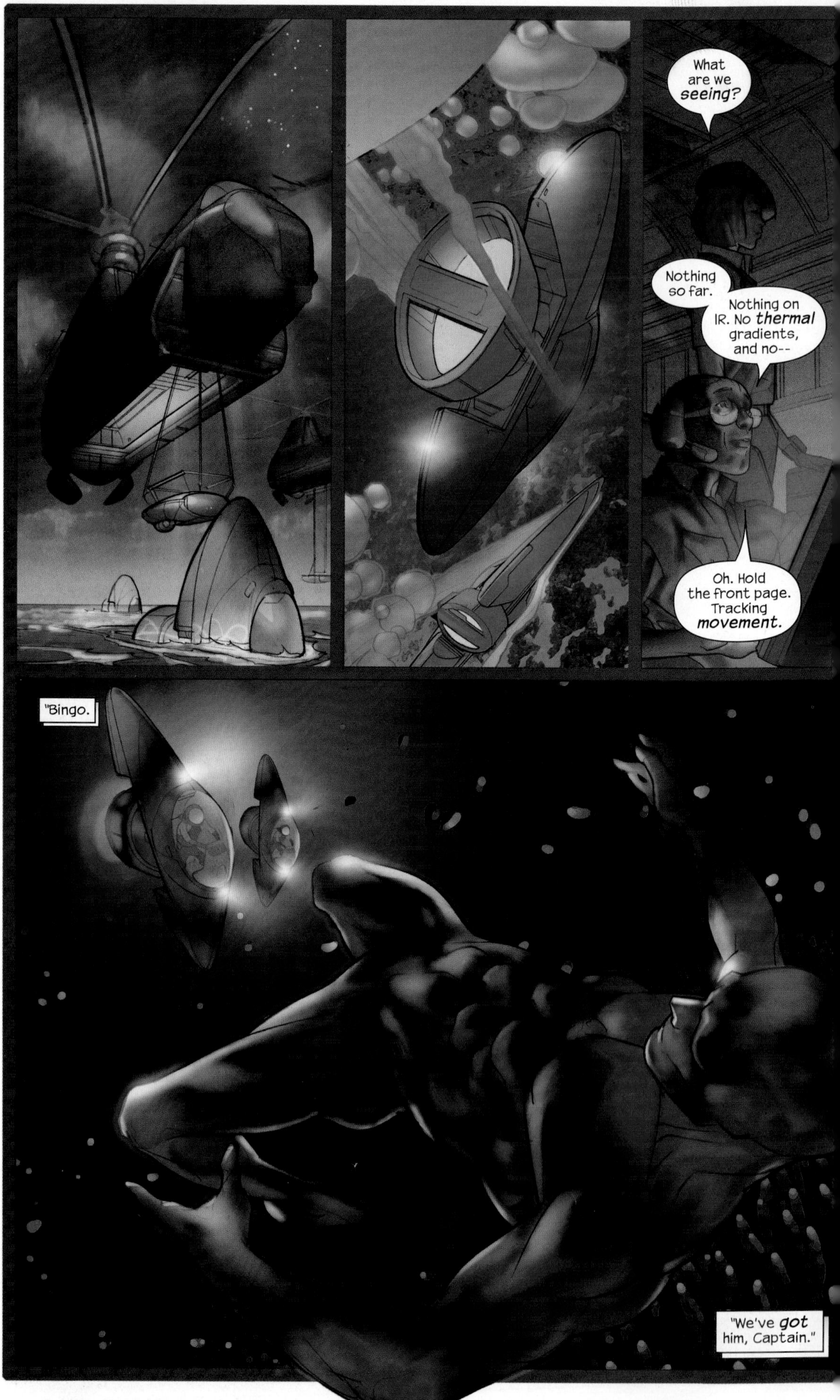
What are we *seeing?*
Nothing so far.
Nothing on IR. No *thermal* gradients, and no--
Oh. Hold the front page. Tracking *movement.*
"Bingo.
"We've *got* him, Captain."

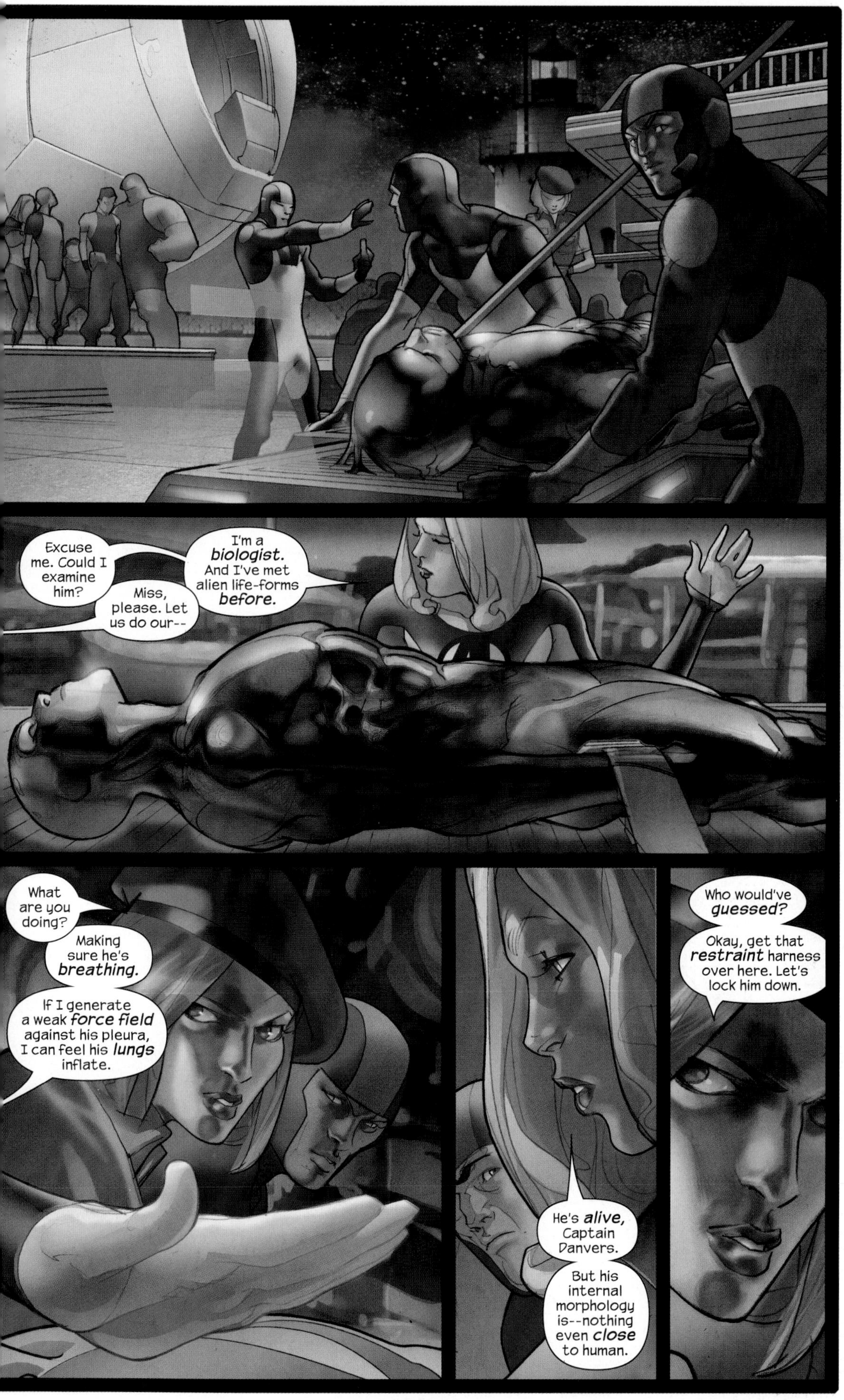
Excuse me. Could I examine him?
Miss, please. Let us do our--
I'm a *biologist.* And I've met alien life-forms *before.*
What are you doing?
Making sure he's *breathing.*
If I generate a weak *force field* against his pleura, I can feel his *lungs* inflate.
He's *alive,* Captain Danvers.
But his internal morphology is--nothing even *close* to human.
Who would've *guessed?*
Okay, get that *restraint* harness over here. Let's lock him down.

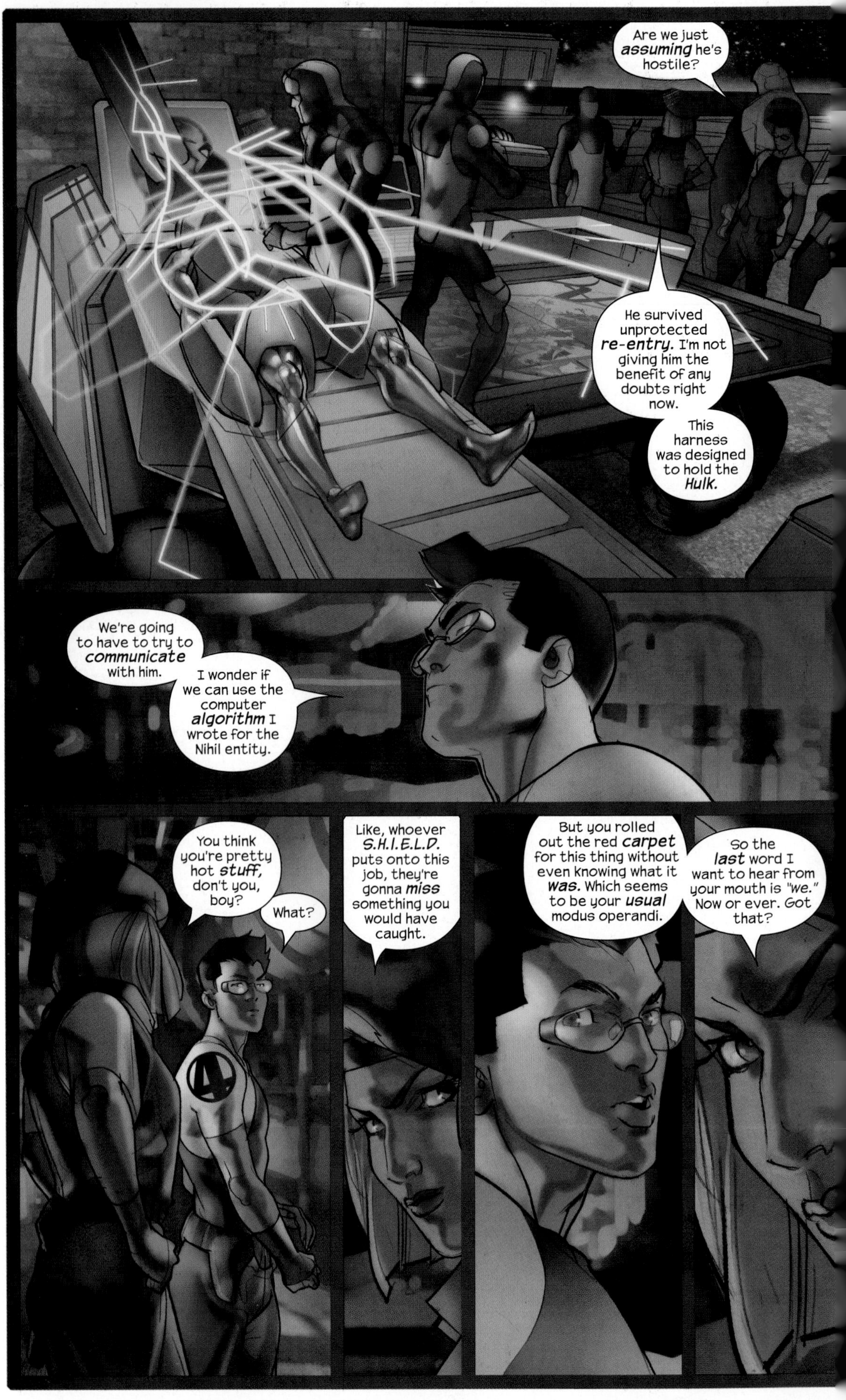

Are we just *assuming* he's hostile?
He survived unprotected *re-entry*. I'm not giving him the benefit of any doubts right now.
This harness was designed to hold the *Hulk*.
We're going to have to try to *communicate* with him.
I wonder if we can use the computer *algorithm* I wrote for the Nihil entity.
You think you're pretty hot *stuff*, don't you, boy?
What?
Like, whoever *S.H.I.E.L.D.* puts onto this job, they're gonna *miss* something you would have caught.
But you rolled out the red *carpet* for this thing without even knowing what it *was*. Which seems to be your *usual* modus operandi.
So the *last* word I want to hear from your mouth is *"we."* Now or ever. Got that?

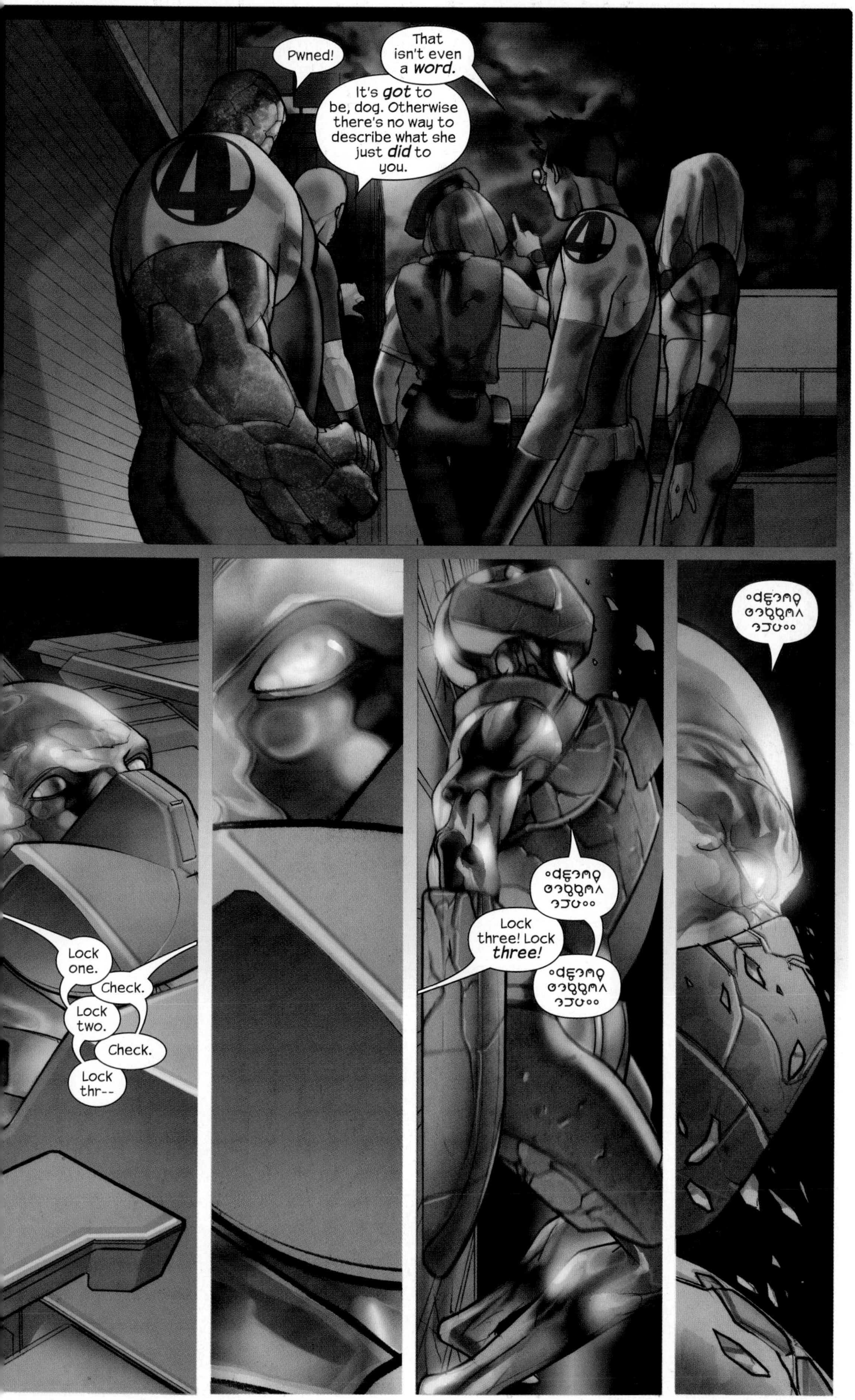
Pwned!
That isn't even a *word.*
It's *got* to be, dog. Otherwise there's no way to describe what she just *did* to you.
Lock one.
Check.
Lock two.
Check.
Lock thr--
Lock three! Lock *three!*

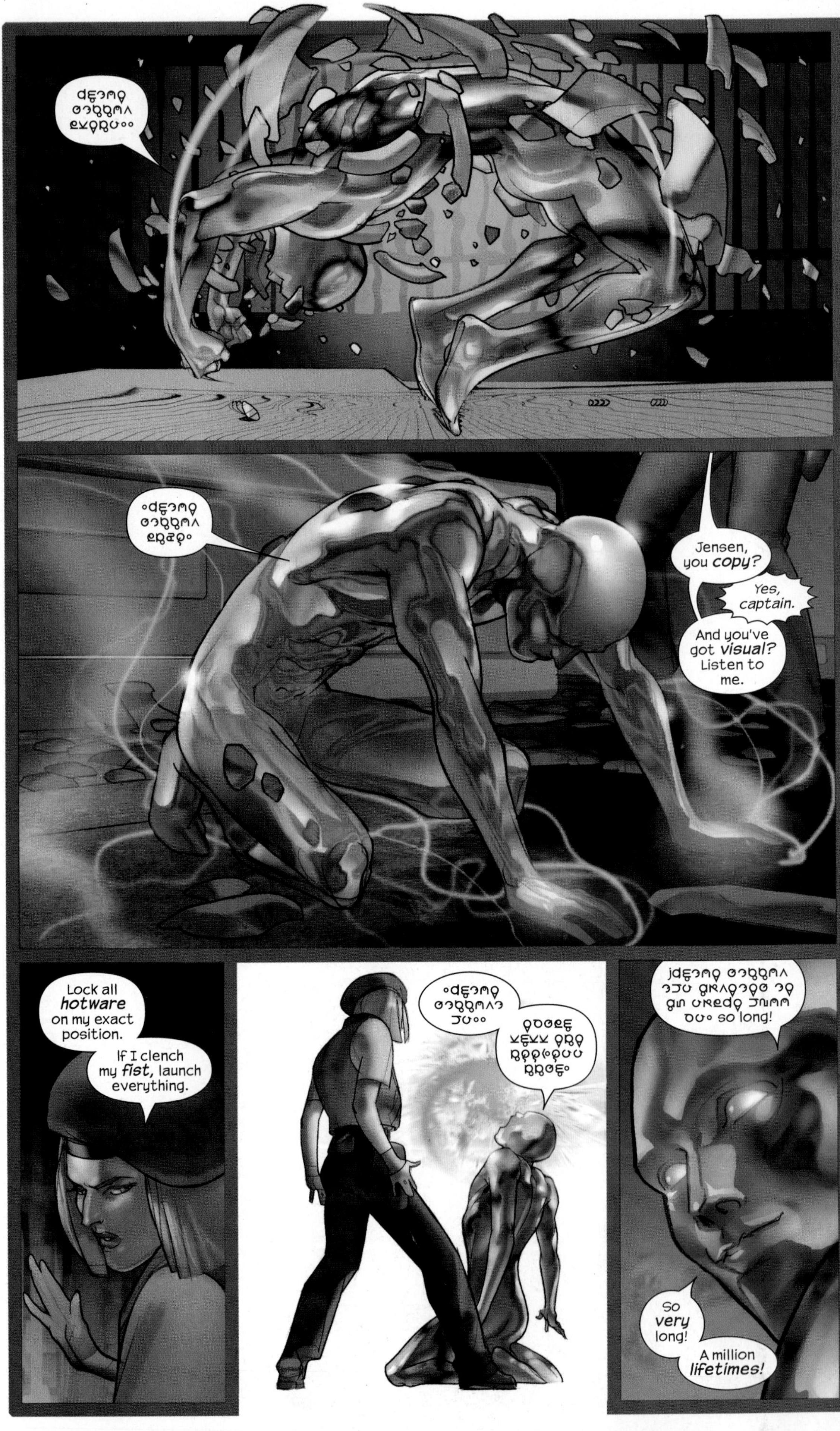

Jensen, you copy?
Yes, captain.
And you've got visual? Listen to me.
Lock all hotware on my exact position.
If I clench my fist, launch everything.
so long!
So very long!
A million lifetimes!

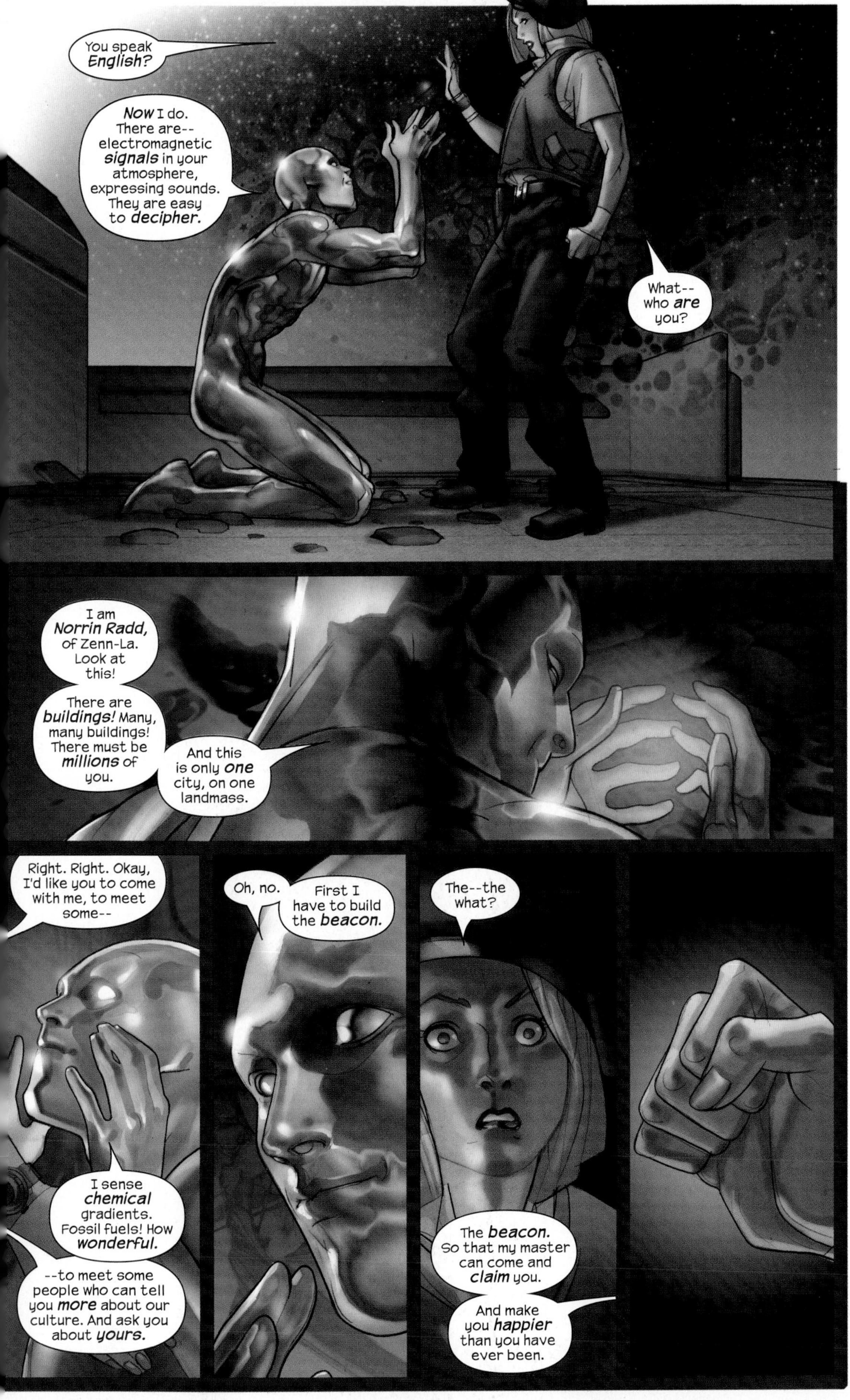
You speak English?
Now I do. There are-- electromagnetic signals in your atmosphere, expressing sounds. They are easy to decipher.
What-- who are you?
I am Norrin Radd, of Zenn-La. Look at this!
There are buildings! Many, many buildings! There must be millions of you.
And this is only one city, on one landmass.
Right. Right. Okay, I'd like you to come with me, to meet some--
I sense chemical gradients. Fossil fuels! How wonderful.
--to meet some people who can tell you more about our culture. And ask you about yours.
Oh, no.
First I have to build the beacon.
The--the what?
The beacon. So that my master can come and claim you.
And make you happier than you have ever been.

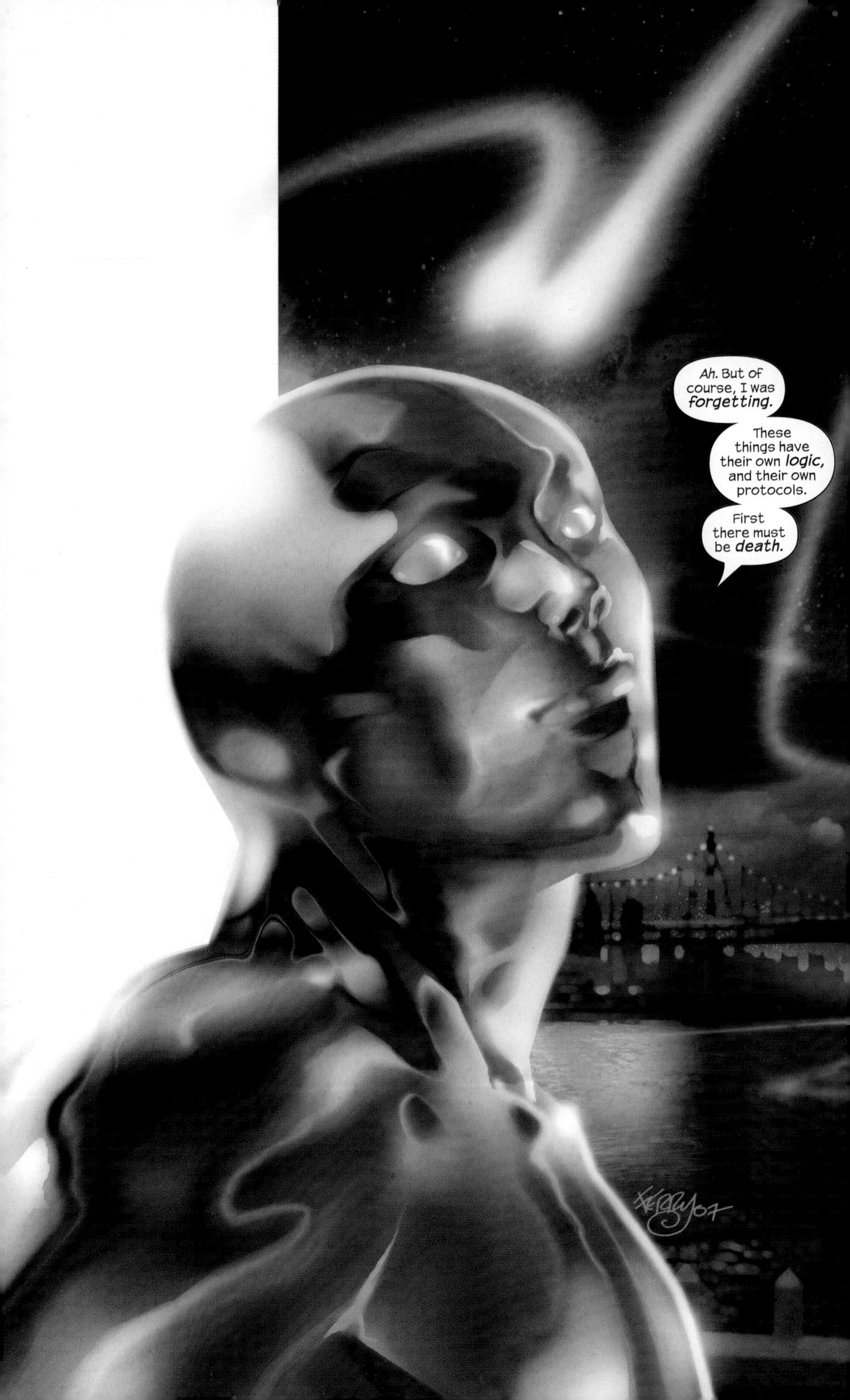
Ah. But of course, I was ***forgetting.***
These things have their own ***logic,*** and their own protocols.
First there must be ***death.***

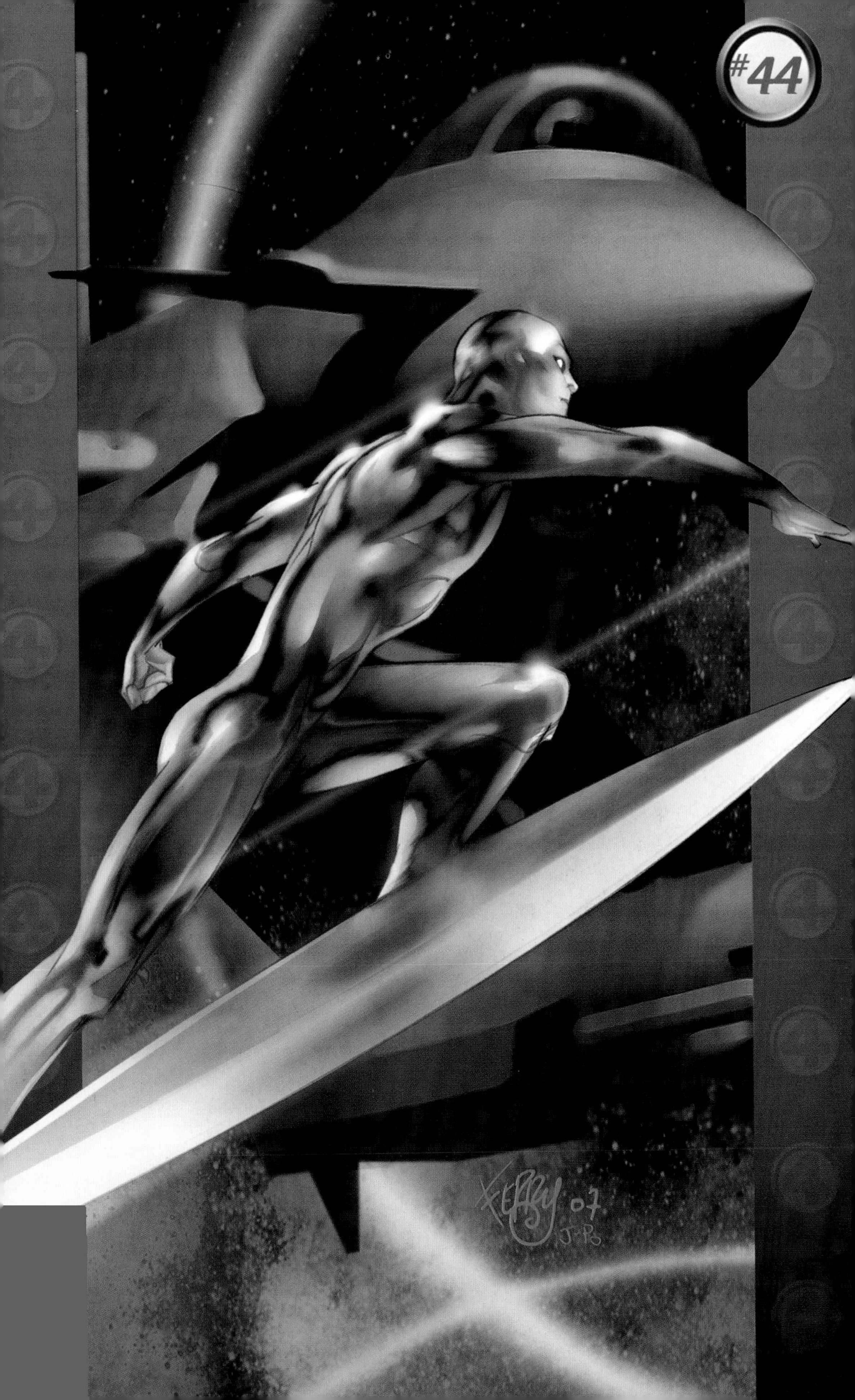
#44

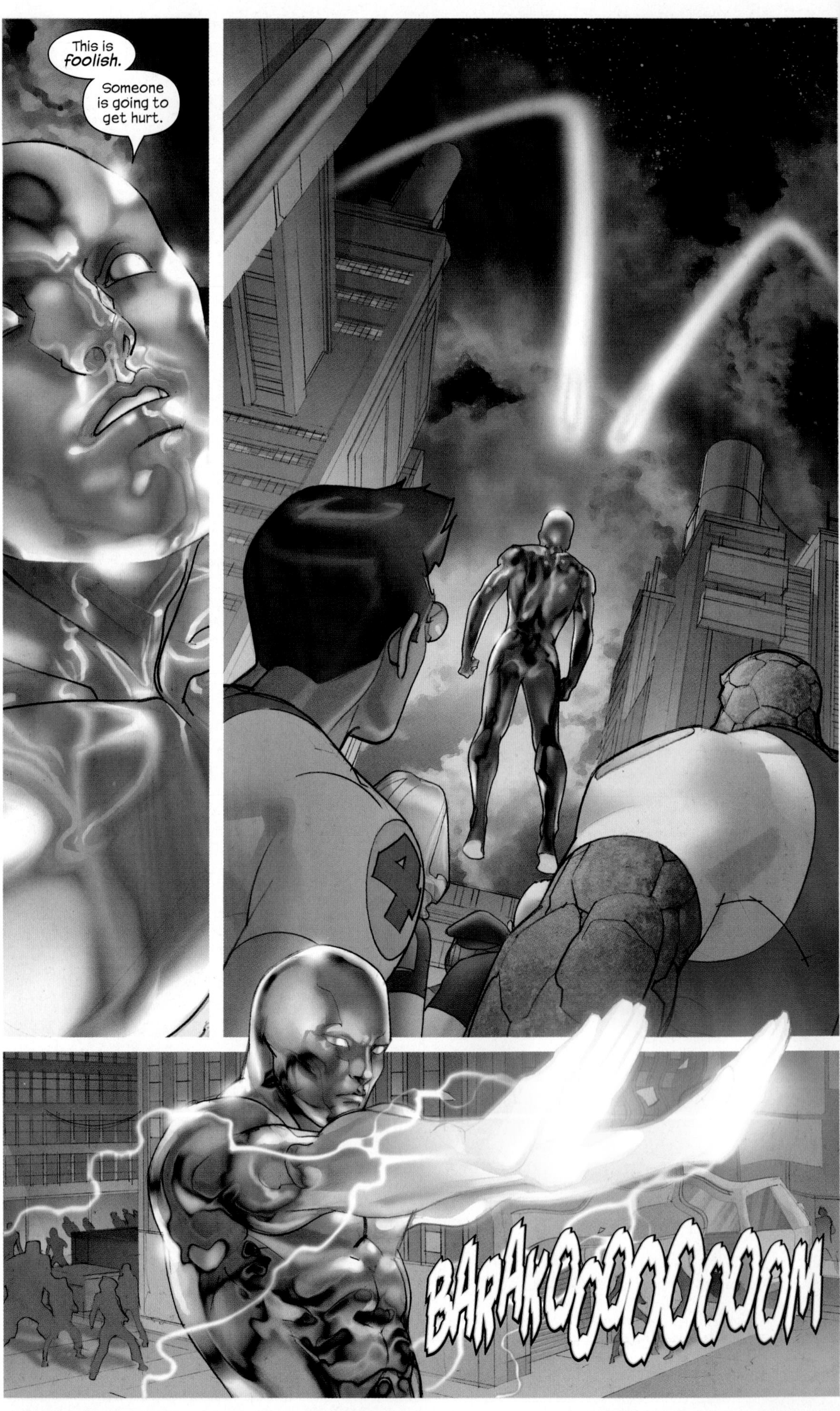
This is foolish.
Someone is going to get hurt.
BARAKOOOOOOOOM

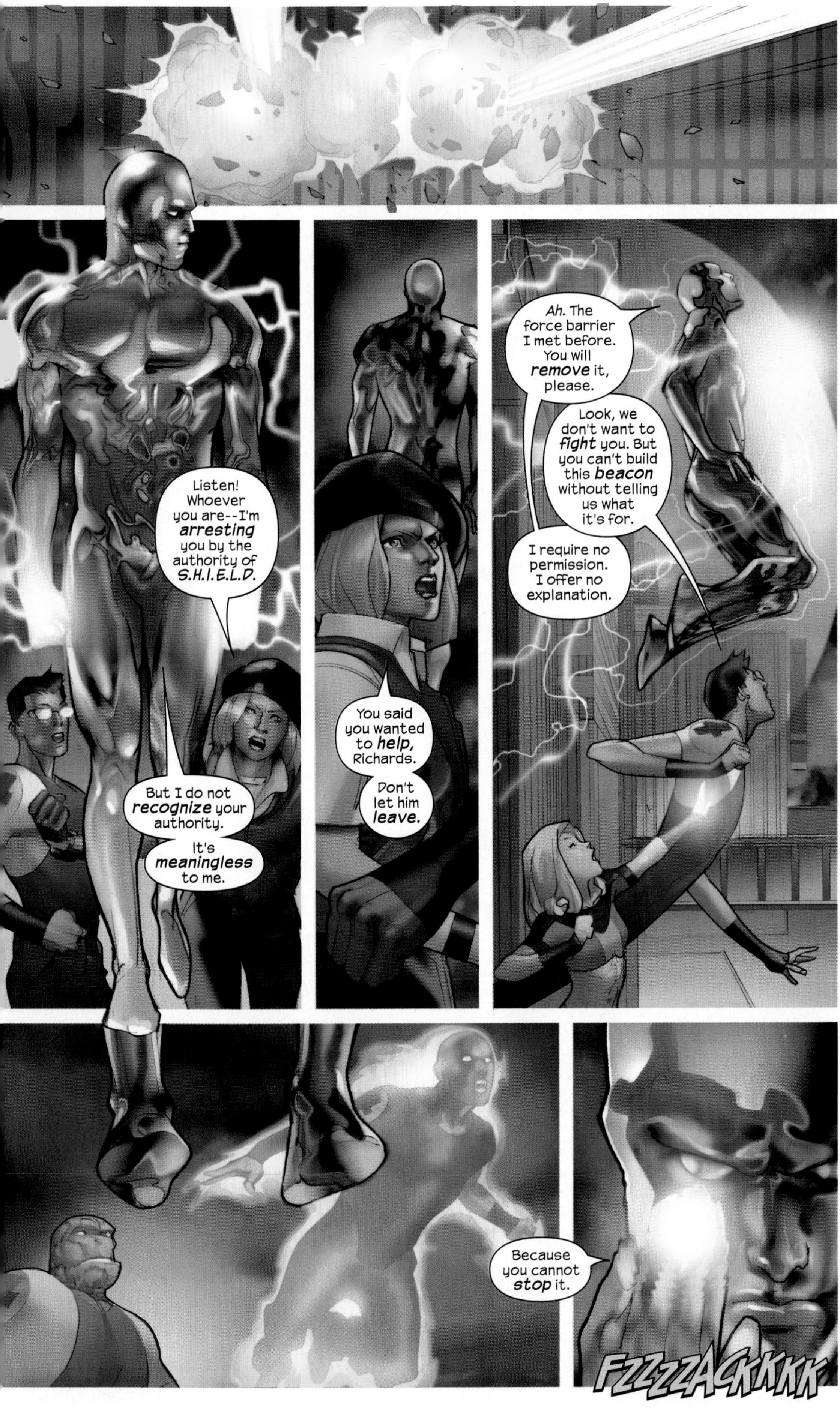
Listen! Whoever you are--I'm arresting you by the authority of S.H.I.E.L.D.
But I do not recognize your authority.
It's meaningless to me.
You said you wanted to help, Richards.
Don't let him leave.
Ah. The force barrier I met before. You will remove it, please.
Look, we don't want to fight you. But you can't build this beacon without telling us what it's for.
I require no permission. I offer no explanation.
Because you cannot stop it.
FZZZZACKKKK

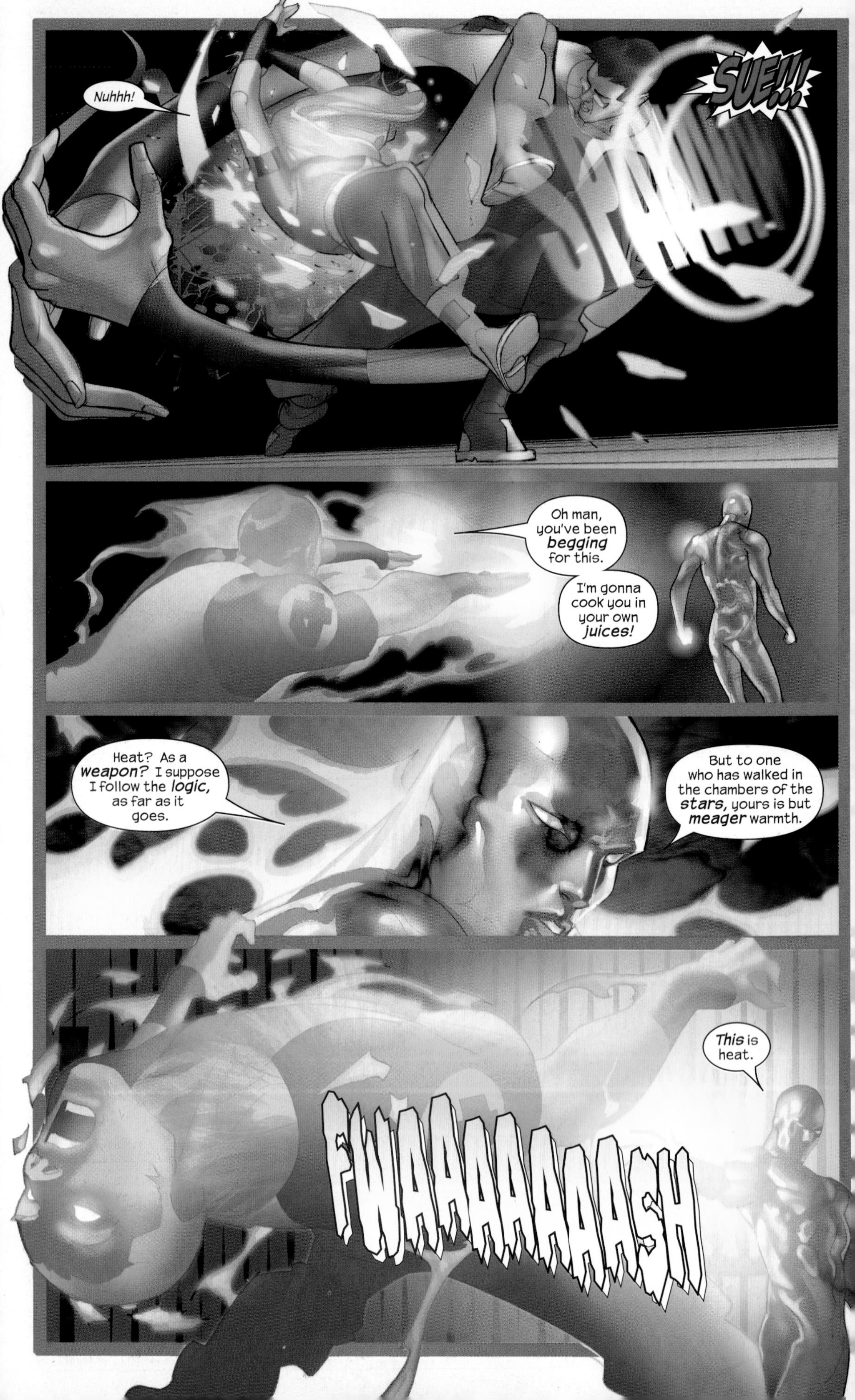
Nuhhh!
SUE!!!
Oh man, you've been *begging* for this.
I'm gonna cook you in your own *juices!*
Heat? As a *weapon?* I suppose I follow the *logic,* as far as it goes.
But to one who has walked in the chambers of the *stars,* yours is but *meager* warmth.
This is heat.
FWAAAAAAAASH

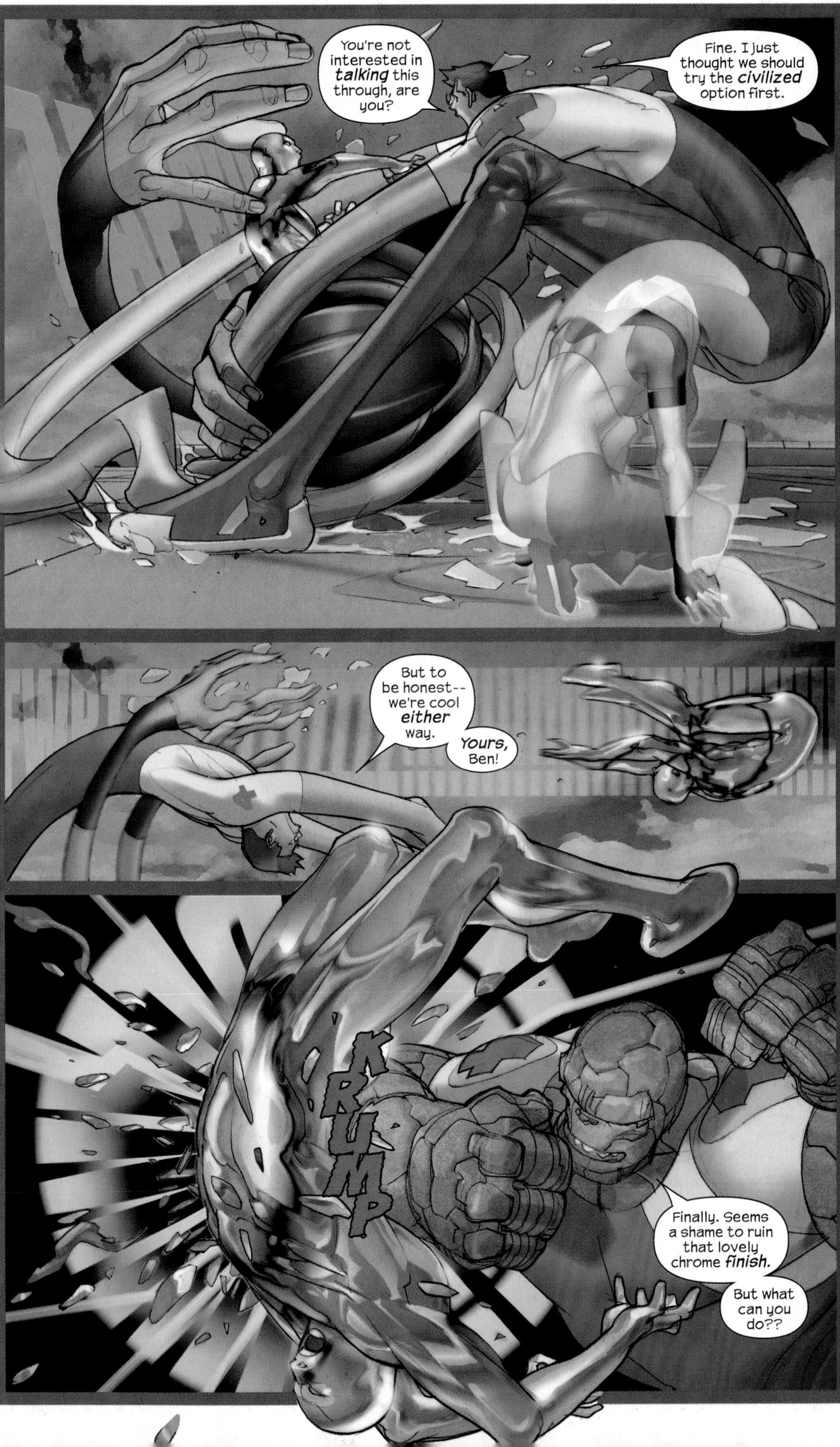
You're not interested in talking this through, are you?
Fine. I just thought we should try the civilized option first.
But to be honest-- we're cool either way.
Yours, Ben!
KRUMP
Finally. Seems a shame to ruin that lovely chrome finish.
But what can you do??

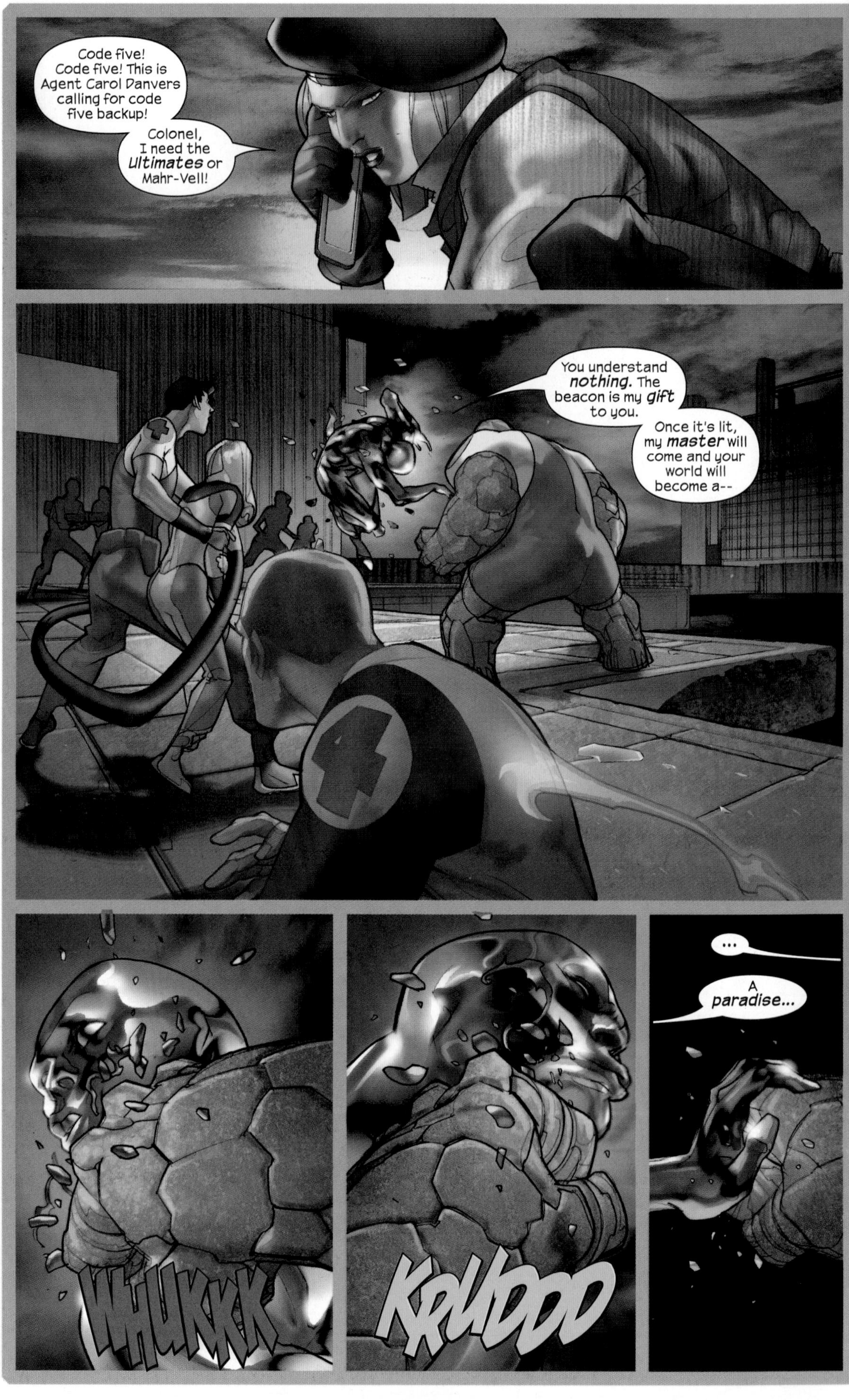
Code five! Code five! This is Agent Carol Danvers calling for code five backup!
Colonel, I need the *Ultimates* or Mahr-Vell!
You understand *nothing.* The beacon is my *gift* to you.
Once it's lit, my *master* will come and your world will become a--
WHUKKK
KRUDDD
...
A *paradise...*

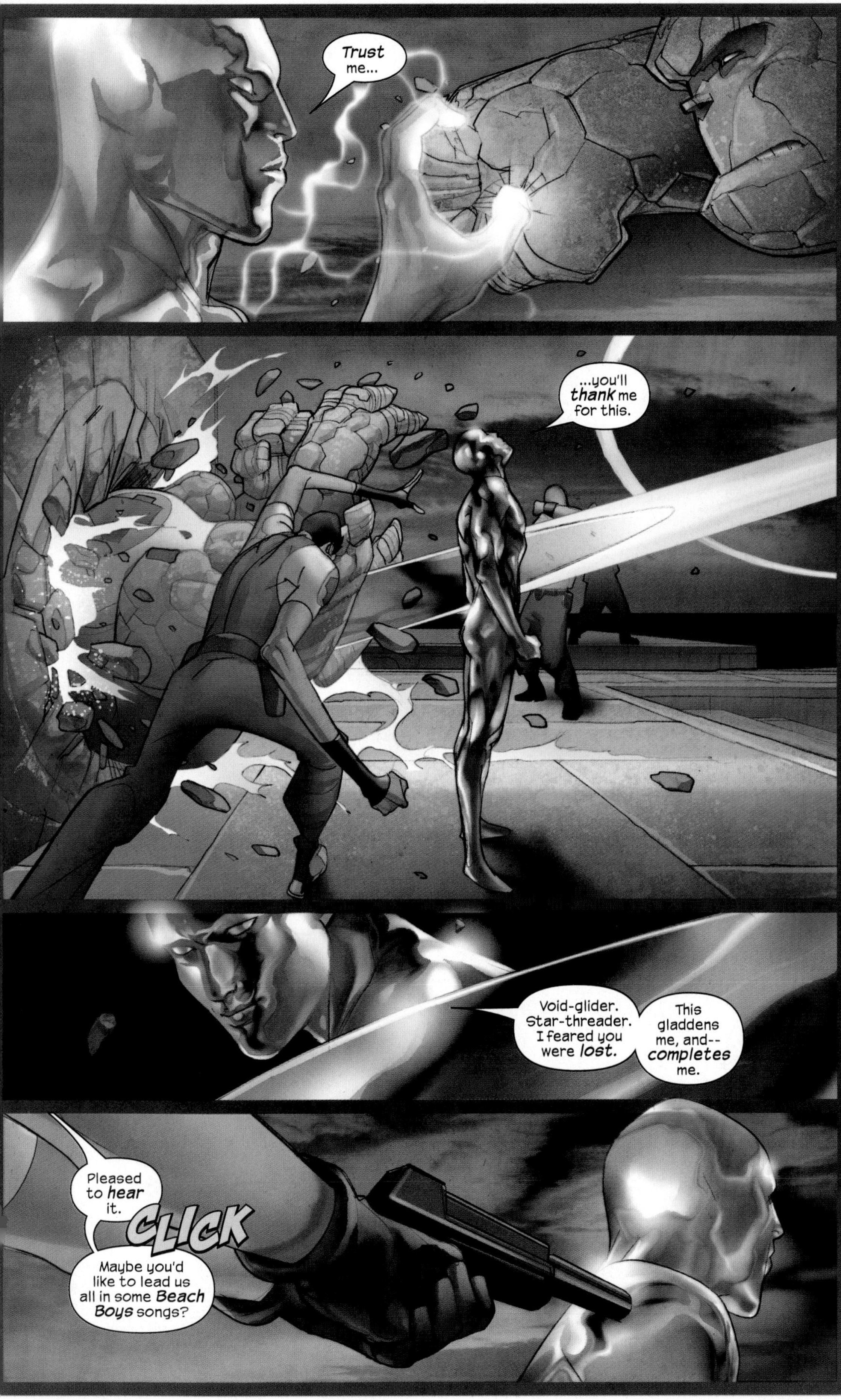
Trust me...
...you'll thank me for this.
Void-glider. Star-threader. I feared you were lost.
This gladdens me, and-- completes me.
Pleased to hear it.
CLICK
Maybe you'd like to lead us all in some Beach Boys songs?

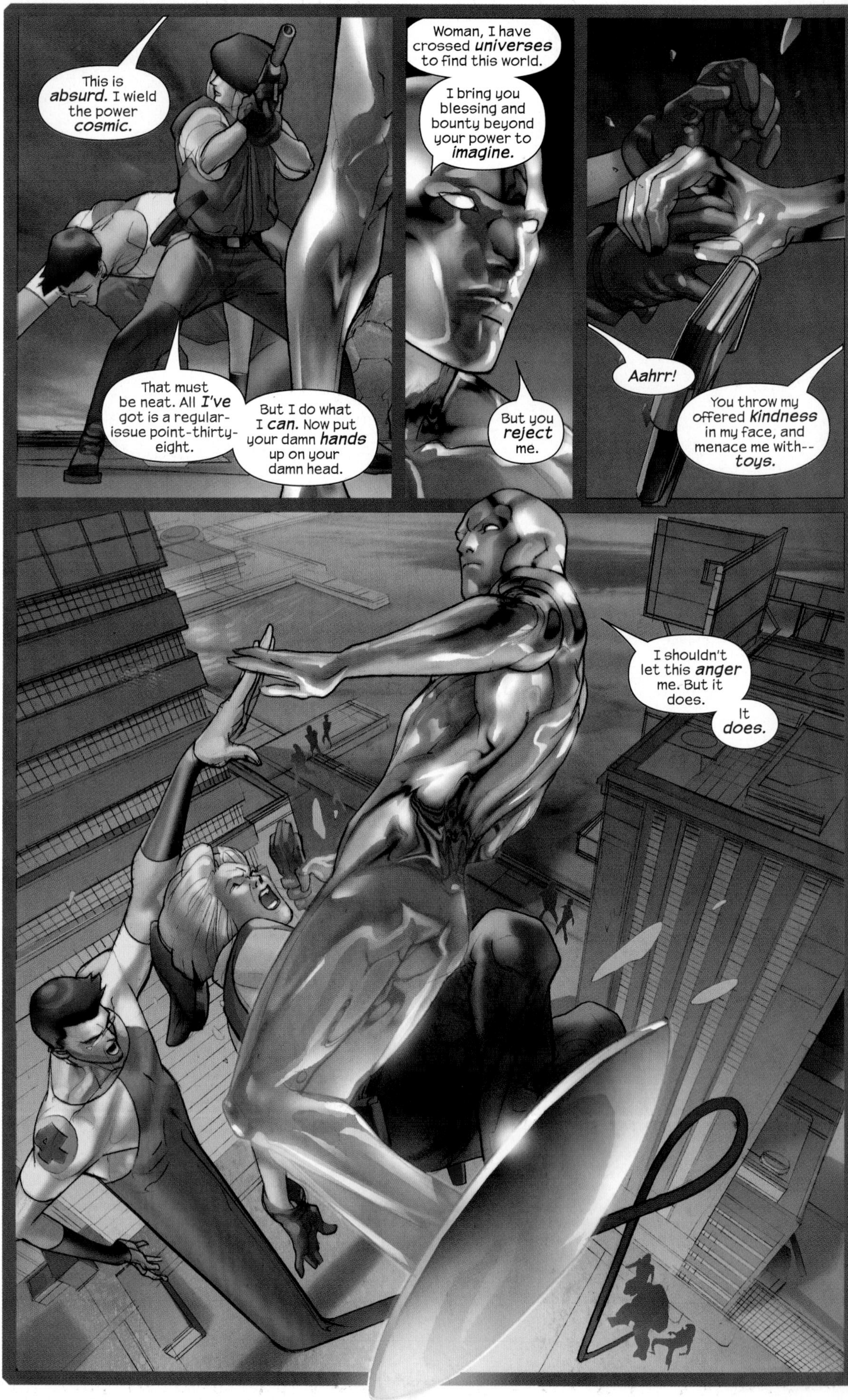
This is absurd. I wield the power cosmic.
That must be neat. All I've got is a regular-issue point-thirty-eight.
But I do what I can. Now put your damn hands up on your damn head.
Woman, I have crossed universes to find this world.
I bring you blessing and bounty beyond your power to imagine.
But you reject me.
Aahrr!
You throw my offered kindness in my face, and menace me with-- toys.
I shouldn't let this anger me. But it does.
It does.

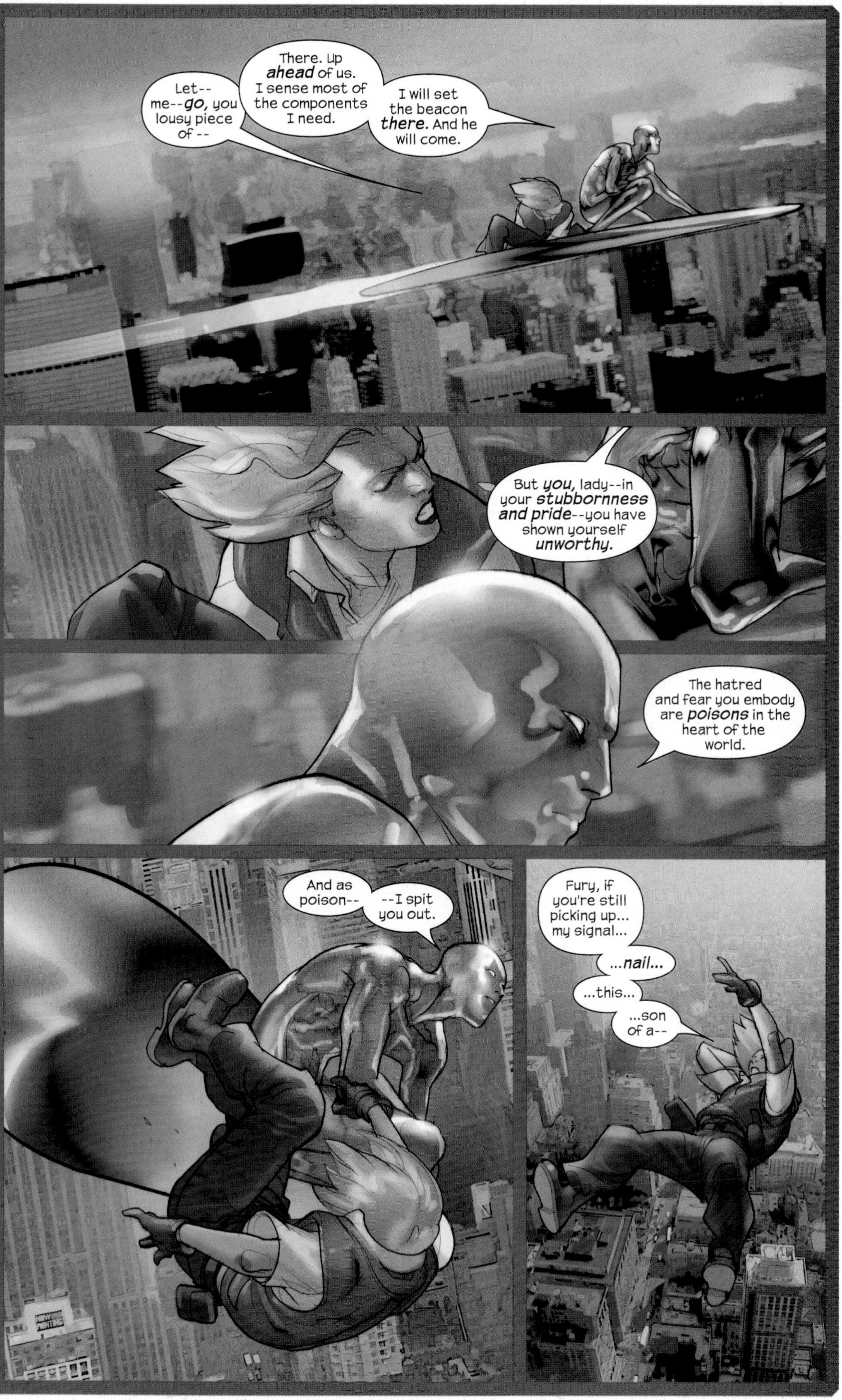
Let-- me--go, you lousy piece of --
There. Up ahead of us. I sense most of the components I need.
I will set the beacon there. And he will come.
But you, lady--in your stubbornness and pride--you have shown yourself unworthy.
The hatred and fear you embody are poisons in the heart of the world.
And as poison--
--I spit you out.
Fury, if you're still picking up... my signal...
...nail...
...this...
...son of a--

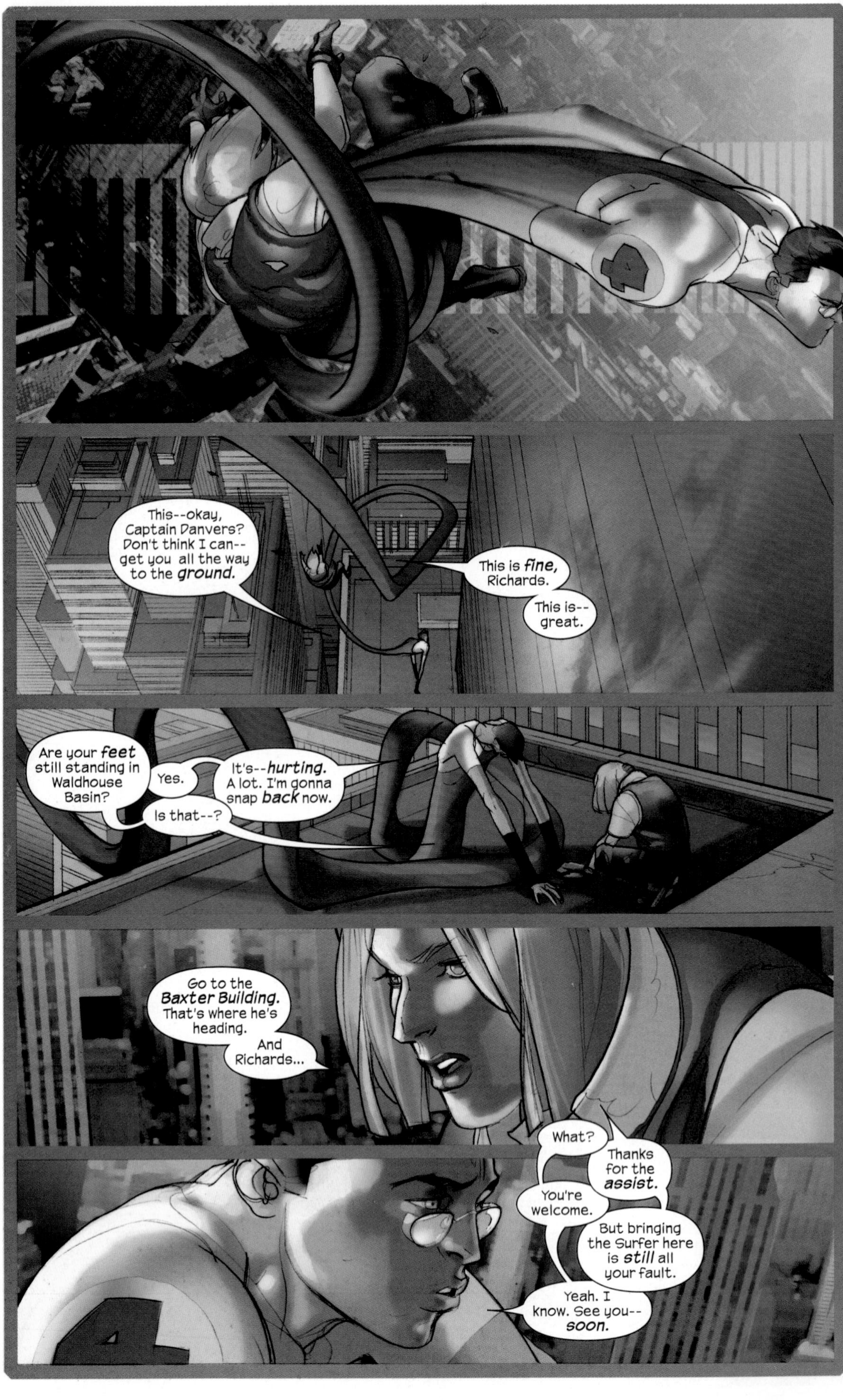
This--okay, Captain Danvers? Don't think I can--get you all the way to the ground.
This is fine, Richards.
This is--great.
Are your feet still standing in Waldhouse Basin?
Yes.
Is that--?
It's--hurting. A lot. I'm gonna snap back now.
Go to the Baxter Building. That's where he's heading.
And Richards...
What?
Thanks for the assist.
You're welcome.
But bringing the Surfer here is still all your fault.
Yeah. I know. See you--soon.

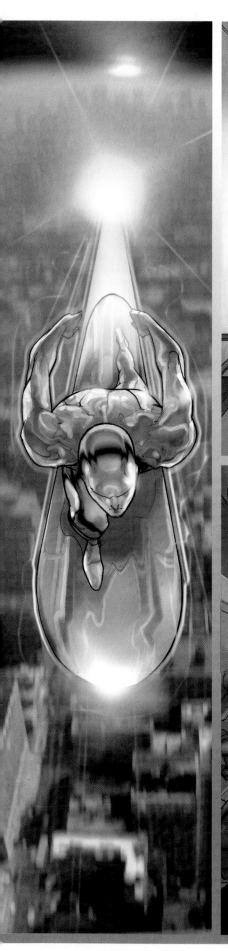

Lieutenant Lumpkin, we've got *incoming,* and it's--

SHOOOOOM

Oh God, he's here! He's *here!*

Unthinking *violence,* yet again.

Master, this world needs you more than I could have *guessed.*

And it *will* have you.

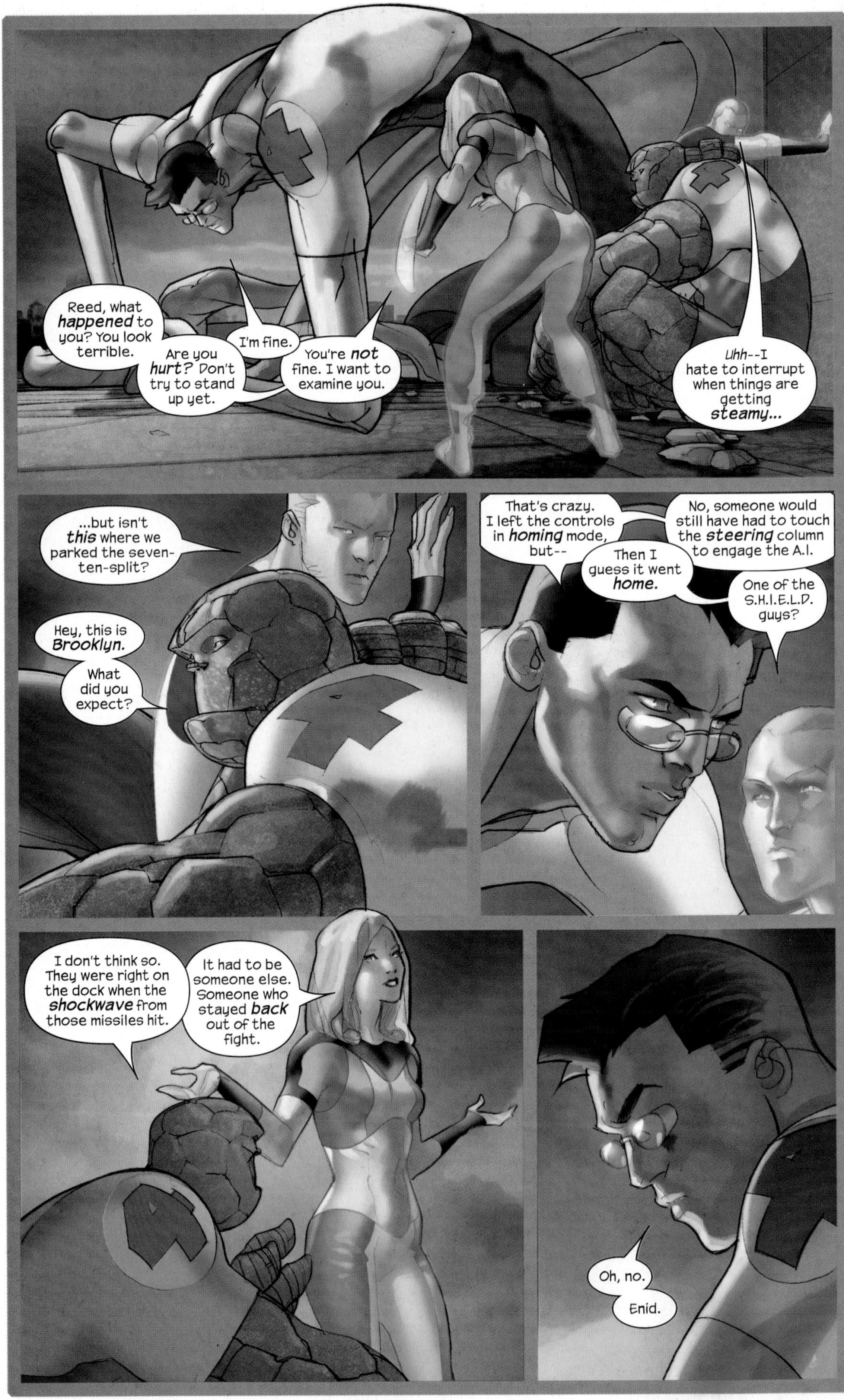
Reed, what happened to you? You look terrible.
I'm fine.
Are you hurt? Don't try to stand up yet.
You're not fine. I want to examine you.
Uhh--I hate to interrupt when things are getting steamy...
...but isn't this where we parked the seven-ten-split?
Hey, this is Brooklyn.
What did you expect?
That's crazy. I left the controls in homing mode, but--
No, someone would still have had to touch the steering column to engage the A.I.
Then I guess it went home.
One of the S.H.I.E.L.D. guys?
I don't think so. They were right on the dock when the shockwave from those missiles hit.
It had to be someone else. Someone who stayed back out of the fight.
Oh, no.
Enid.

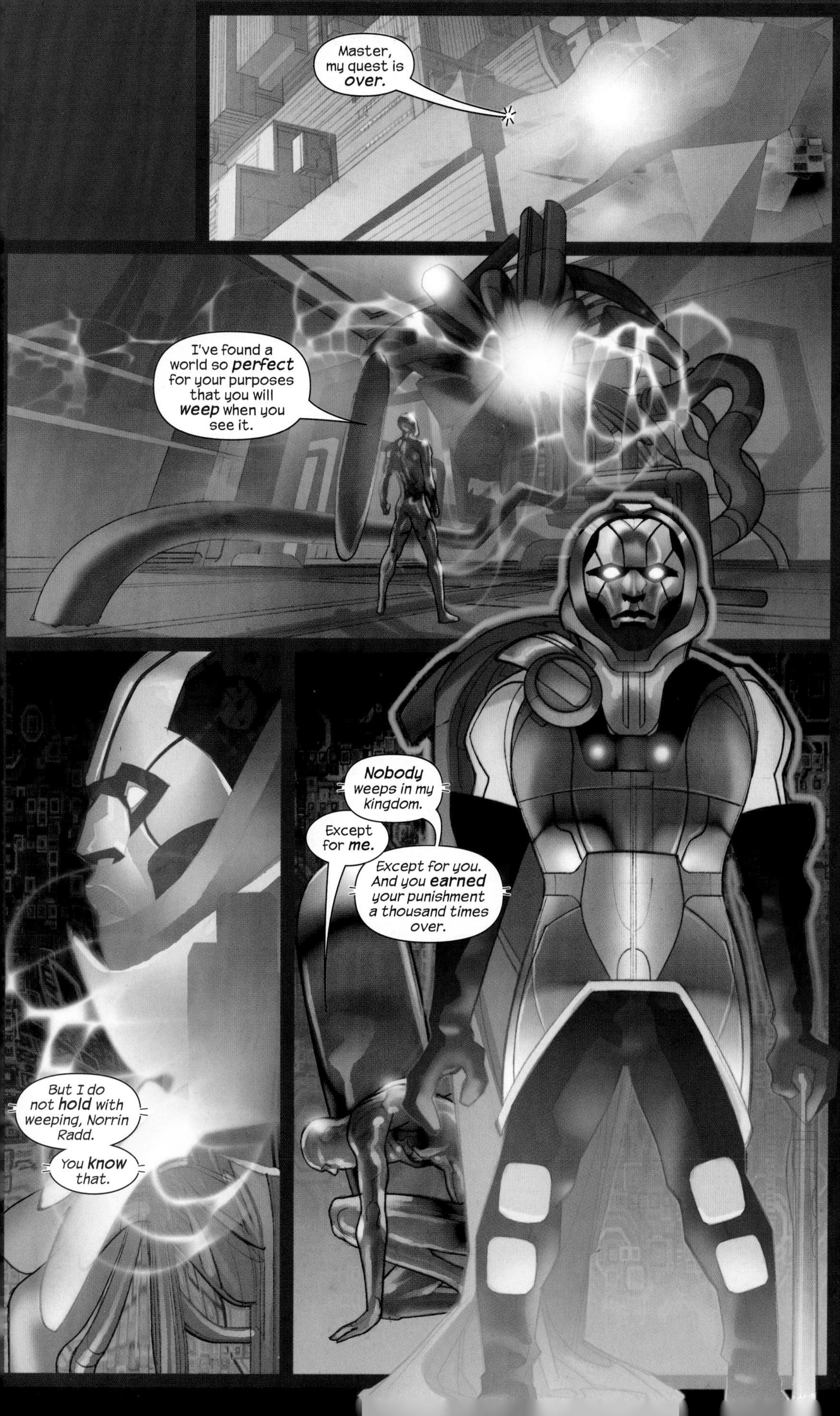
Master, my quest is over.
I've found a world so perfect for your purposes that you will weep when you see it.
But I do not hold with weeping, Norrin Radd.
You know that.
Nobody weeps in my kingdom.
Except for me.
Except for you. And you earned your punishment a thousand times over.

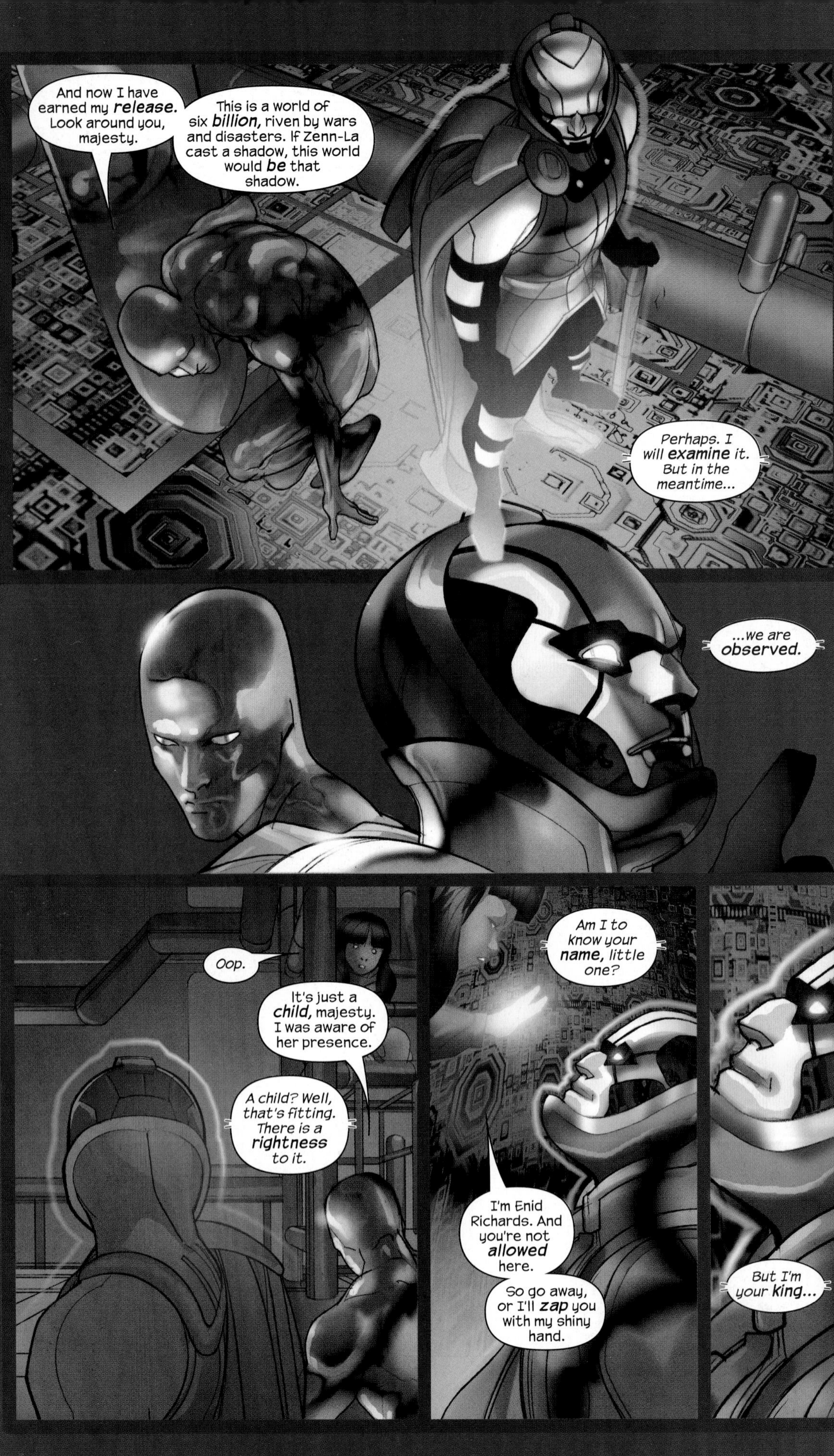

And now I have earned my **release.** Look around you, majesty.
This is a world of six **billion,** riven by wars and disasters. If Zenn-La cast a shadow, this world would **be** that shadow.
Perhaps. I will **examine** it. But in the meantime...
...we are **observed.**
Oop.
It's just a **child,** majesty. I was aware of her presence.
A child? Well, that's fitting. There is a **rightness** to it.
Am I to know your **name,** little one?
I'm Enid Richards. And you're not **allowed** here.
So go away, or I'll **zap** you with my shiny hand.
But I'm your **king...**

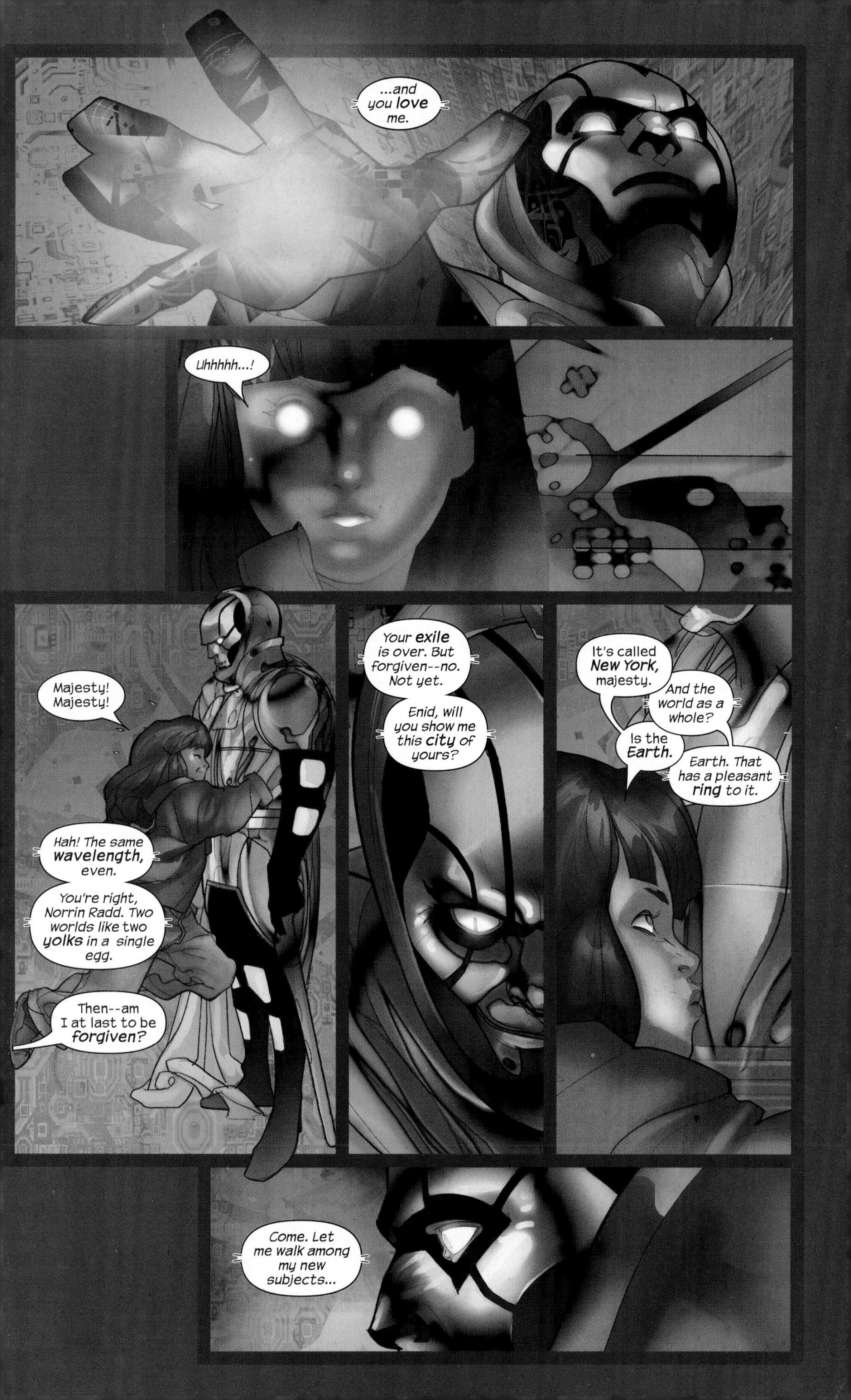
...and you love me.
Uhhhhh...!
Majesty! Majesty!
Hah! The same wavelength, even.
You're right, Norrin Radd. Two worlds like two yolks in a single egg.
Then--am I at last to be forgiven?
Your exile is over. But forgiven--no. Not yet.
Enid, will you show me this city of yours?
It's called New York, majesty.
And the world as a whole?
Is the Earth.
Earth. That has a pleasant ring to it.
Come. Let me walk among my new subjects...

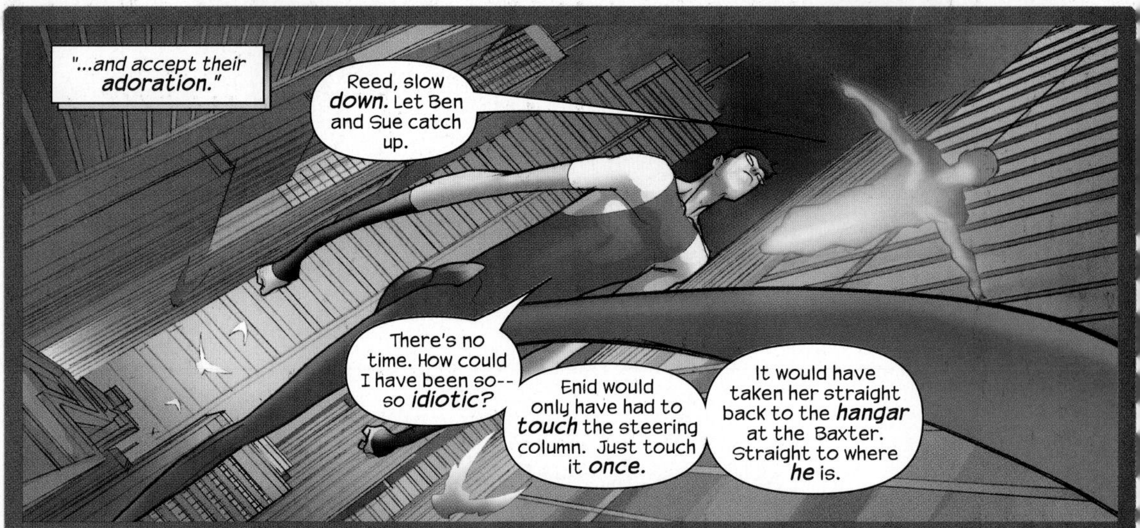
"...and accept their adoration."
Reed, slow down. Let Ben and Sue catch up.
There's no time. How could I have been so-- so idiotic?
Enid would only have had to touch the steering column. Just touch it once.
It would have taken her straight back to the hangar at the Baxter. Straight to where he is.

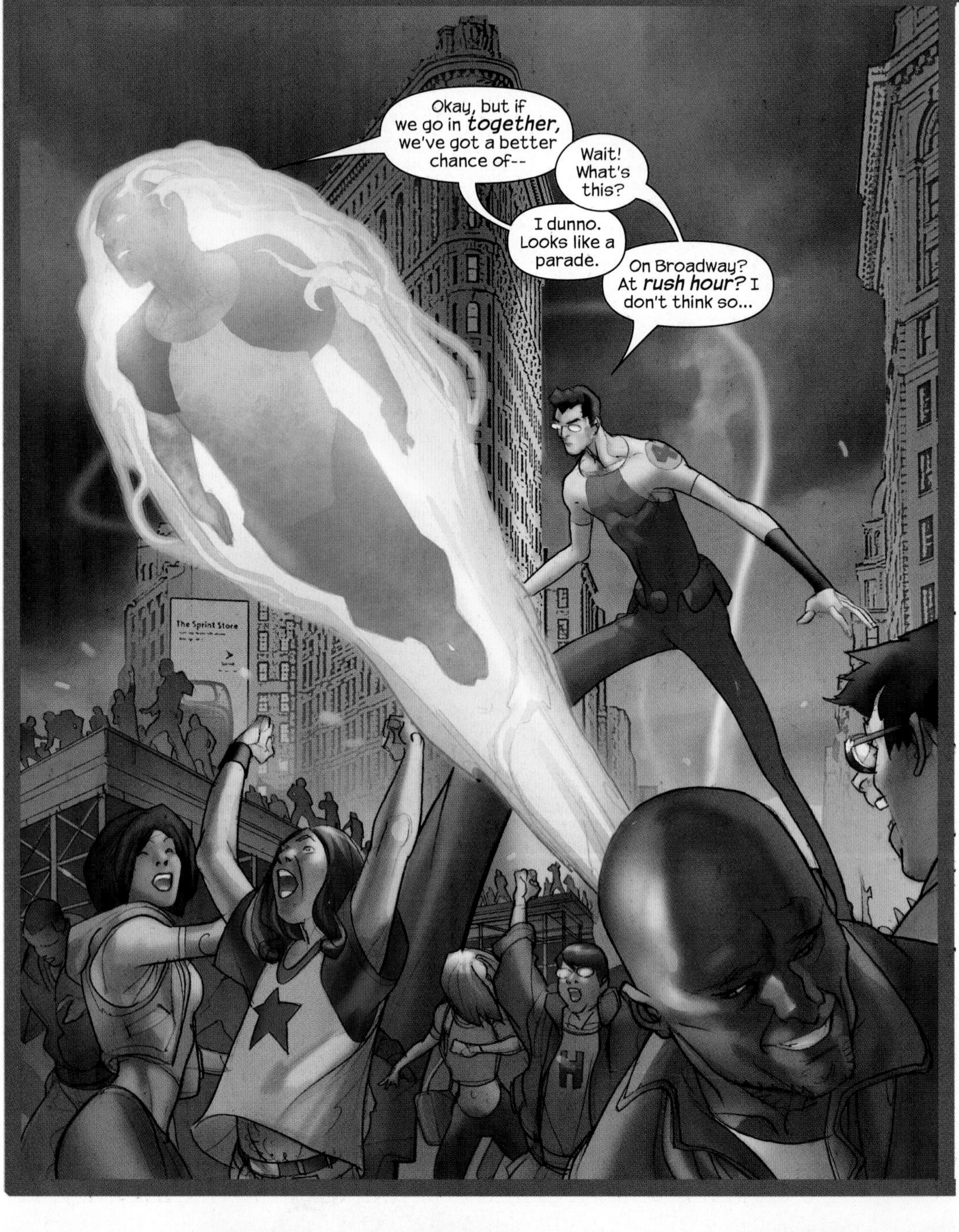
Okay, but if we go in together, we've got a better chance of--
Wait! What's this?
I dunno. Looks like a parade.
On Broadway? At rush hour? I don't think so...
The Sprint Store

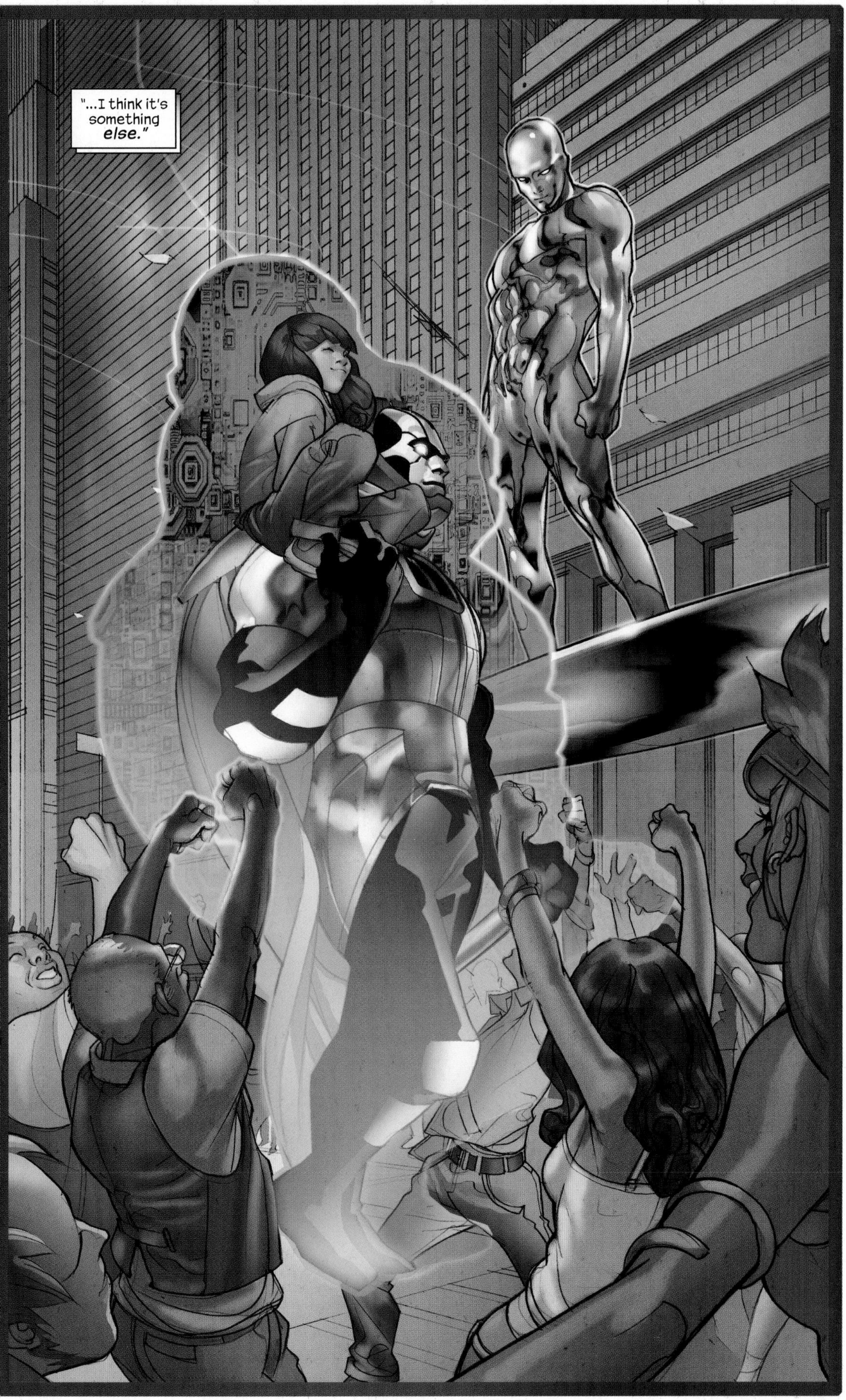
"...I think it's something *else.*"

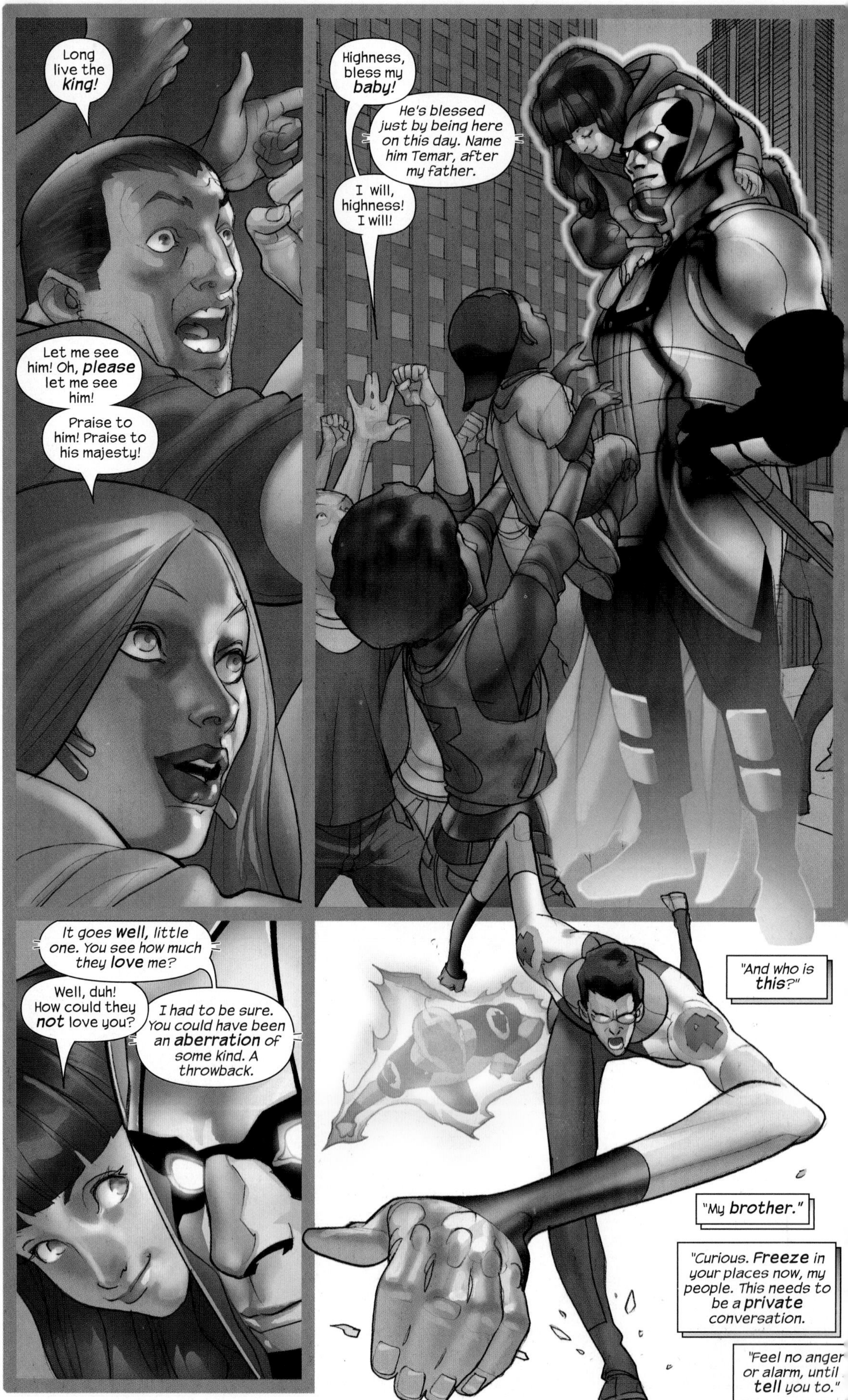

Long live the king!
Let me see him! Oh, please let me see him!
Praise to him! Praise to his majesty!
Highness, bless my baby!
He's blessed just by being here on this day. Name him Temar, after my father.
I will, highness! I will!
It goes well, little one. You see how much they love me?
Well, duh! How could they not love you?
I had to be sure. You could have been an aberration of some kind. A throwback.
"And who is this?"
"My brother."
"Curious. Freeze in your places now, my people. This needs to be a private conversation.
"Feel no anger or alarm, until I tell you to."

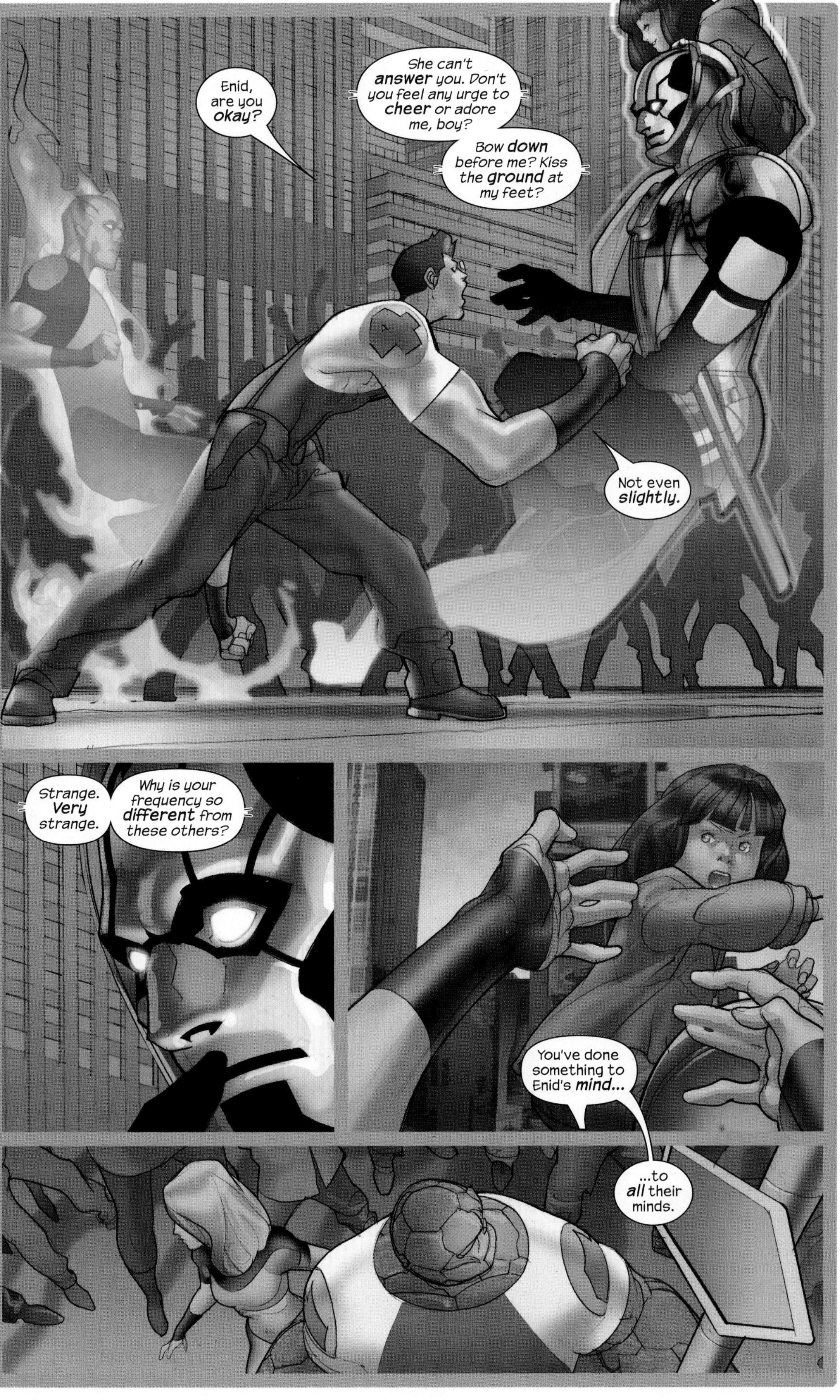
Enid, are you **okay**?
She can't **answer** you. Don't you feel any urge to **cheer** or adore me, boy?
Bow **down** before me? Kiss the **ground** at my feet?
Not even **slightly**.
Strange. **Very** strange.
Why is your frequency so **different** from these others?
You've done something to Enid's **mind**...
...to **all** their minds.

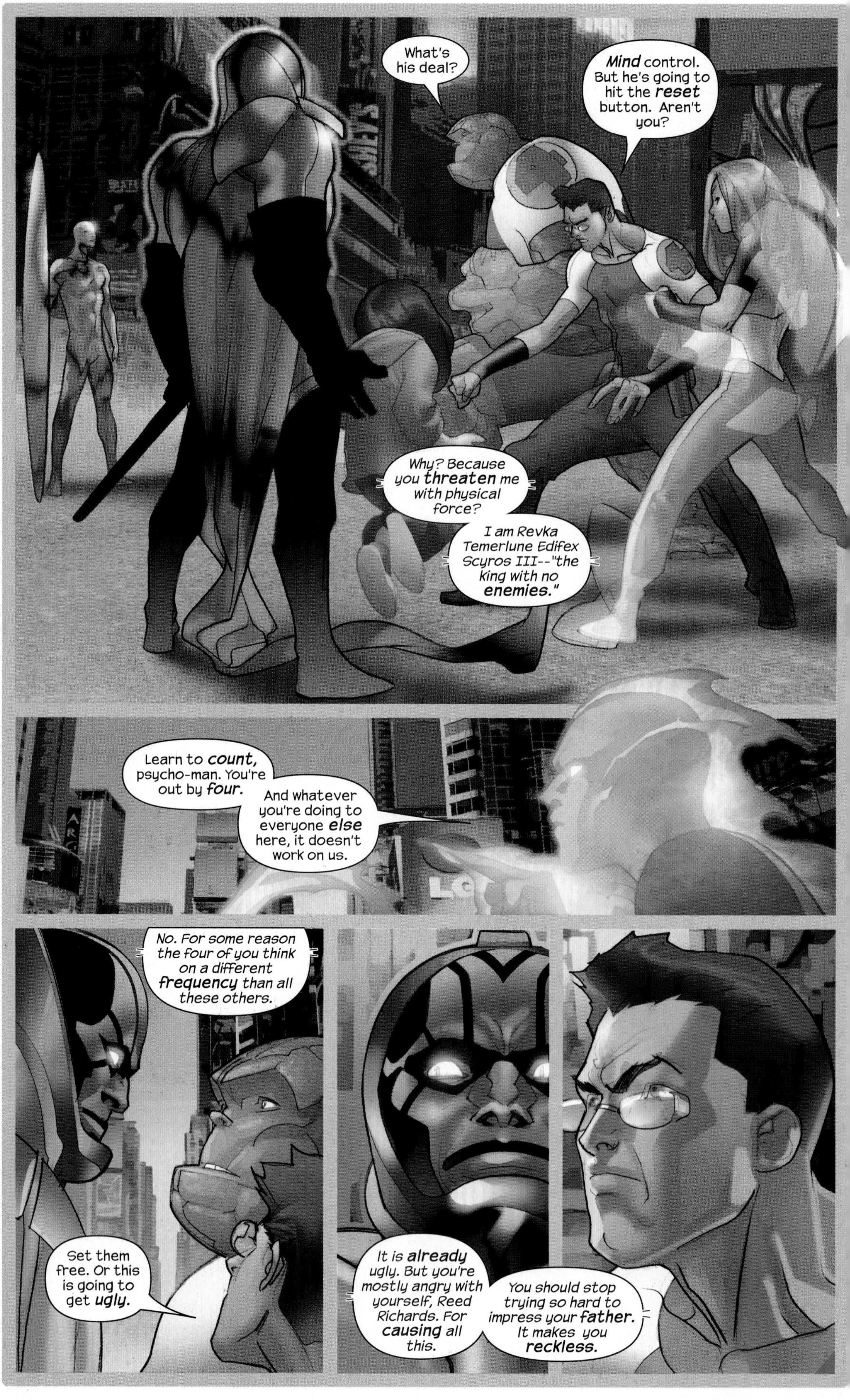
What's his deal?
Mind control. But he's going to hit the reset button. Aren't you?
Why? Because you threaten me with physical force?
I am Revka Temerlune Edifex Scyros III--"the king with no enemies."
Learn to count, psycho-man. You're out by four.
And whatever you're doing to everyone else here, it doesn't work on us.
No. For some reason the four of you think on a different frequency than all these others.
Set them free. Or this is going to get ugly.
It is already ugly. But you're mostly angry with yourself, Reed Richards. For causing all this.
You should stop trying so hard to impress your father. It makes you reckless.

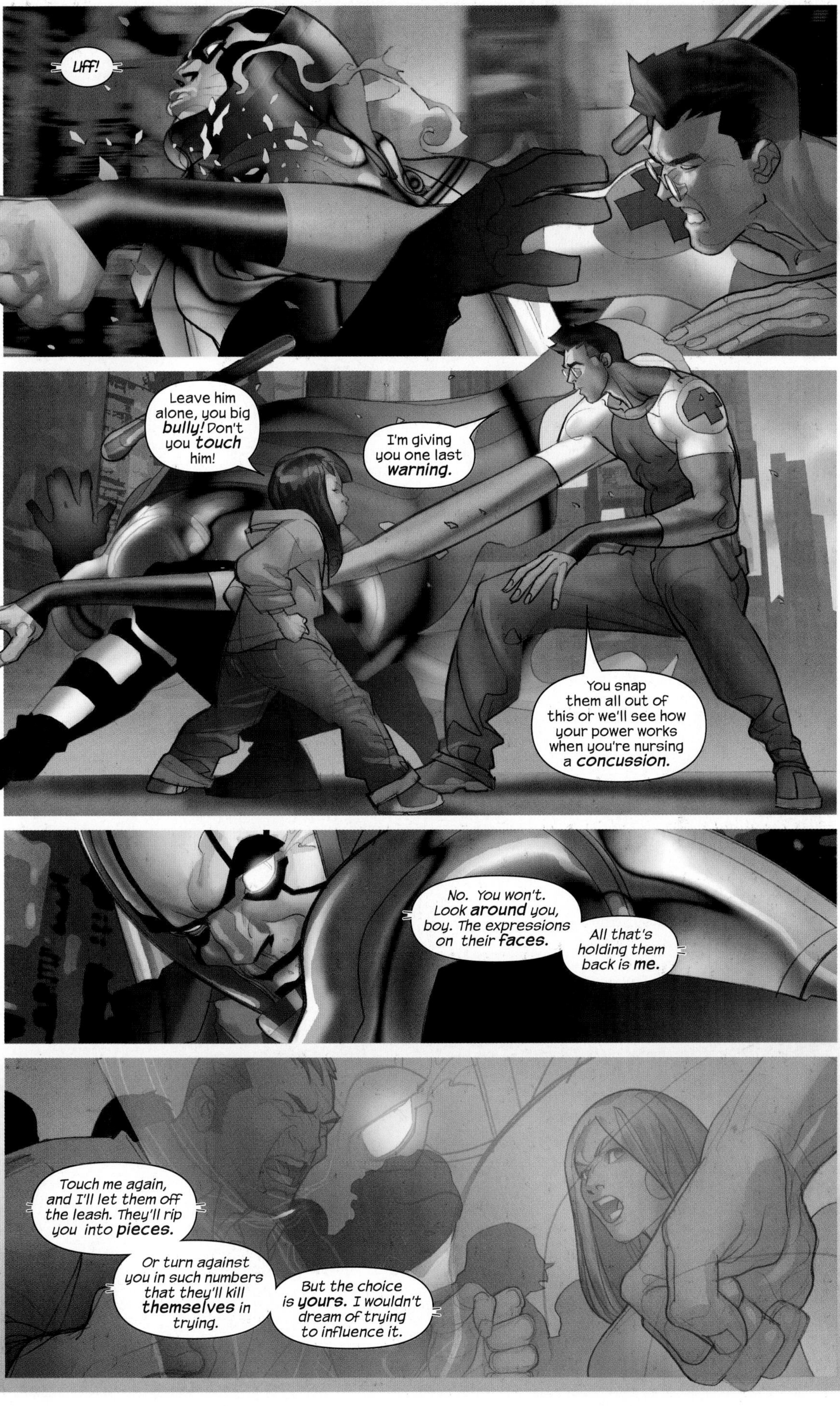
UFF!
Leave him alone, you big bully! Don't you touch him!
I'm giving you one last warning.
You snap them all out of this or we'll see how your power works when you're nursing a concussion.
No. You won't. Look around you, boy. The expressions on their faces.
All that's holding them back is me.
Touch me again, and I'll let them off the leash. They'll rip you into pieces.
Or turn against you in such numbers that they'll kill themselves in trying.
But the choice is yours. I wouldn't dream of trying to influence it.

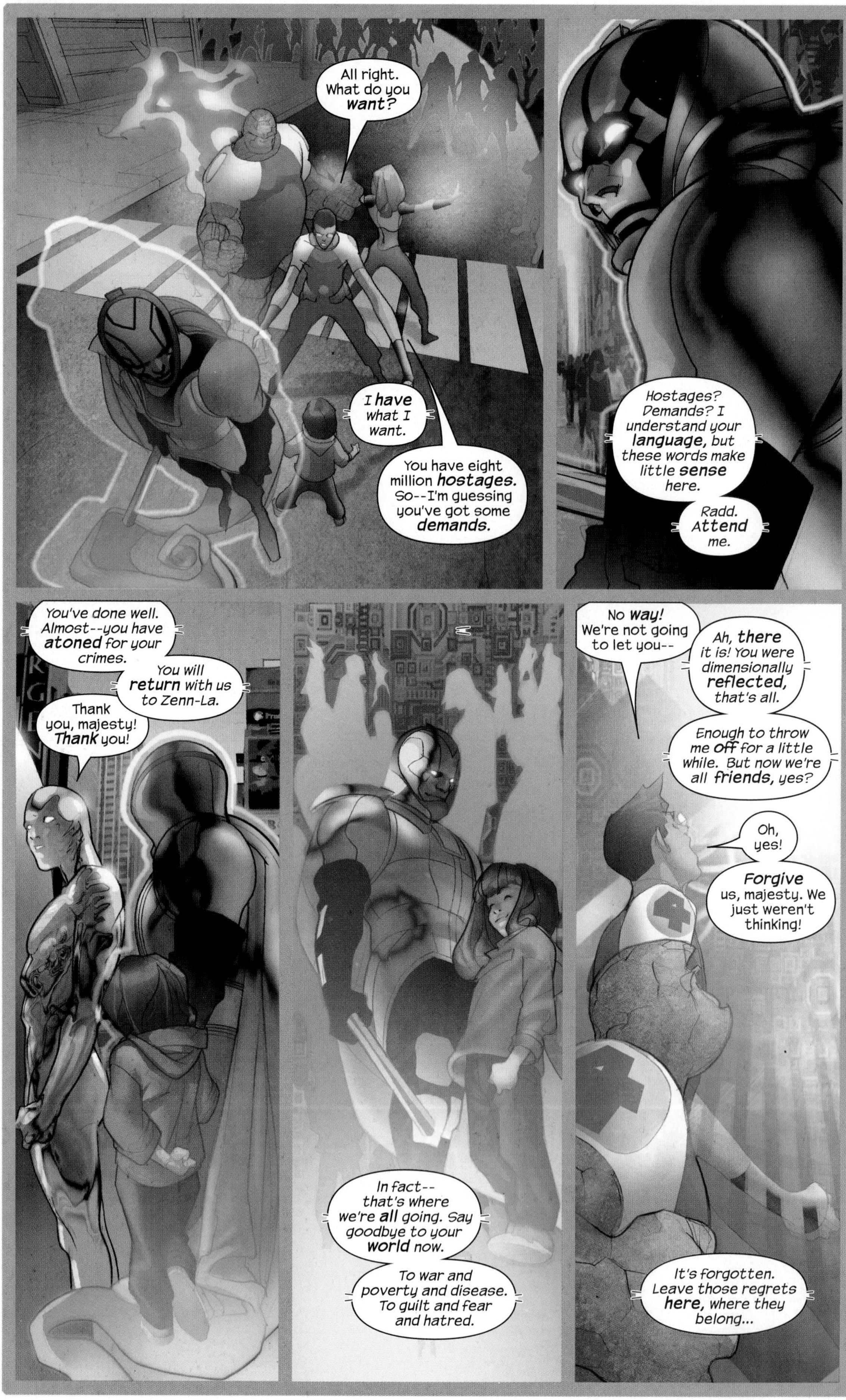
All right. What do you want?
I have what I want.
You have eight million hostages. So--I'm guessing you've got some demands.
Hostages? Demands? I understand your language, but these words make little sense here.
Radd. Attend me.
You've done well. Almost--you have atoned for your crimes.
You will return with us to Zenn-La.
Thank you, majesty! Thank you!
In fact--that's where we're all going. Say goodbye to your world now.
To war and poverty and disease. To guilt and fear and hatred.
No way! We're not going to let you--
Ah, there it is! You were dimensionally reflected, that's all.
Enough to throw me off for a little while. But now we're all friends, yes?
Oh, yes!
Forgive us, majesty. We just weren't thinking!
It's forgotten. Leave those regrets here, where they belong...

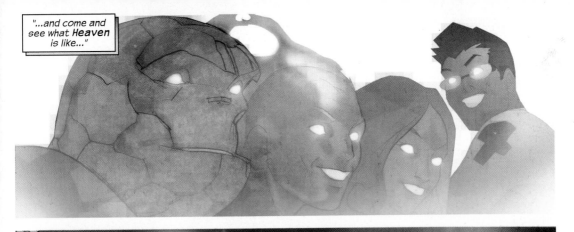

"...and come and see what *Heaven* is like..."

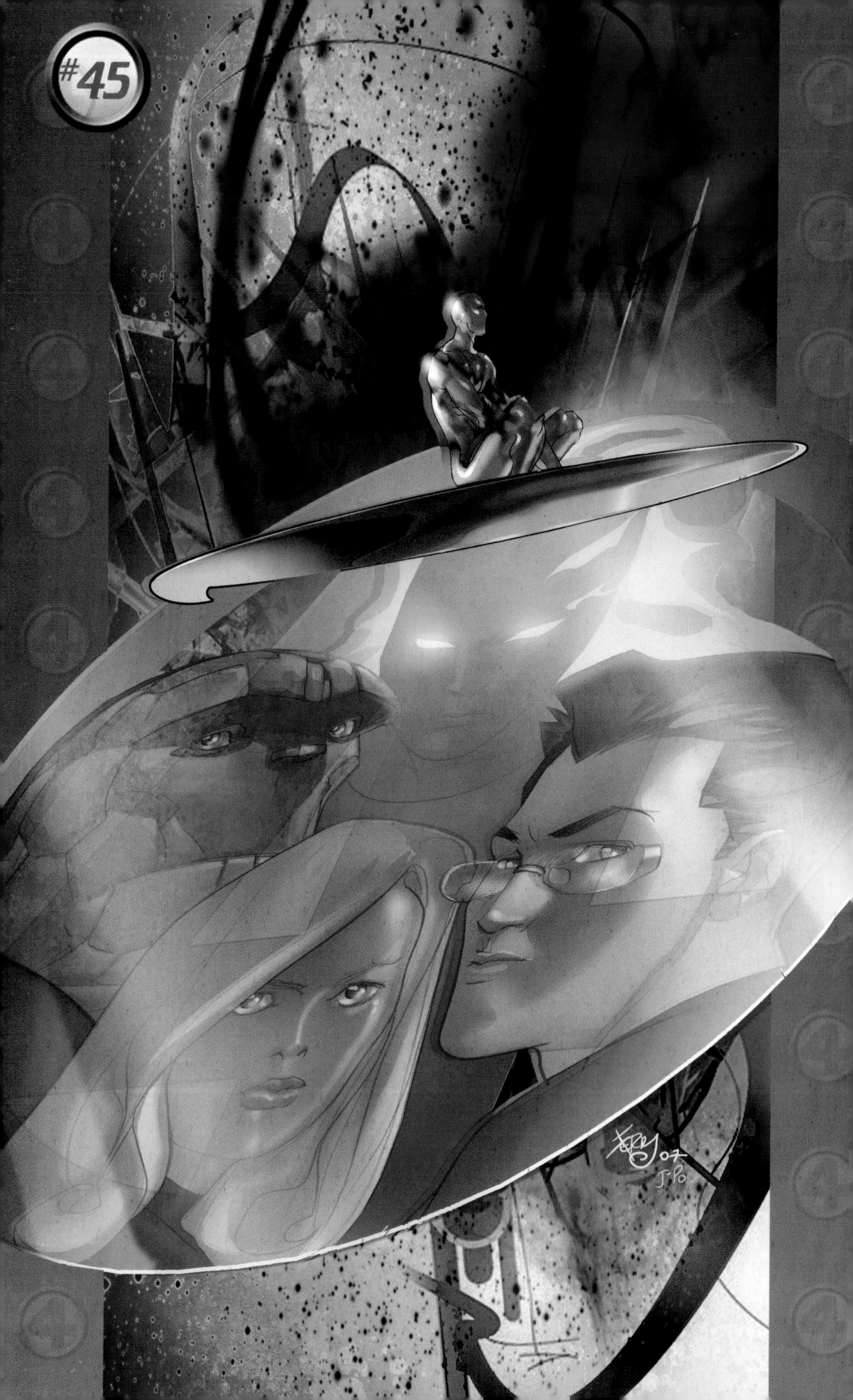
#45

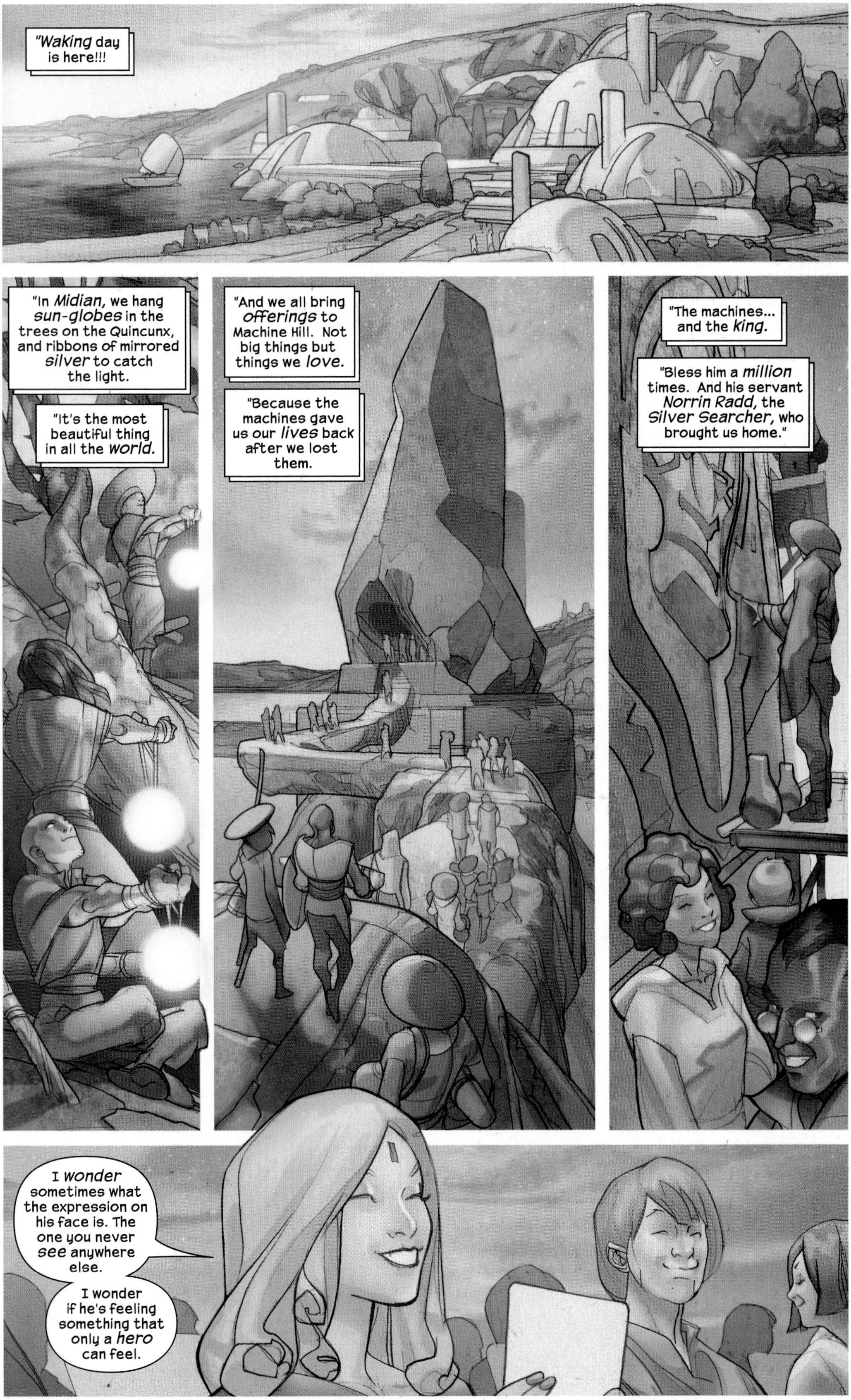
"Waking day is here!!!
"In Midian, we hang sun-globes in the trees on the Quincunx, and ribbons of mirrored silver to catch the light.
"It's the most beautiful thing in all the world.
"And we all bring offerings to Machine Hill. Not big things but things we love.
"Because the machines gave us our lives back after we lost them.
"The machines... and the king.
"Bless him a million times. And his servant Norrin Radd, the Silver Searcher, who brought us home."
I wonder sometimes what the expression on his face is. The one you never see anywhere else.
I wonder if he's feeling something that only a hero can feel.

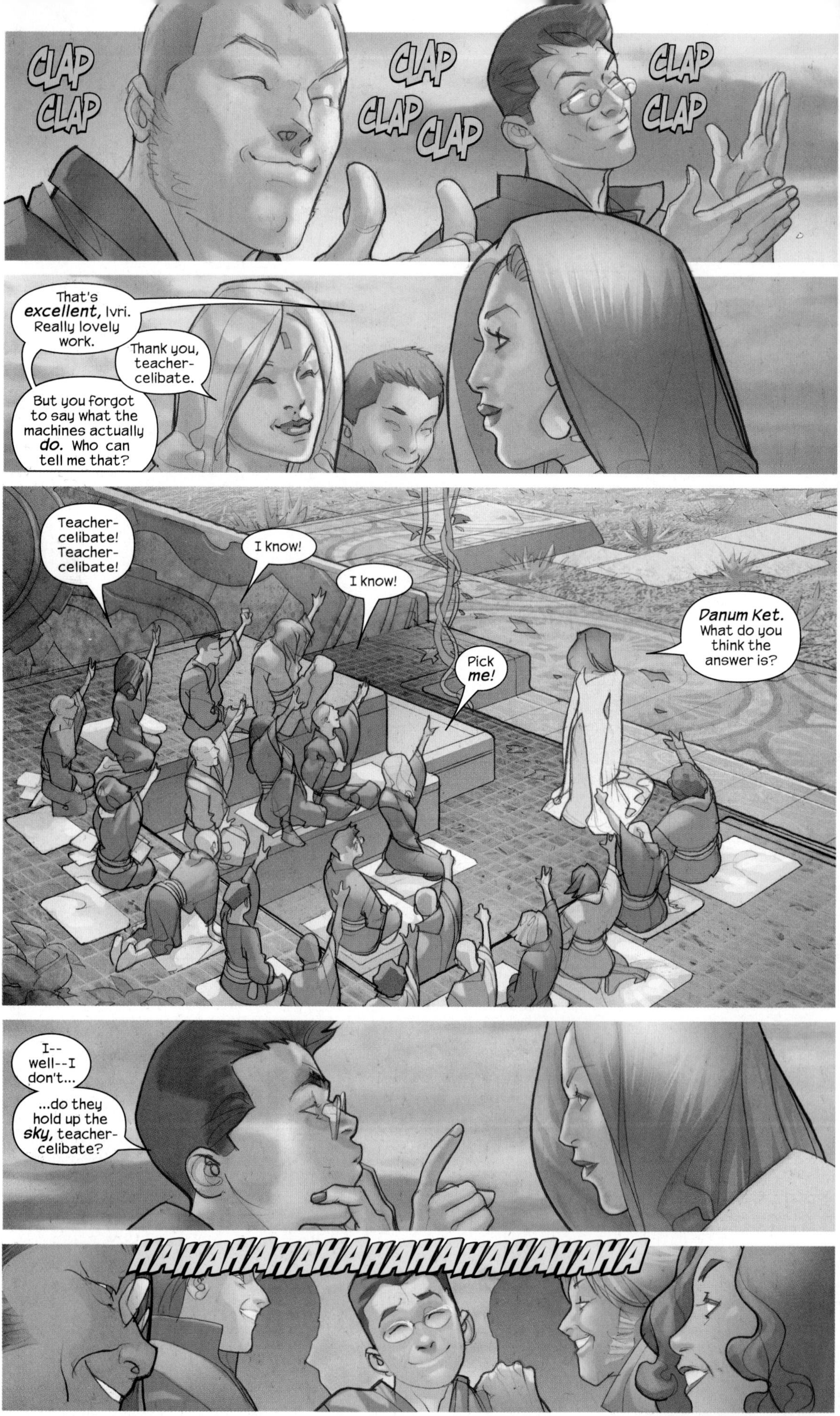
CLAP CLAP
CLAP CLAP CLAP
CLAP CLAP
That's excellent, Ivri. Really lovely work.
Thank you, teacher-celibate.
But you forgot to say what the machines actually do. Who can tell me that?
Teacher-celibate! Teacher-celibate!
I know!
I know!
Pick me!
Danum Ket. What do you think the answer is?
I-- well--I don't...
...do they hold up the sky, teacher-celibate?
HAHAHAHAHAHAHAHAHAHAHAHAHA

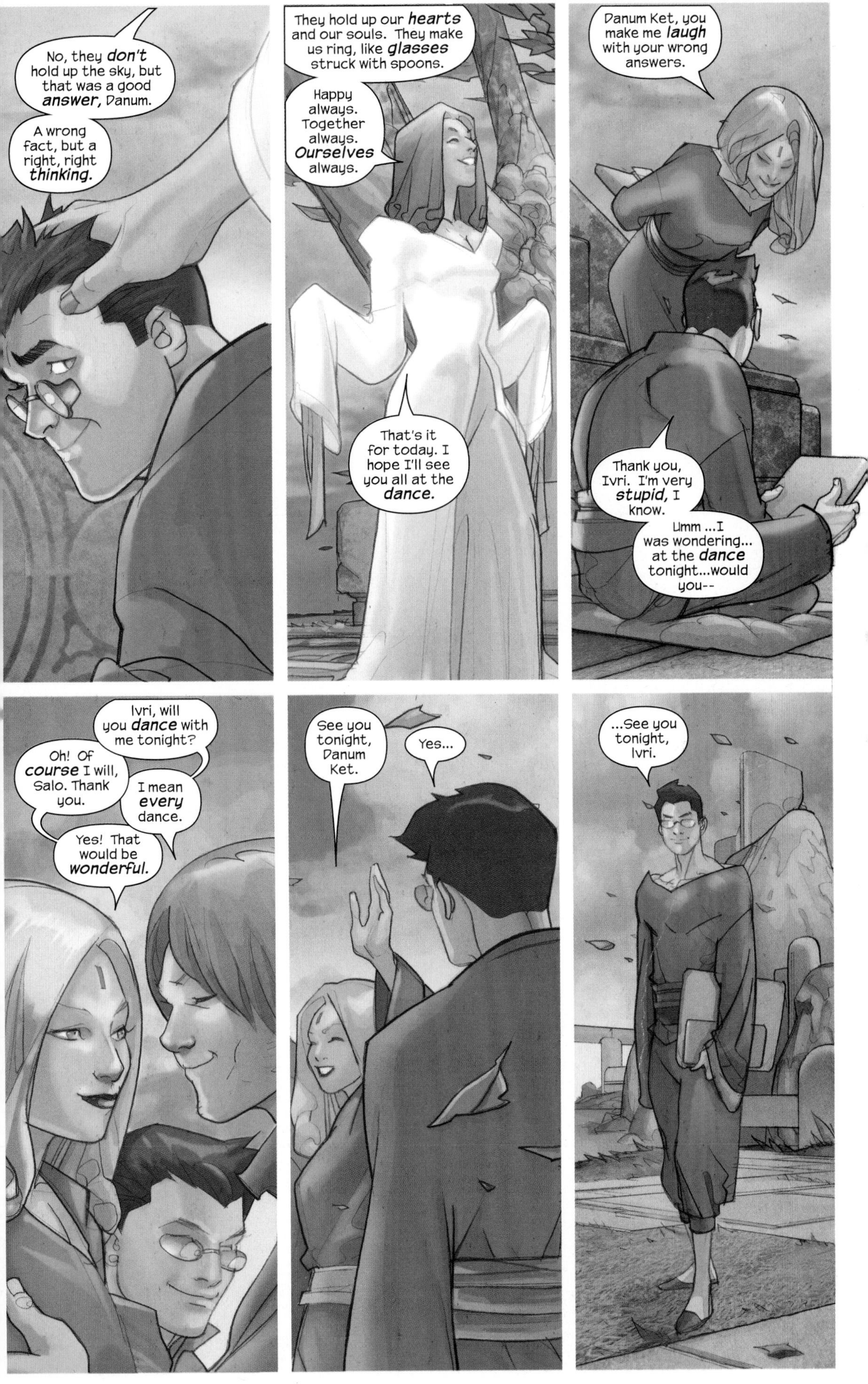
No, they don't hold up the sky, but that was a good answer, Danum.
A wrong fact, but a right, right thinking.
They hold up our hearts and our souls. They make us ring, like glasses struck with spoons.
Happy always. Together always. Ourselves always.
That's it for today. I hope I'll see you all at the dance.
Danum Ket, you make me laugh with your wrong answers.
Thank you, Ivri. I'm very stupid, I know.
Umm ...I was wondering... at the dance tonight...would you--
Ivri, will you dance with me tonight?
Oh! Of course I will, Salo. Thank you.
I mean every dance.
Yes! That would be wonderful.
See you tonight, Danum Ket.
Yes...
...See you tonight, Ivri.

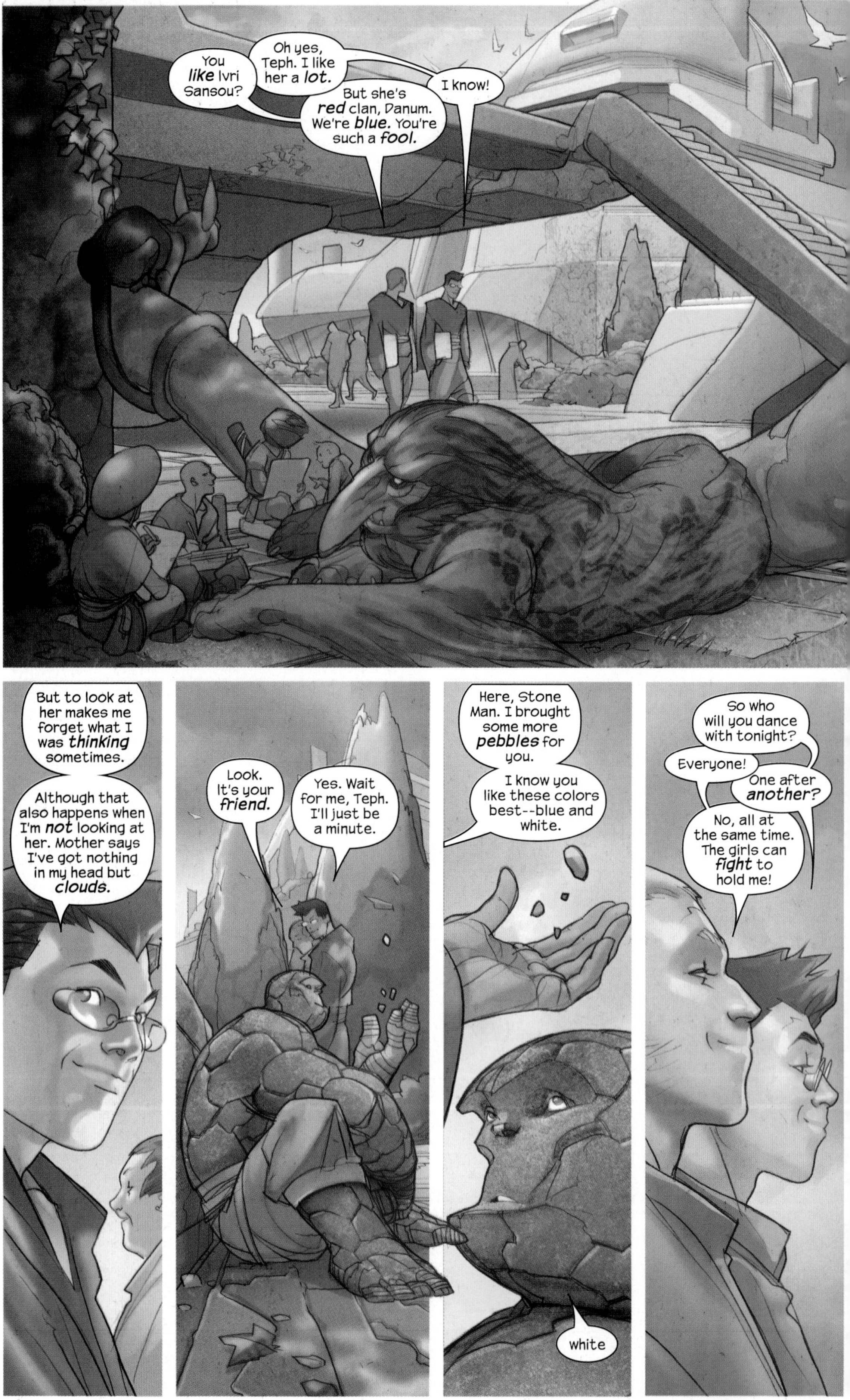
You like Ivri Sansou?
Oh yes, Teph. I like her a lot.
But she's red clan, Danum. We're blue. You're such a fool.
I know!
But to look at her makes me forget what I was thinking sometimes.
Although that also happens when I'm not looking at her. Mother says I've got nothing in my head but clouds.
Look. It's your friend.
Yes. Wait for me, Teph. I'll just be a minute.
Here, Stone Man. I brought some more pebbles for you.
I know you like these colors best--blue and white.
white
So who will you dance with tonight?
Everyone!
One after another?
No, all at the same time. The girls can fight to hold me!

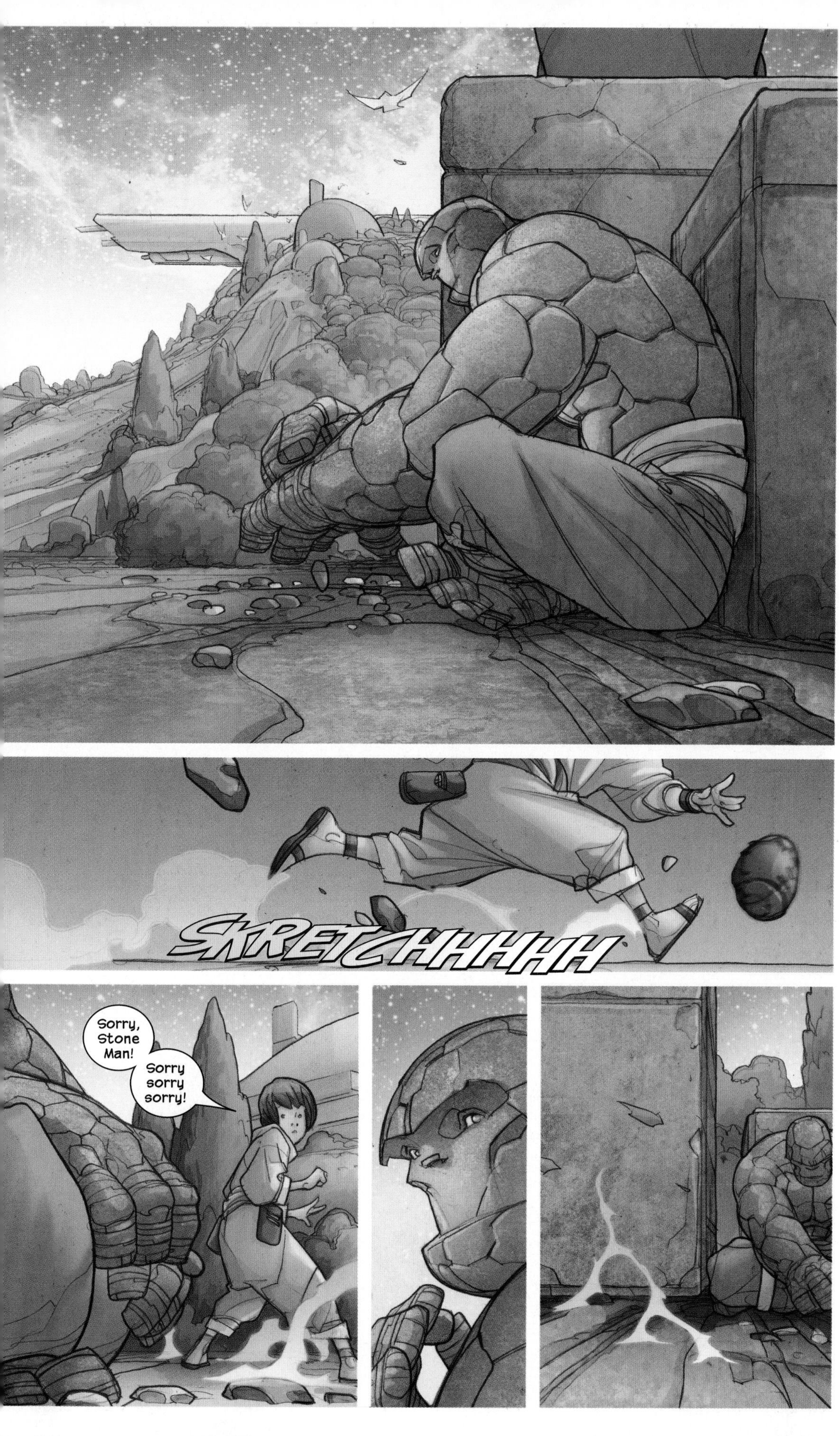
SKRETCHHHHHH
Sorry, Stone Man!
Sorry sorry sorry!

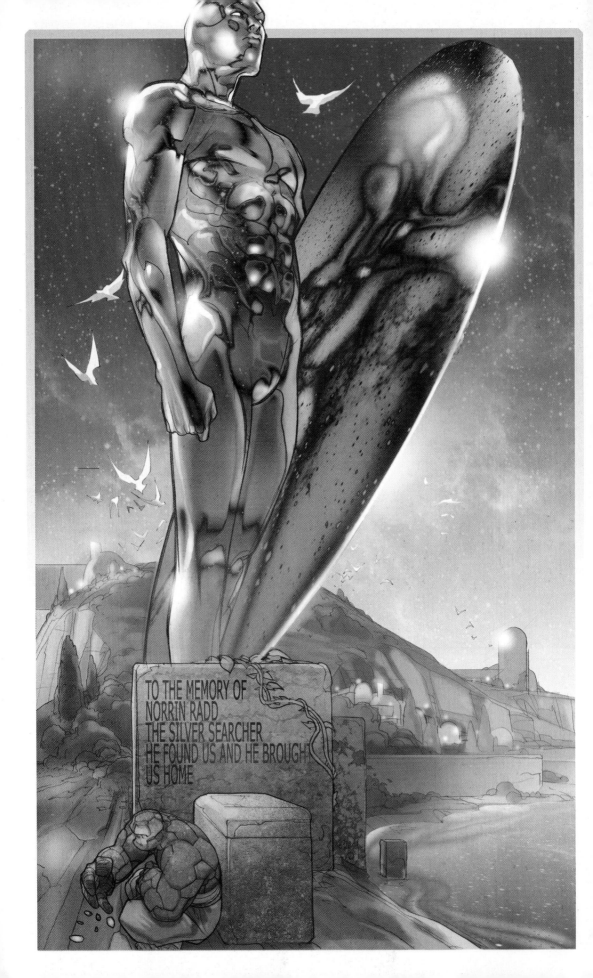

TO THE MEMORY OF
NORRIN RADD
THE SILVER SEARCHER
HE FOUND US AND HE BROUGHT
US HOME

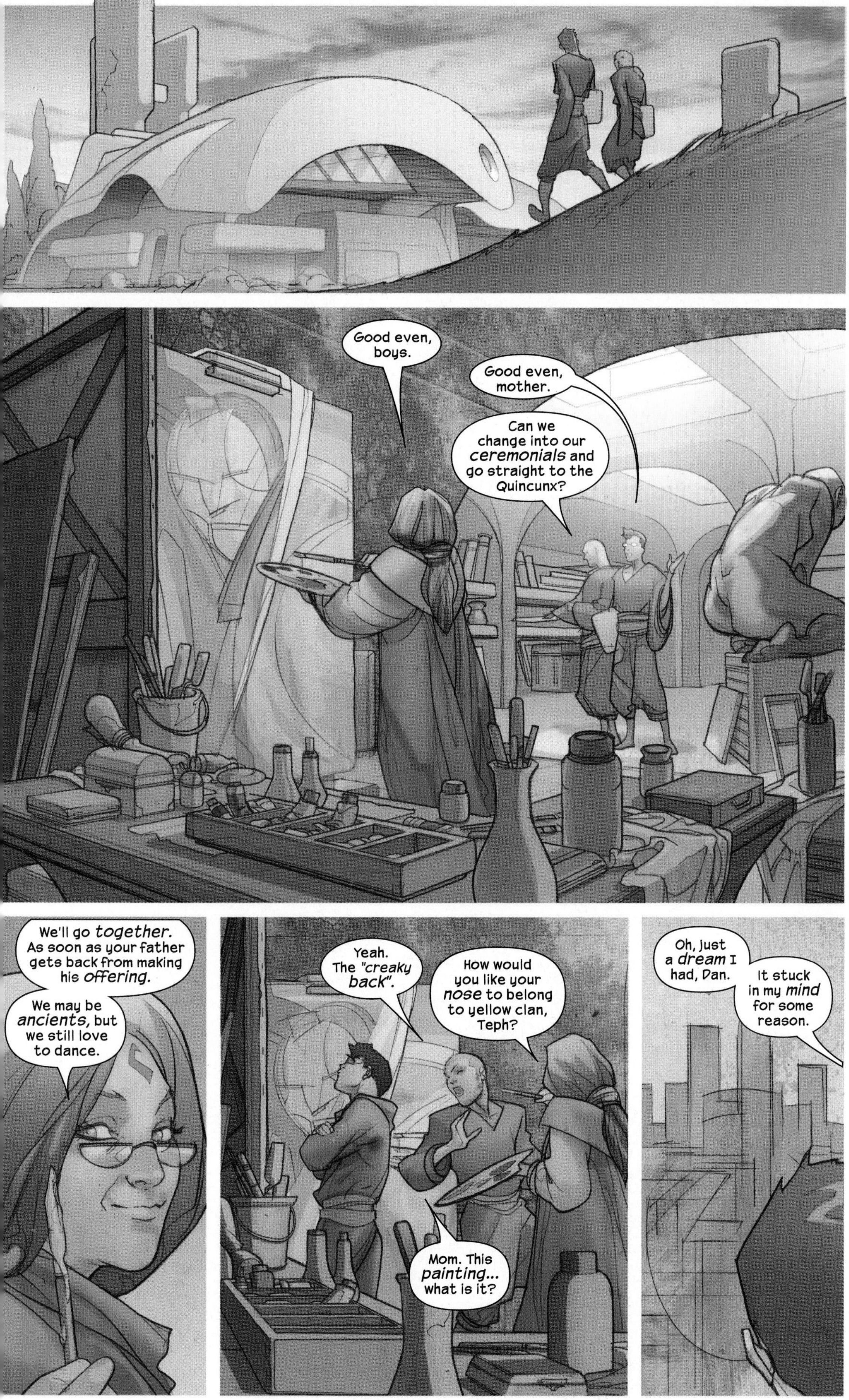
Good even, boys.
Good even, mother.
Can we change into our *ceremonials* and go straight to the Quincunx?
We'll go *together.* As soon as your father gets back from making his *offering.*
We may be *ancients,* but we still love to dance.
Yeah. The "*creaky back*".
How would you like your *nose* to belong to yellow clan, Teph?
Mom. This *painting...* what is it?
Oh, just a *dream* I had, Dan.
It stuck in my *mind* for some reason.

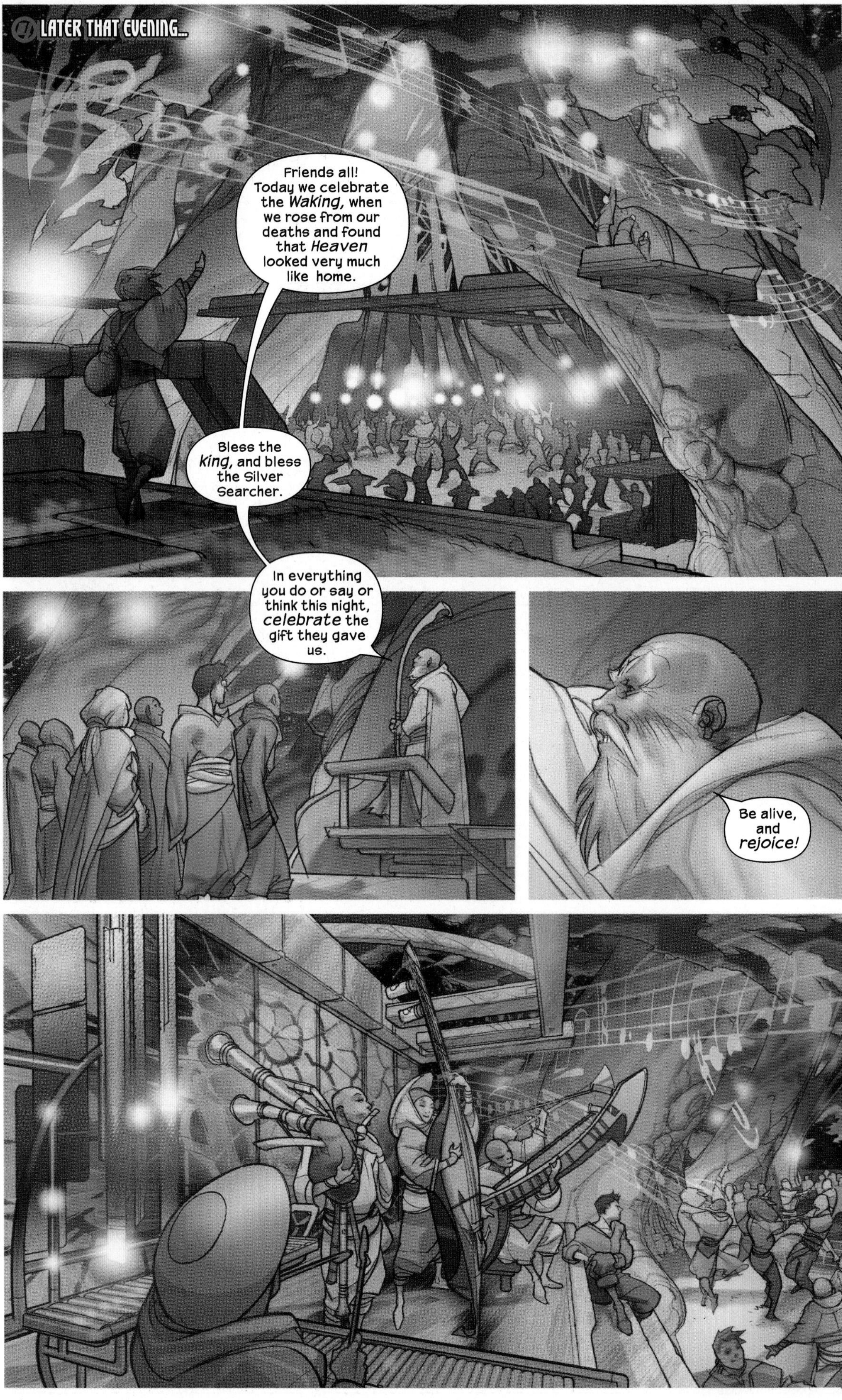
LATER THAT EVENING...
Friends all! Today we celebrate the *Waking,* when we rose from our deaths and found that *Heaven* looked very much like home.
Bless the *King,* and bless the Silver Searcher.
In everything you do or say or think this night, *celebrate* the gift they gave us.
Be alive, and *rejoice!*

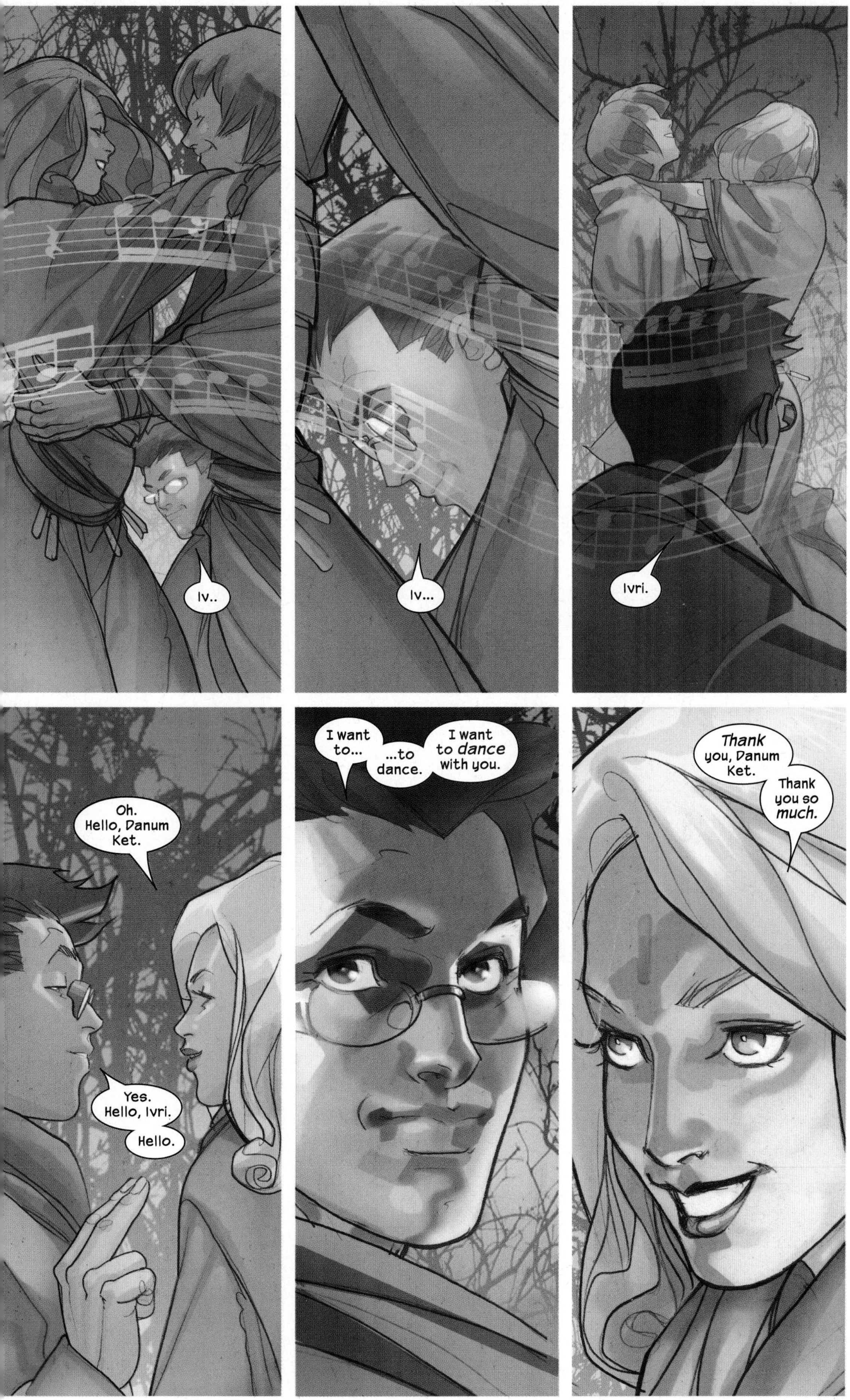
Iv..
Iv...
Ivri.
Oh. Hello, Danum Ket.
Yes. Hello, Ivri.
Hello.
I want to...
...to dance.
I want to *dance* with you.
Thank you, Danum Ket.
Thank you so *much.*

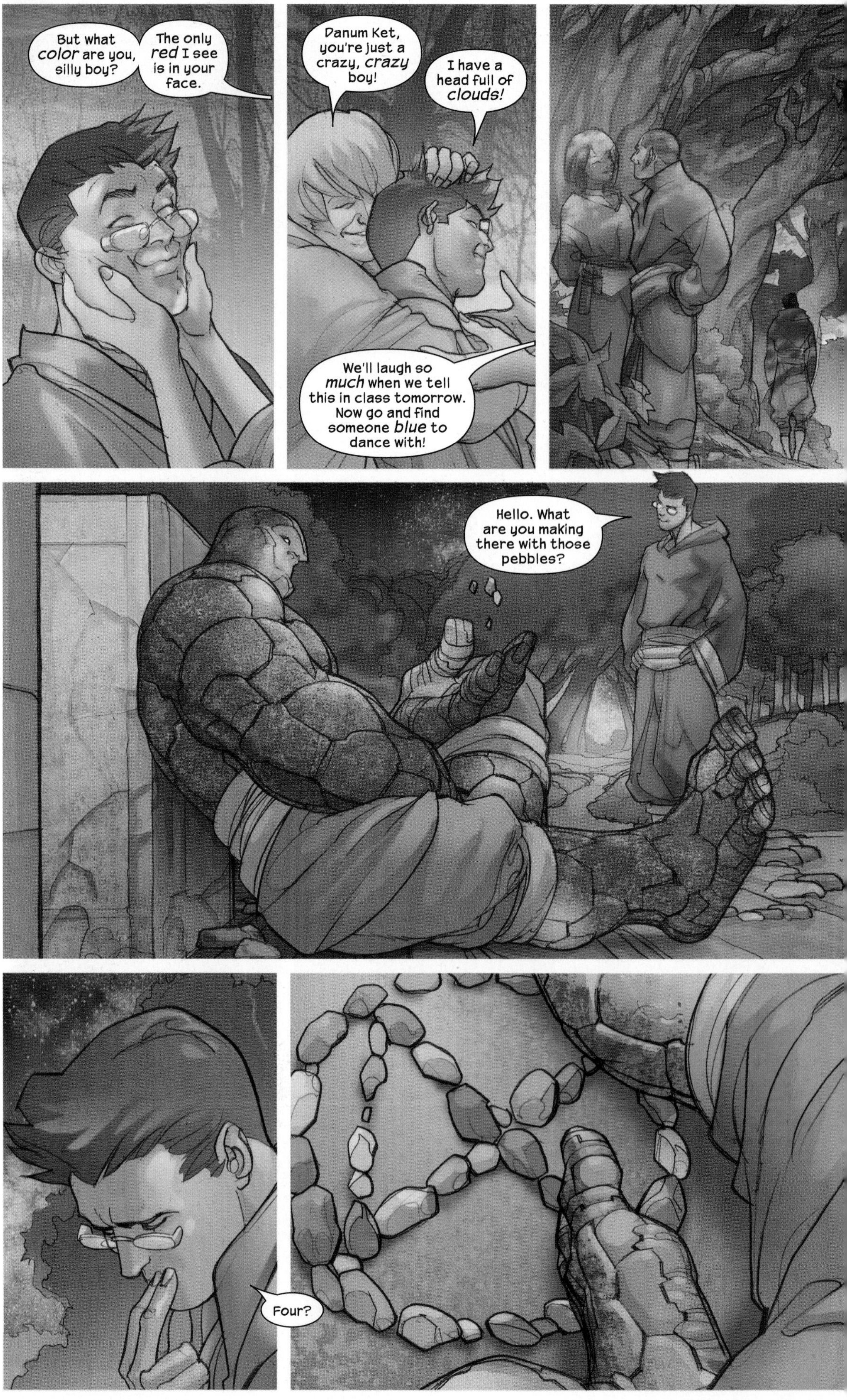
But what *color* are you, silly boy?
The only *red* I see is in your face.
Danum Ket, you're just a crazy, *crazy* boy!
I have a head full of *clouds!*
We'll laugh so *much* when we tell this in class tomorrow. Now go and find someone *blue* to dance with!
Hello. What are you making there with those pebbles?
Four?

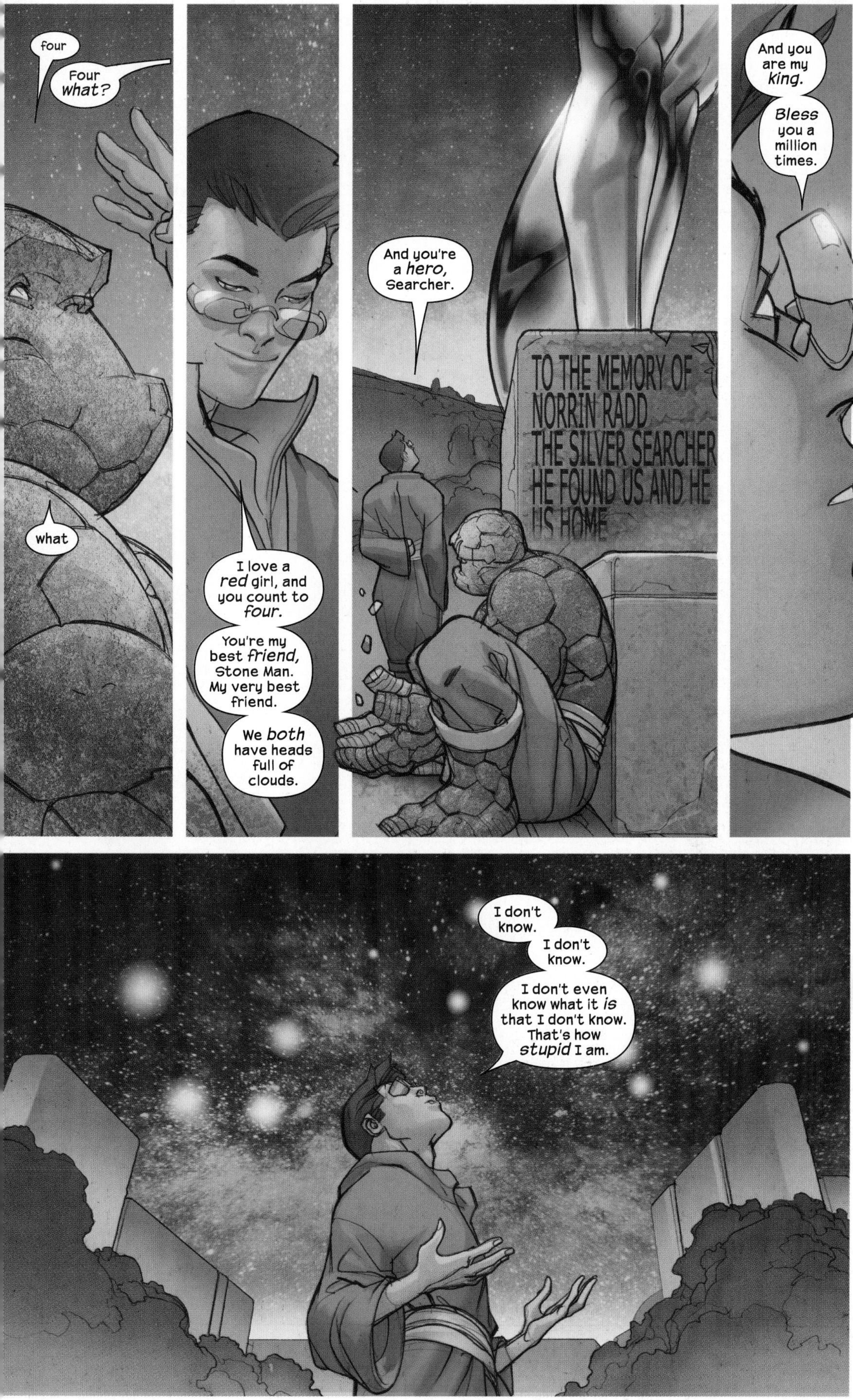
four
Four what?
what
I love a red girl, and you count to four.
You're my best friend, Stone Man. My very best friend.
We both have heads full of clouds.
And you're a hero, Searcher.
TO THE MEMORY OF
NORRIN RADD
THE SILVER SEARCHER
HE FOUND US AND HE
US HOME
And you are my king.
Bless you a million times.
I don't know.
I don't know.
I don't even know what it is that I don't know. That's how stupid I am.

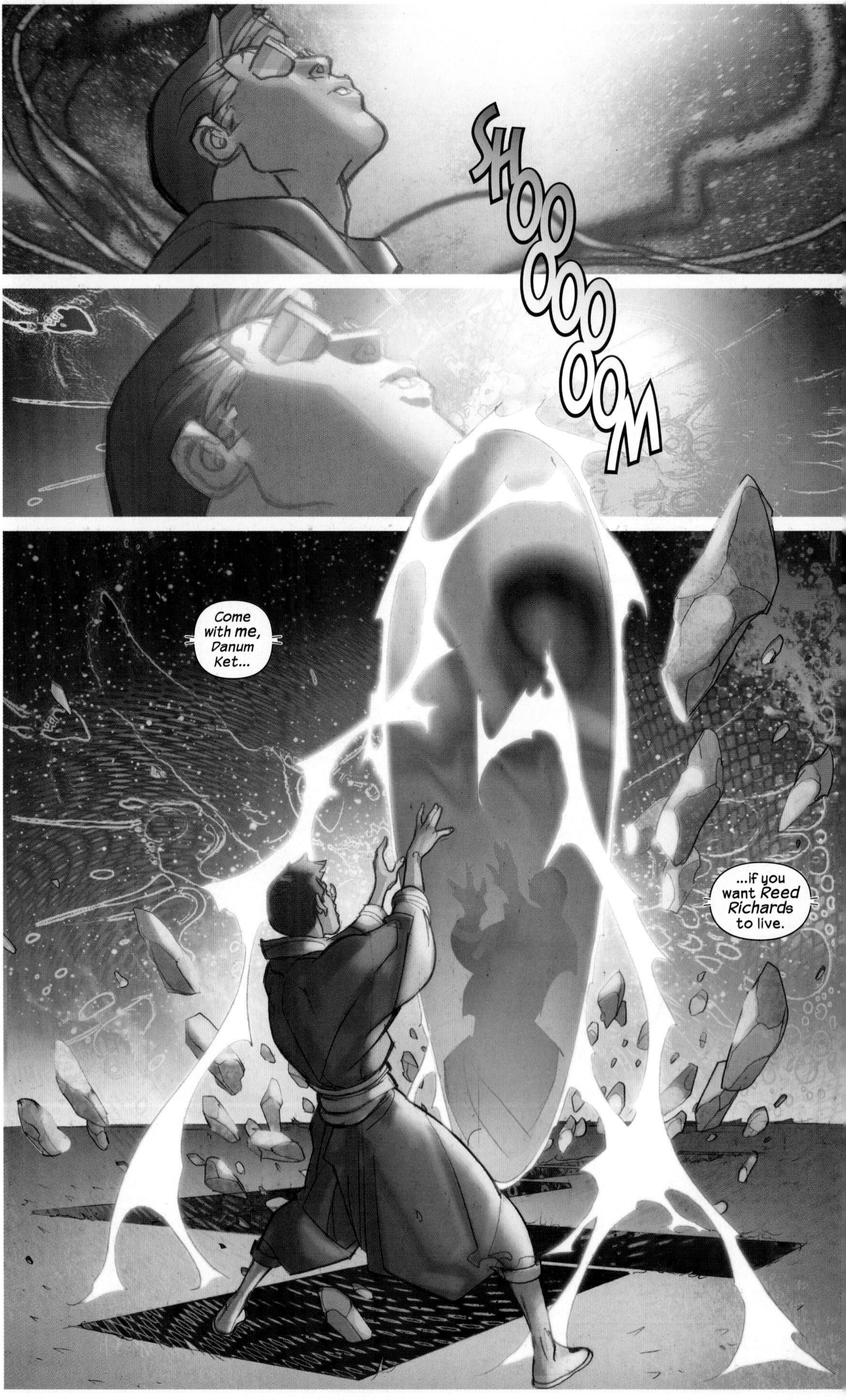
SHOOOOOOM
Come with me, Danum Ket...
...if you want Reed Richards to live.

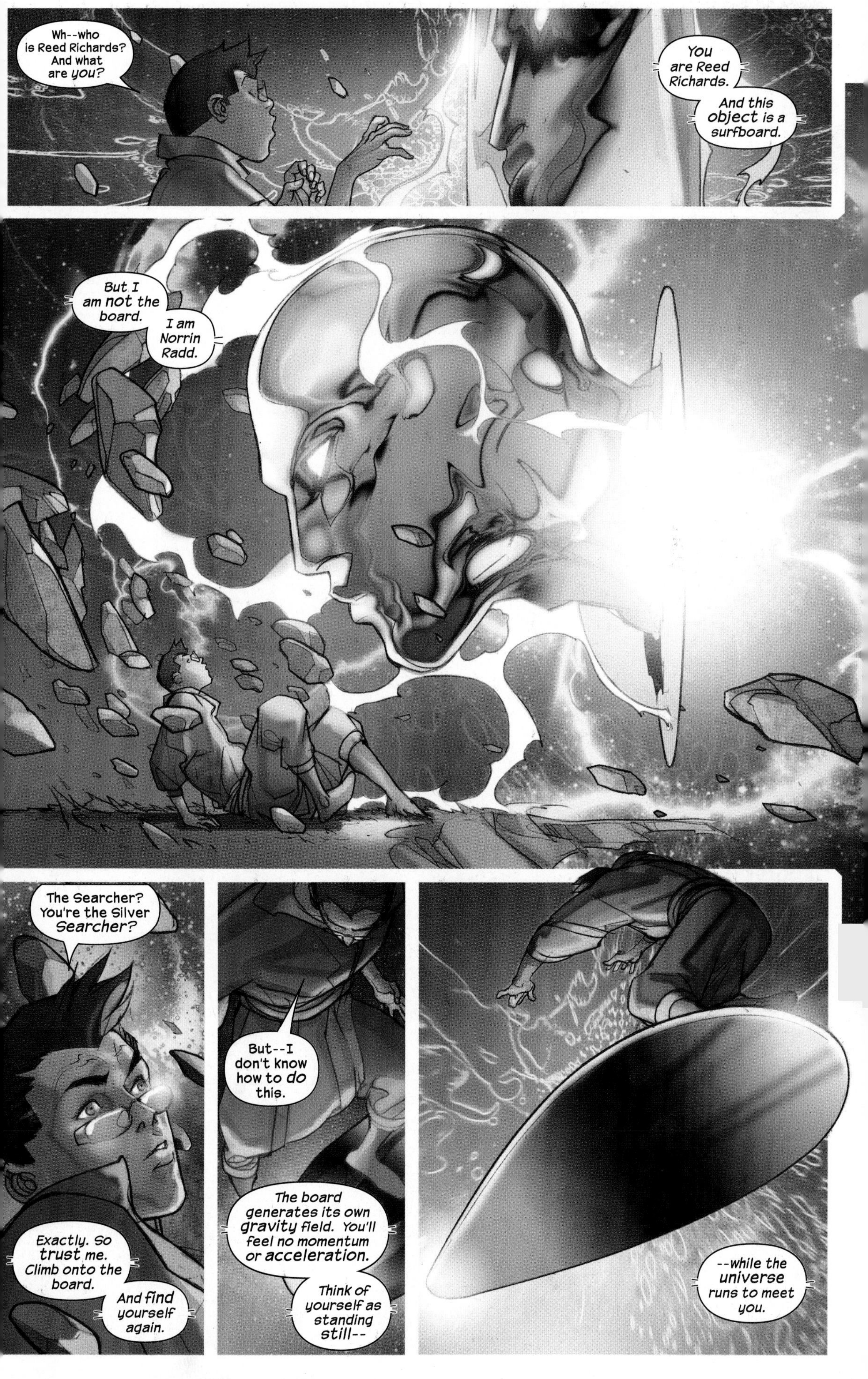
Wh--who is Reed Richards? And what are you?
You are Reed Richards.
And this object is a surfboard.
But I am not the board.
I am Norrin Radd.
The Searcher? You're the Silver Searcher?
Exactly. So trust me. Climb onto the board.
And find yourself again.
But--I don't know how to do this.
The board generates its own gravity field. You'll feel no momentum or acceleration.
Think of yourself as standing still--
--while the universe runs to meet you.

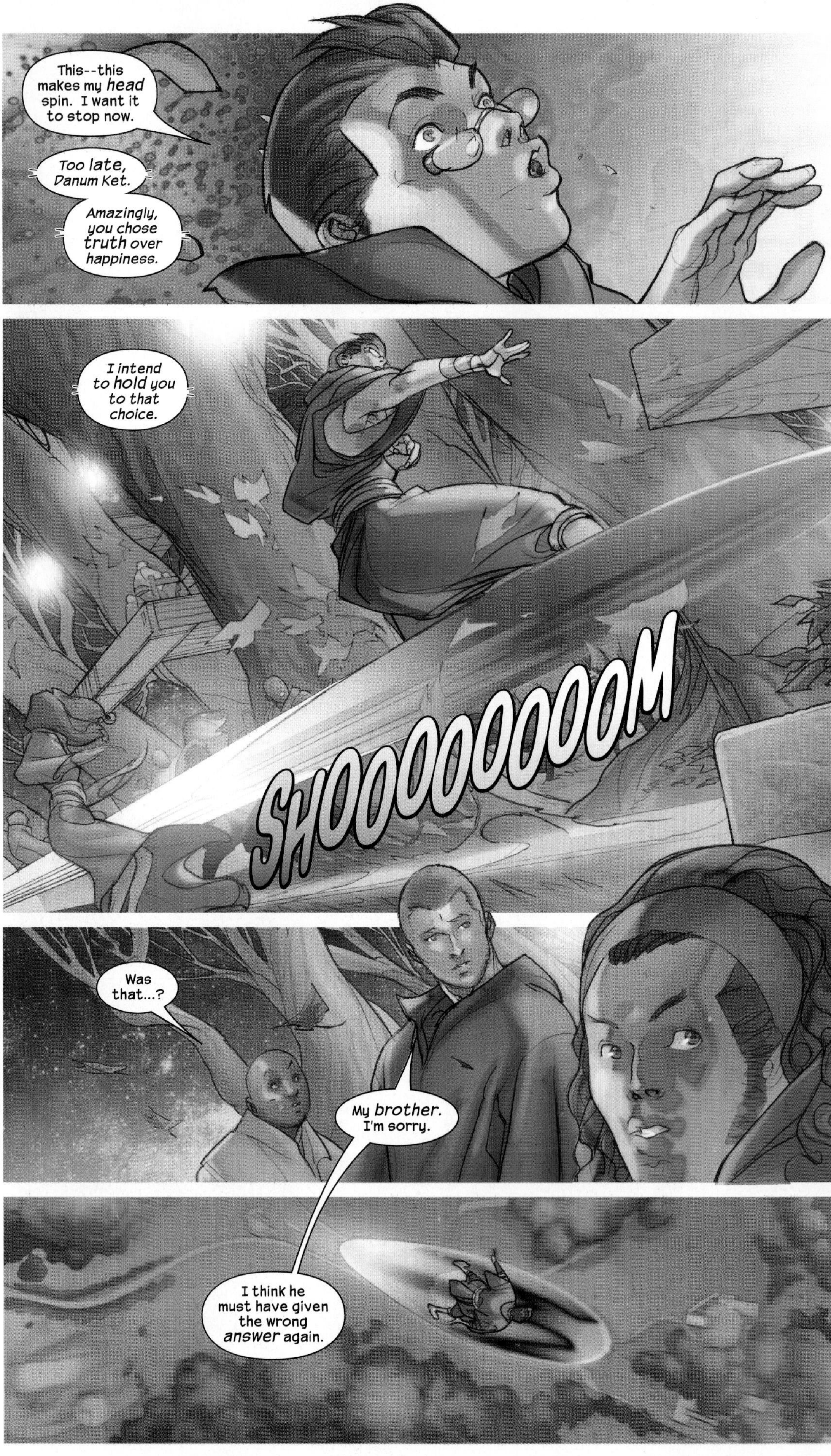
This--this makes my head spin. I want it to stop now.
Too late, Danum Ket.
Amazingly, you chose truth over happiness.
I intend to hold you to that choice.
SHOOOOOOOOM
Was that...?
My brother. I'm sorry.
I think he must have given the wrong answer again.

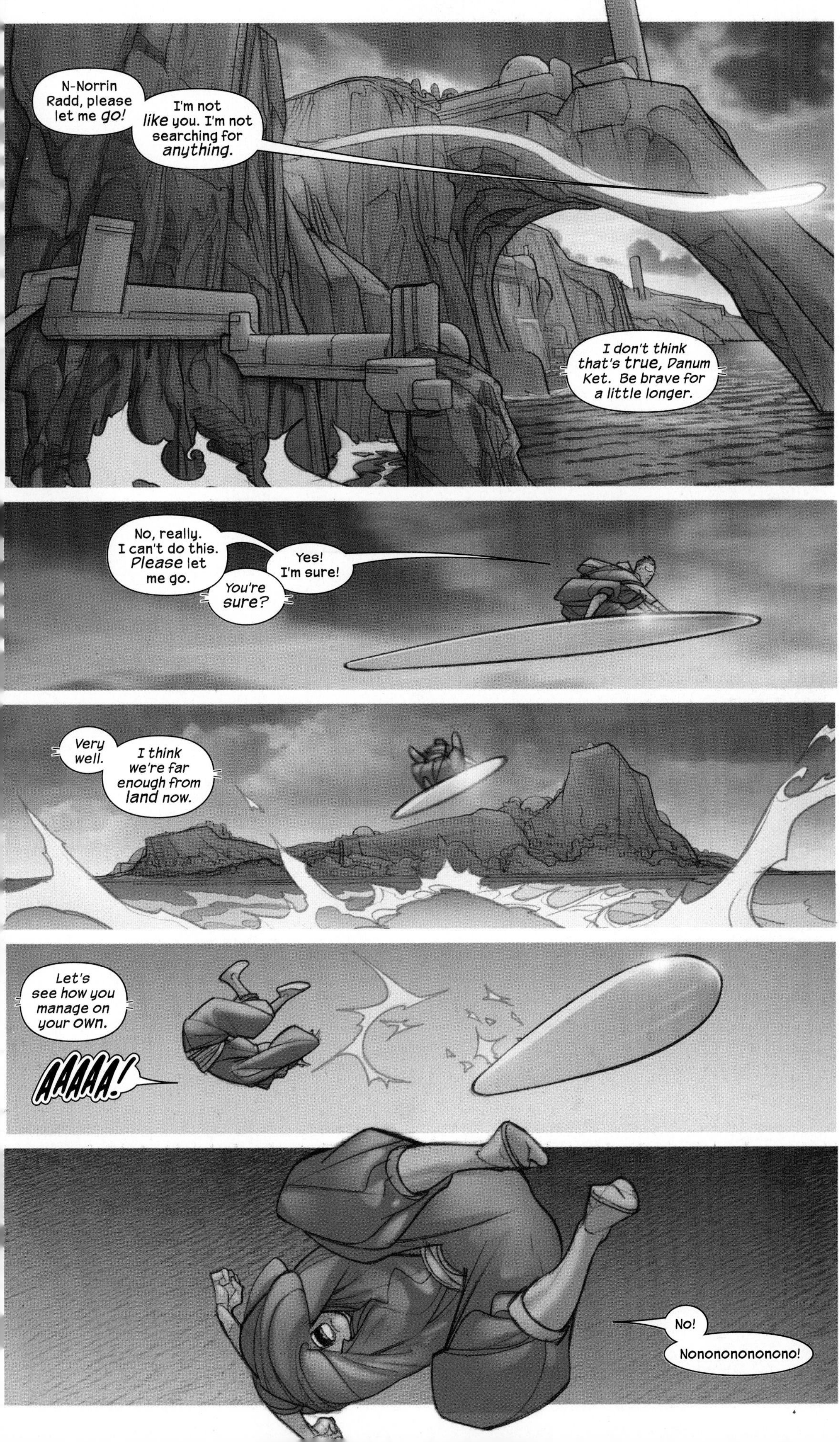

N-Norrin Radd, please let me go!
I'm not like you. I'm not searching for anything.
I don't think that's true, Danum Ket. Be brave for a little longer.
No, really. I can't do this. Please let me go.
You're sure?
Yes! I'm sure!
Very well.
I think we're far enough from land now.
Let's see how you manage on your own.
AAAAA!
No!
Nononononononono!

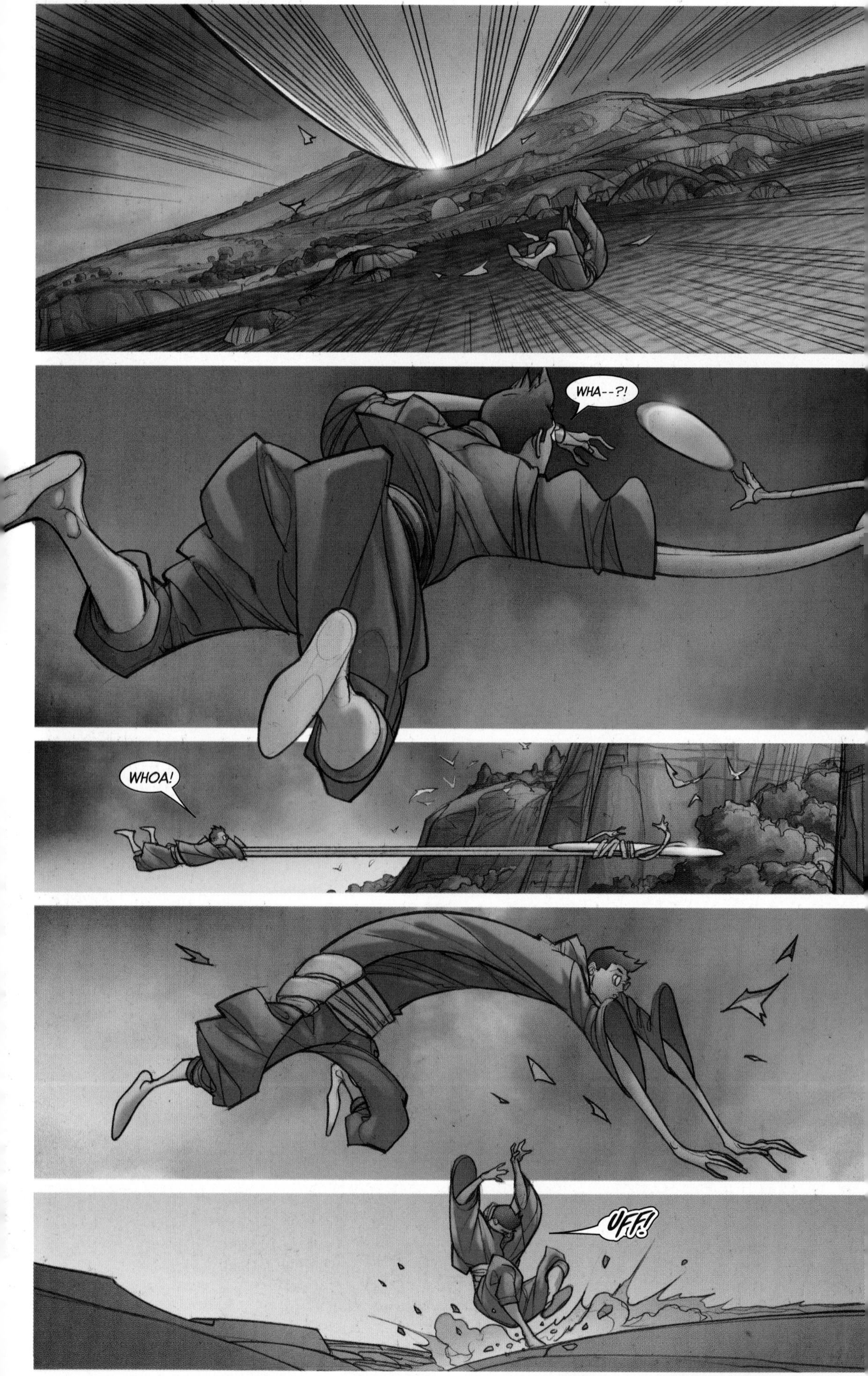
WHA--?!
WHOA!
UFF!

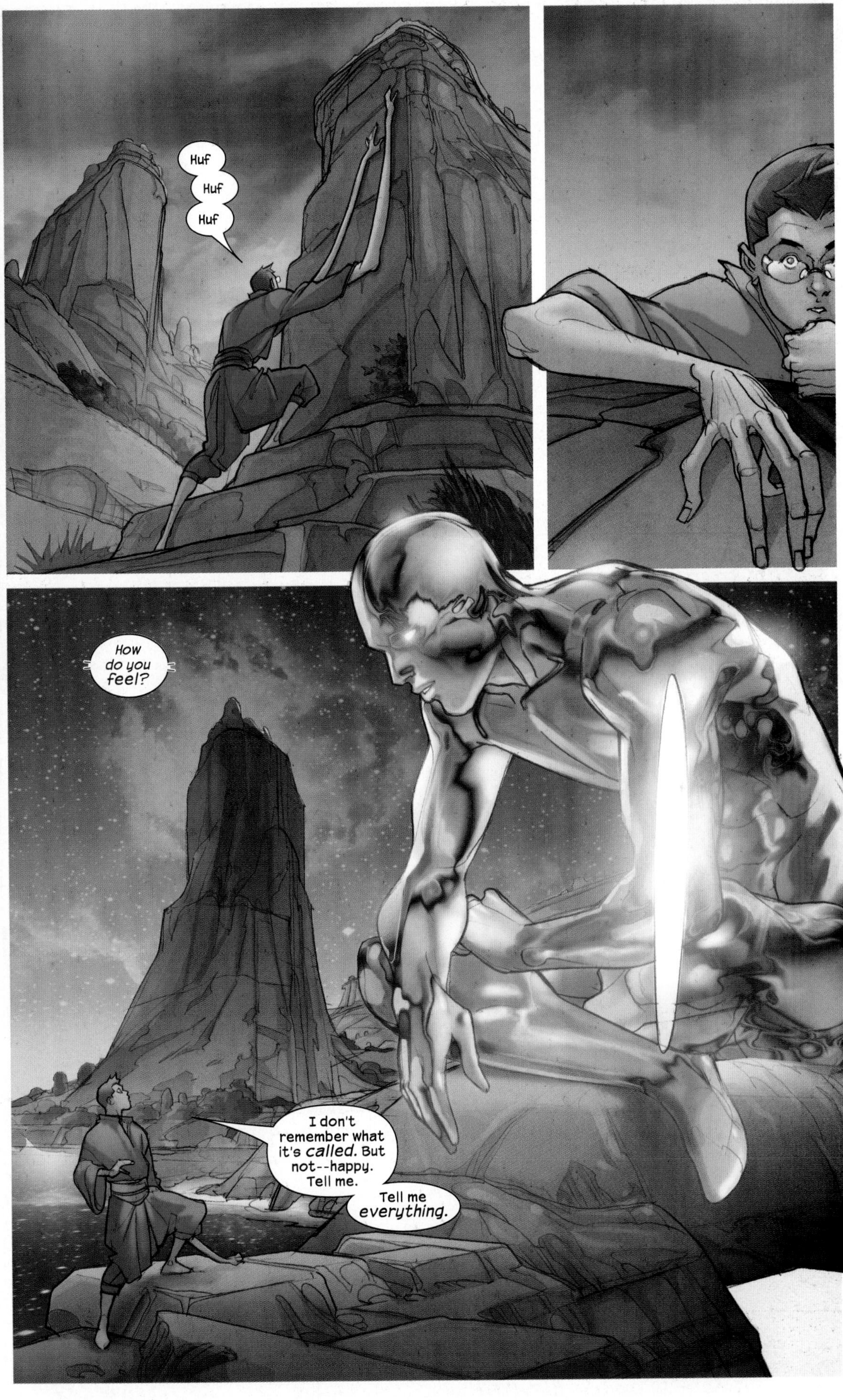

Huf
Huf
Huf
How do you feel?
I don't remember what it's called. But not--happy. Tell me.
Tell me everything.

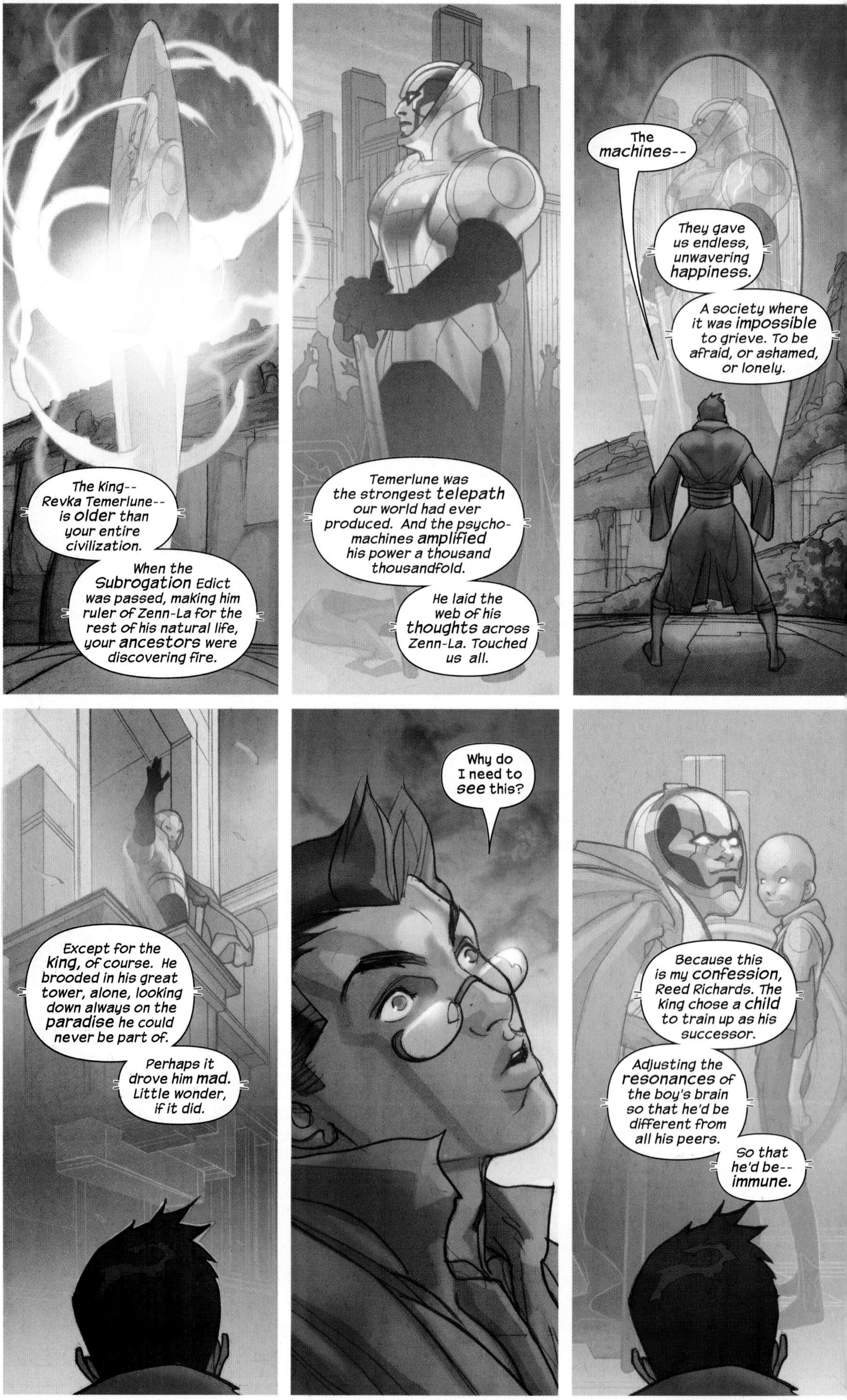
The king--
Revka Temerlune--
is older than
your entire
civilization.
When the Subrogation Edict was passed, making him ruler of Zenn-La for the rest of his natural life, your ancestors were discovering fire.
Temerlune was the strongest telepath our world had ever produced. And the psycho-machines amplified his power a thousand thousandfold.
He laid the web of his thoughts across Zenn-La. Touched us all.
The machines--
They gave us endless, unwavering happiness.
A society where it was impossible to grieve. To be afraid, or ashamed, or lonely.
Except for the king, of course. He brooded in his great tower, alone, looking down always on the paradise he could never be part of.
Perhaps it drove him mad. Little wonder, if it did.
Why do I need to see this?
Because this is my confession, Reed Richards. The king chose a child to train up as his successor.
Adjusting the resonances of the boy's brain so that he'd be different from all his peers.
So that he'd be-- immune.

You.

Me. I grew up outside the cocoon, looking in at other people's shallow, perpetual joy.

It was hard. Eventually-- unbearable.

And so I convinced myself that endless happiness was a tyranny. A curse.

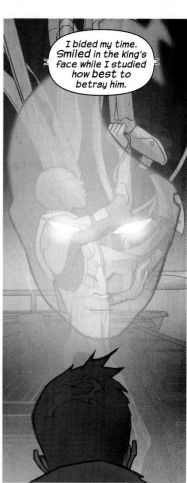

I bided my time. Smiled in the king's face while I studied how best to betray him.

One day I drugged his wine, and while he slept I turned off the machines.

I thought there would be revolution. I thought the people would thank me, and make me king in his place.

But they couldn't bear to see the world as it was. They were like-- addicts in sudden, terrible withdrawal.

They went mad. Killed themselves and each other, in their millions.

My God.

But you said this was--

Thousands of *years* ago. Yes. Temerlune had made himself *immortal* already, by surgical means.

Now he made *me* immortal too, as part of my punishment.

And he took away my *immunity*. Made me his slave.

Sent me out into the *void*, with hermetically sealed skin and a star-core for a heart.

To *search* forever, until I found another race to populate Zenn-La.

Earth. You found Earth.

Good. The memories are *returning* to you, now that I've brought you outside the machines' effective *radius*.

I paid for one sin with *another* just as big, Richards.

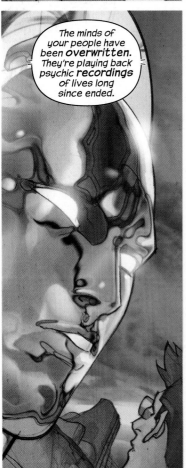

The minds of your people have been *overwritten*. They're playing back psychic *recordings* of lives long since ended.

Zenn-La's last generation, *preserved* in the machines' infallible memories--and now *reborn*.

Infallible?

We'll *see*.

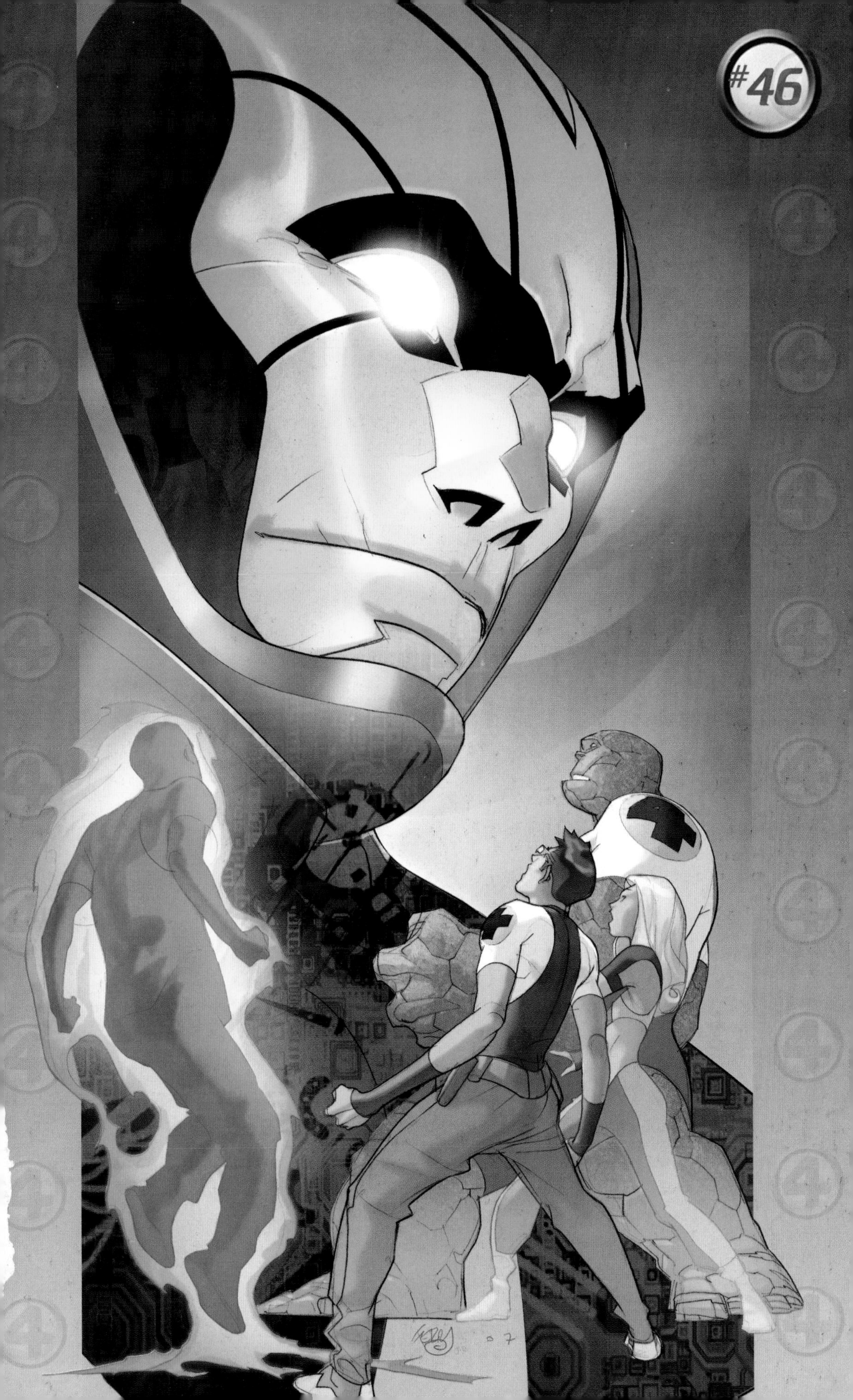
#46

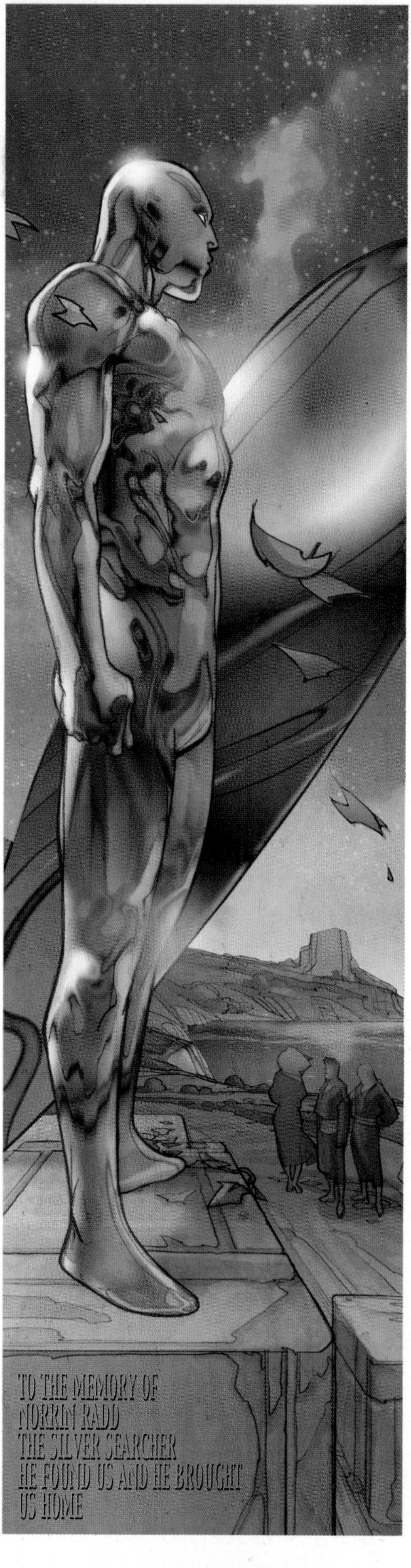
TO THE MEMORY OF
NORRIN RADD
THE SILVER SEARCHER
HE FOUND US AND HE BROUGHT
US HOME

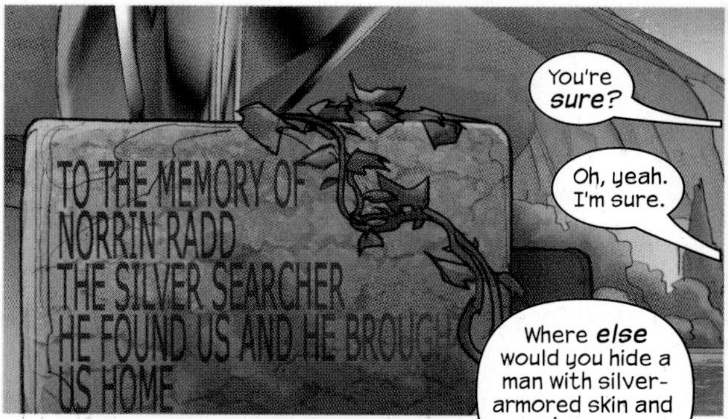
TO THE MEMORY OF
NORRIN RADD
THE SILVER SEARCHER
HE FOUND US AND HE BROUGH
US HOME
You're *sure*?
Oh, yeah. I'm sure.
Where *else* would you hide a man with silver-armored skin and a *star-core* for a heart?

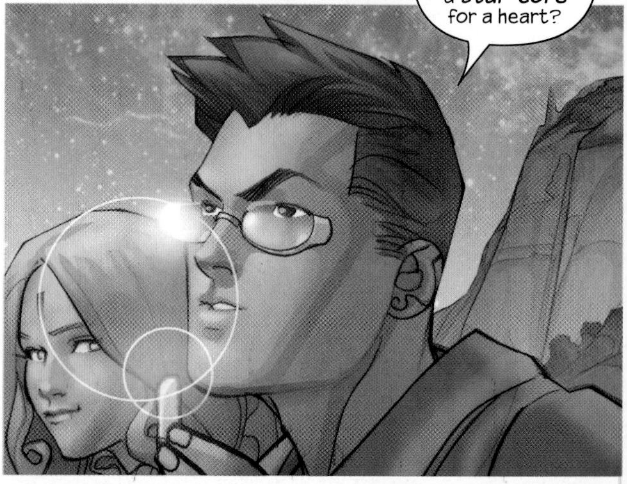

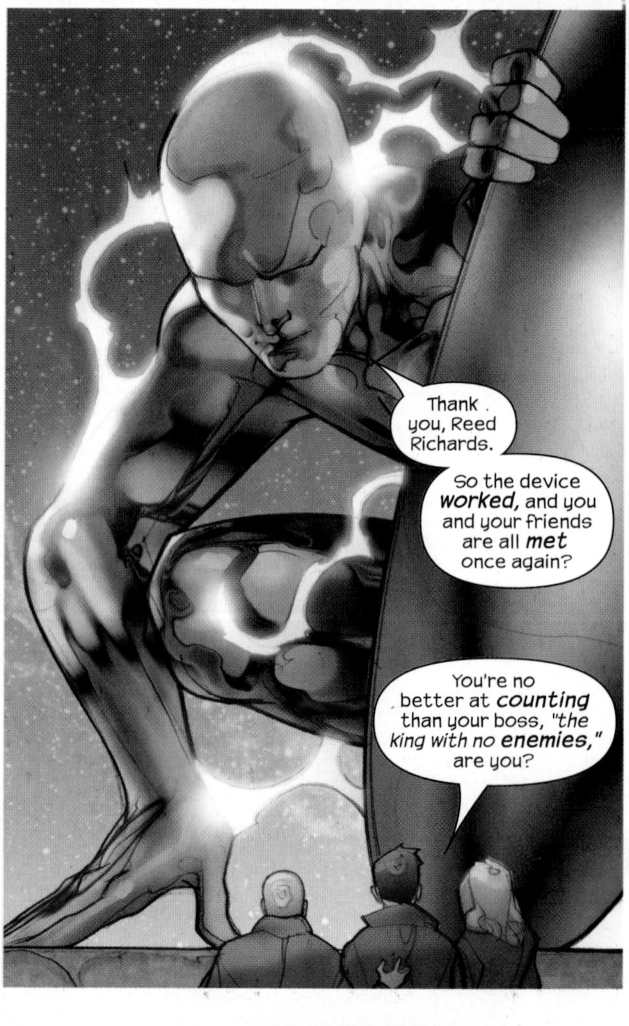
Thank you, Reed Richards.
So the device *worked,* and you and your friends are all *met* once again?
You're no better at *counting* than your boss, *"the king with no enemies,"* are you?

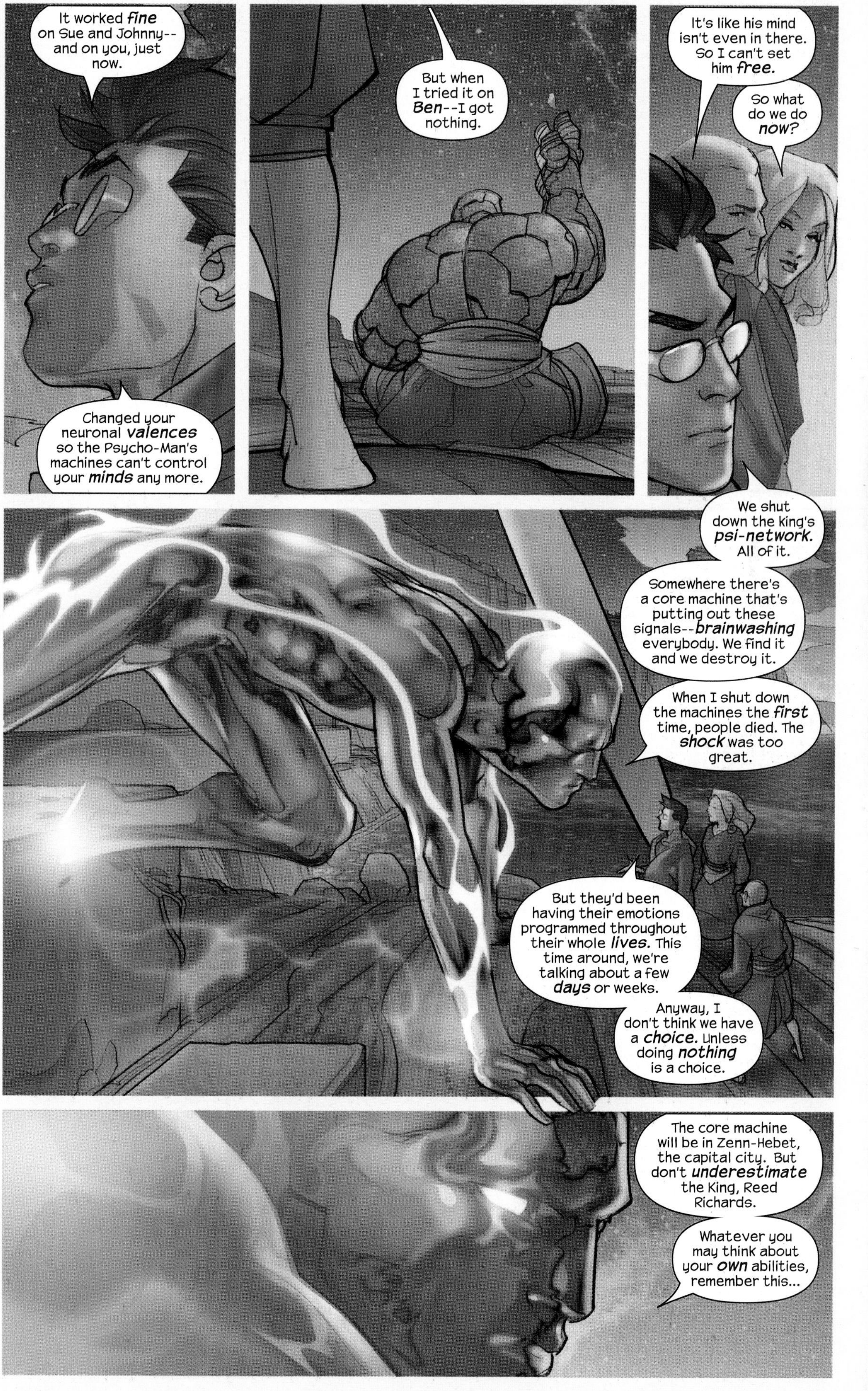
It worked fine on Sue and Johnny-- and on you, just now.
Changed your neuronal valences so the Psycho-Man's machines can't control your minds any more.
But when I tried it on Ben--I got nothing.
It's like his mind isn't even in there. So I can't set him free.
So what do we do now?
We shut down the king's psi-network. All of it.
Somewhere there's a core machine that's putting out these signals--brainwashing everybody. We find it and we destroy it.
When I shut down the machines the first time, people died. The shock was too great.
But they'd been having their emotions programmed throughout their whole lives. This time around, we're talking about a few days or weeks.
Anyway, I don't think we have a choice. Unless doing nothing is a choice.
The core machine will be in Zenn-Hebet, the capital city. But don't underestimate the King, Reed Richards.
Whatever you may think about your own abilities, remember this...

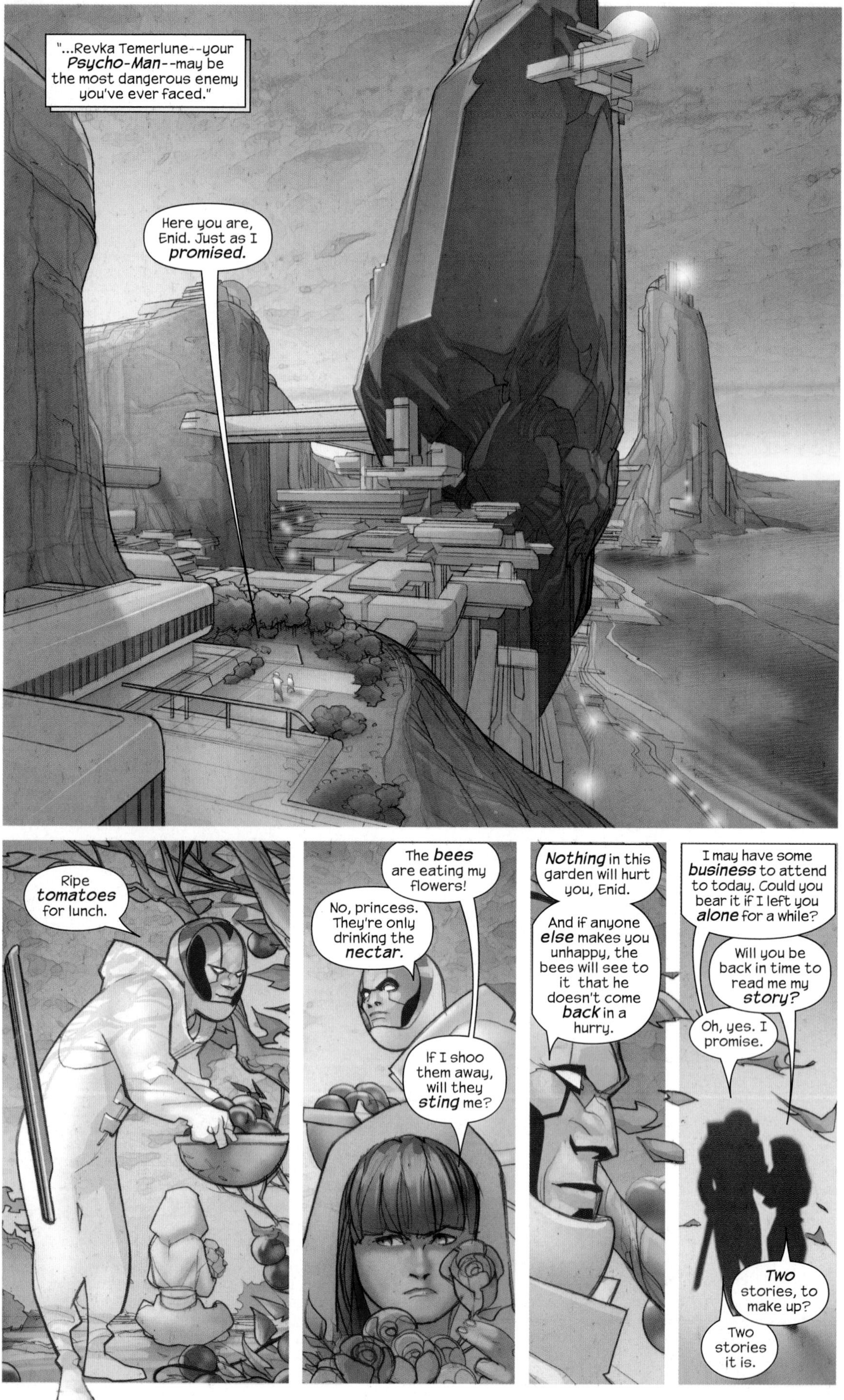
"...Revka Temerlune--your Psycho-Man--may be the most dangerous enemy you've ever faced."
Here you are, Enid. Just as I promised.
Ripe tomatoes for lunch.
The bees are eating my flowers!
No, princess. They're only drinking the nectar.
If I shoo them away, will they sting me?
Nothing in this garden will hurt you, Enid.
And if anyone else makes you unhappy, the bees will see to it that he doesn't come back in a hurry.
I may have some business to attend to today. Could you bear it if I left you alone for a while?
Will you be back in time to read me my story?
Oh, yes. I promise.
Two stories, to make up?
Two stories it is.

I thought capital cities were meant to have a *cosmopolitan* vibe.

Why is everyone *staring* at us?

My face is one that every *child* on Zenn-La knows, Johnny Storm. Even a *glimpse* of my silvery skin arouses excitement.

Your friend Ben is also somewhat out of the *ordinary*.

Fortunately, the *mind-web* keeps everyone happy and docile. This is the best-mannered mob I've ever seen.

I'm not reading any unusual *power* usage, though. We'll have to find the core machine some *other* way.

You think we should search *door-to-door*?

Or maybe just head on up the *hill* toward the big, black skyscraper?

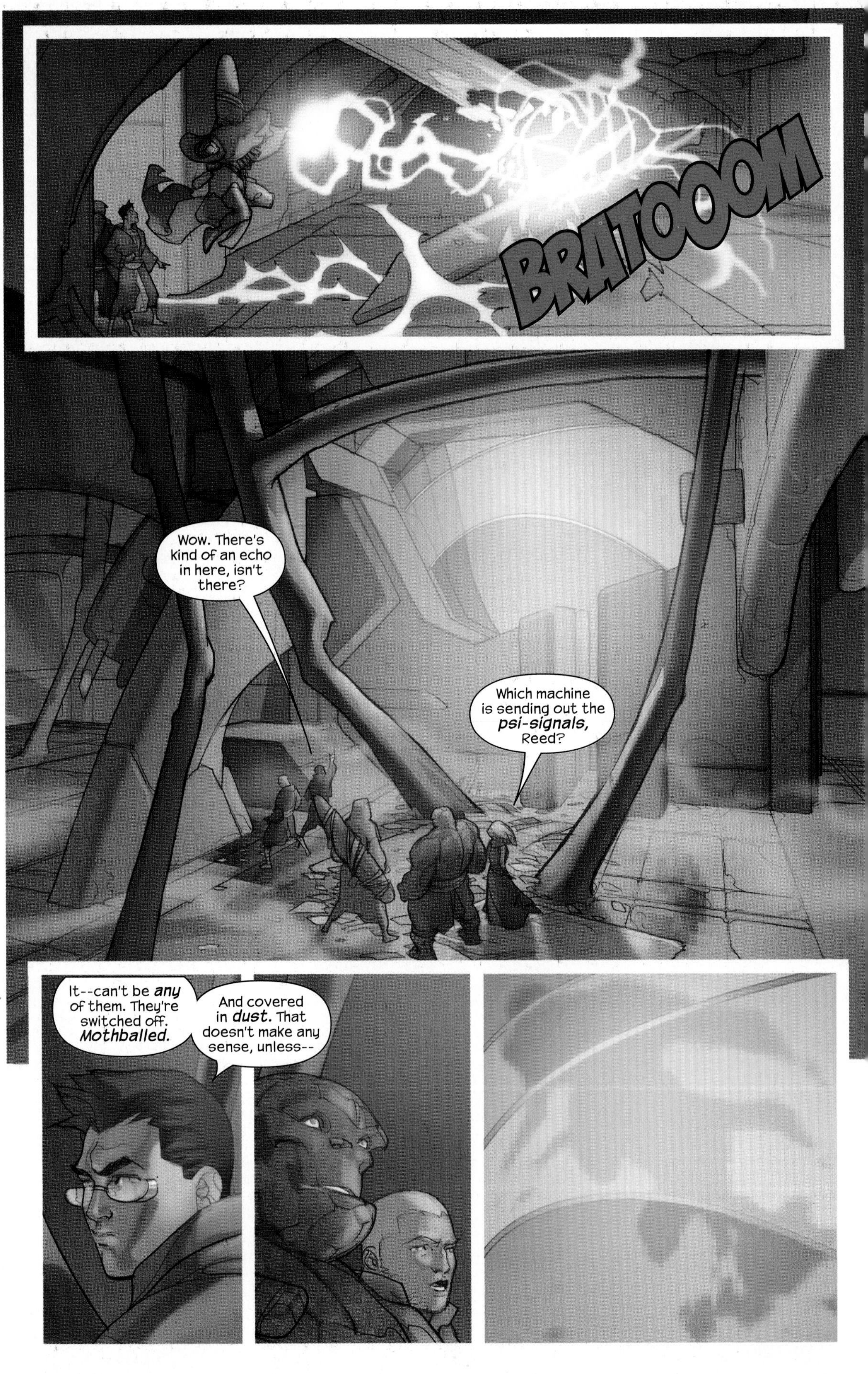
BRATOOOM
Wow. There's kind of an echo in here, isn't there?
Which machine is sending out the *psi-signals,* Reed?
It--can't be *any* of them. They're switched off. *Mothballed.*
And covered in *dust.* That doesn't make any sense, unless--

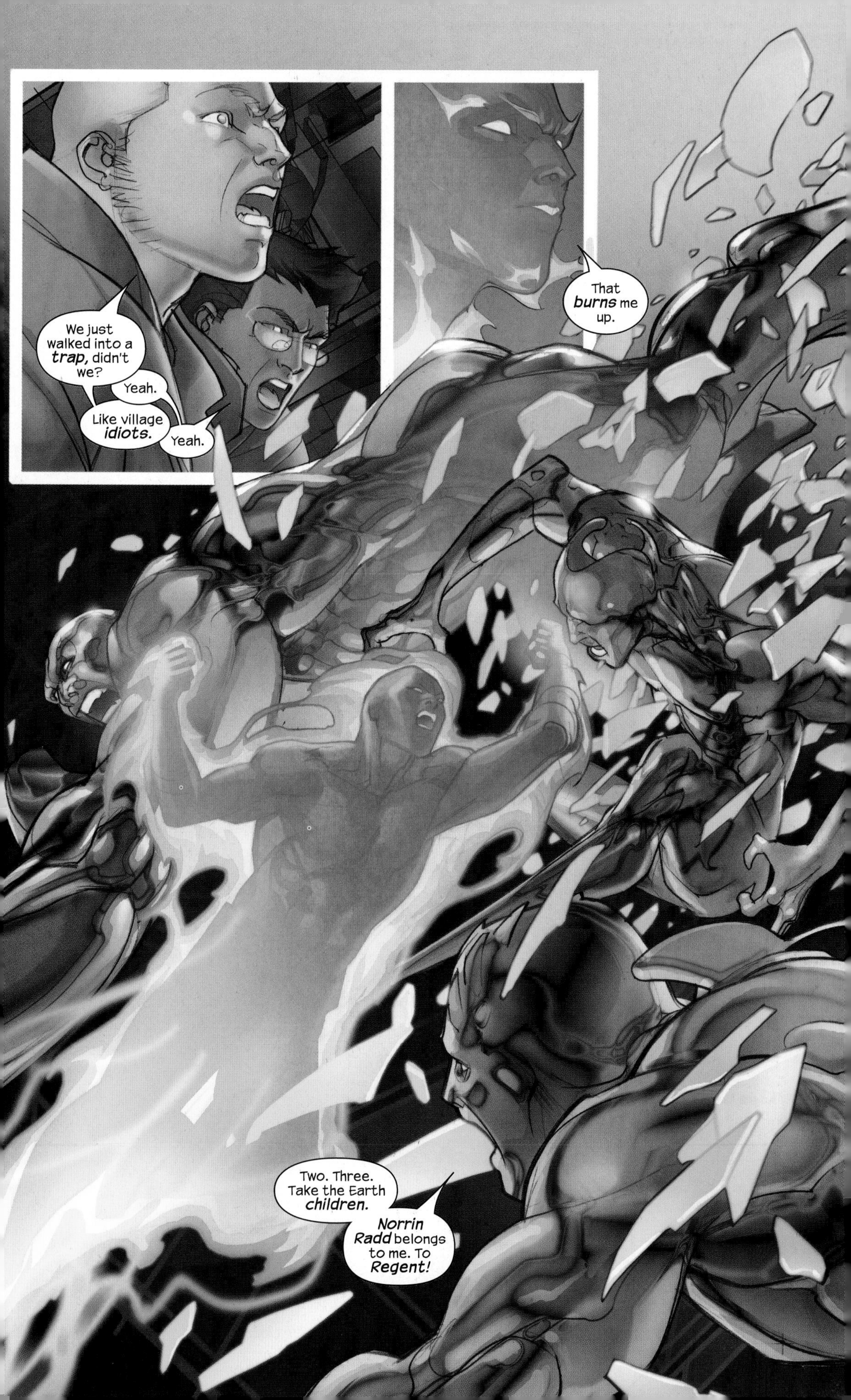
We just walked into a trap, didn't we?
Yeah.
Like village idiots.
Yeah.
That burns me up.
Two. Three. Take the Earth children.
Norrin Radd belongs to me. To Regent!

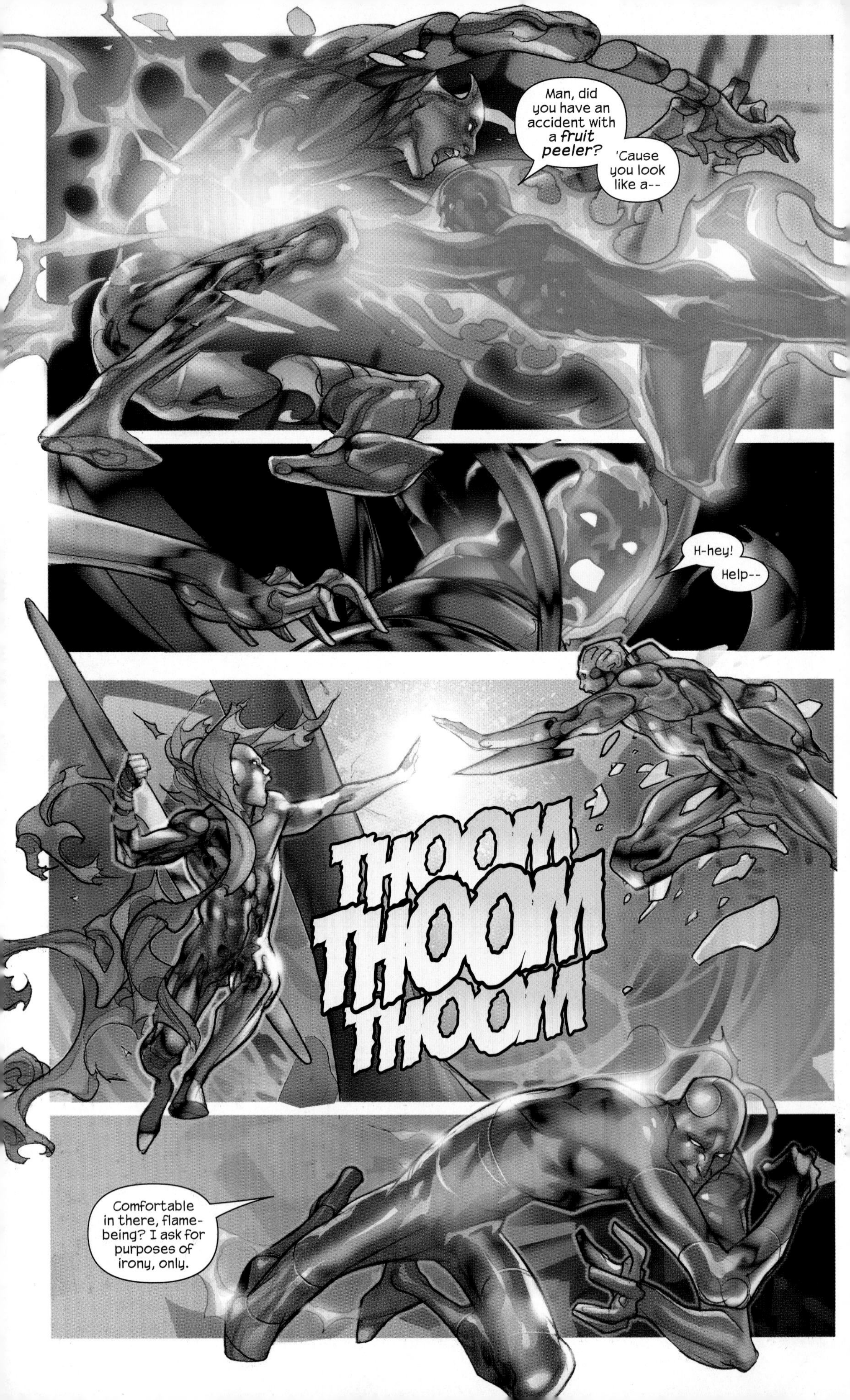

Man, did you have an accident with a *fruit peeler?*
'Cause you look like a--
H-hey!
Help--
THOOM THOOM THOOM
Comfortable in there, flame-being? I ask for purposes of irony, only.

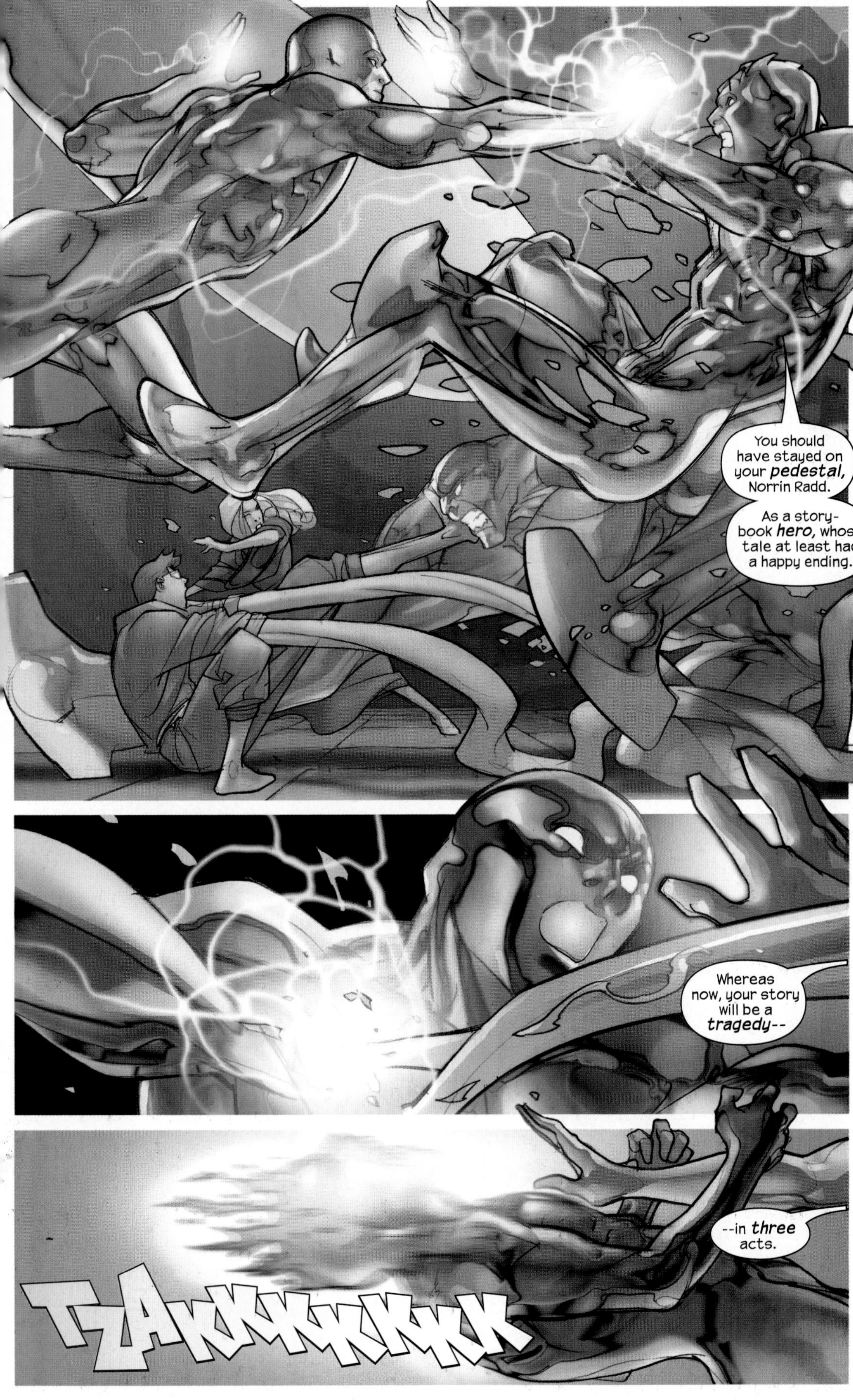
You should have stayed on your *pedestal,* Norrin Radd.
As a story-book *hero,* whose tale at least had a happy ending.
Whereas now, your story will be a *tragedy*--
--in *three* acts.
TZAKKKKKKKKK

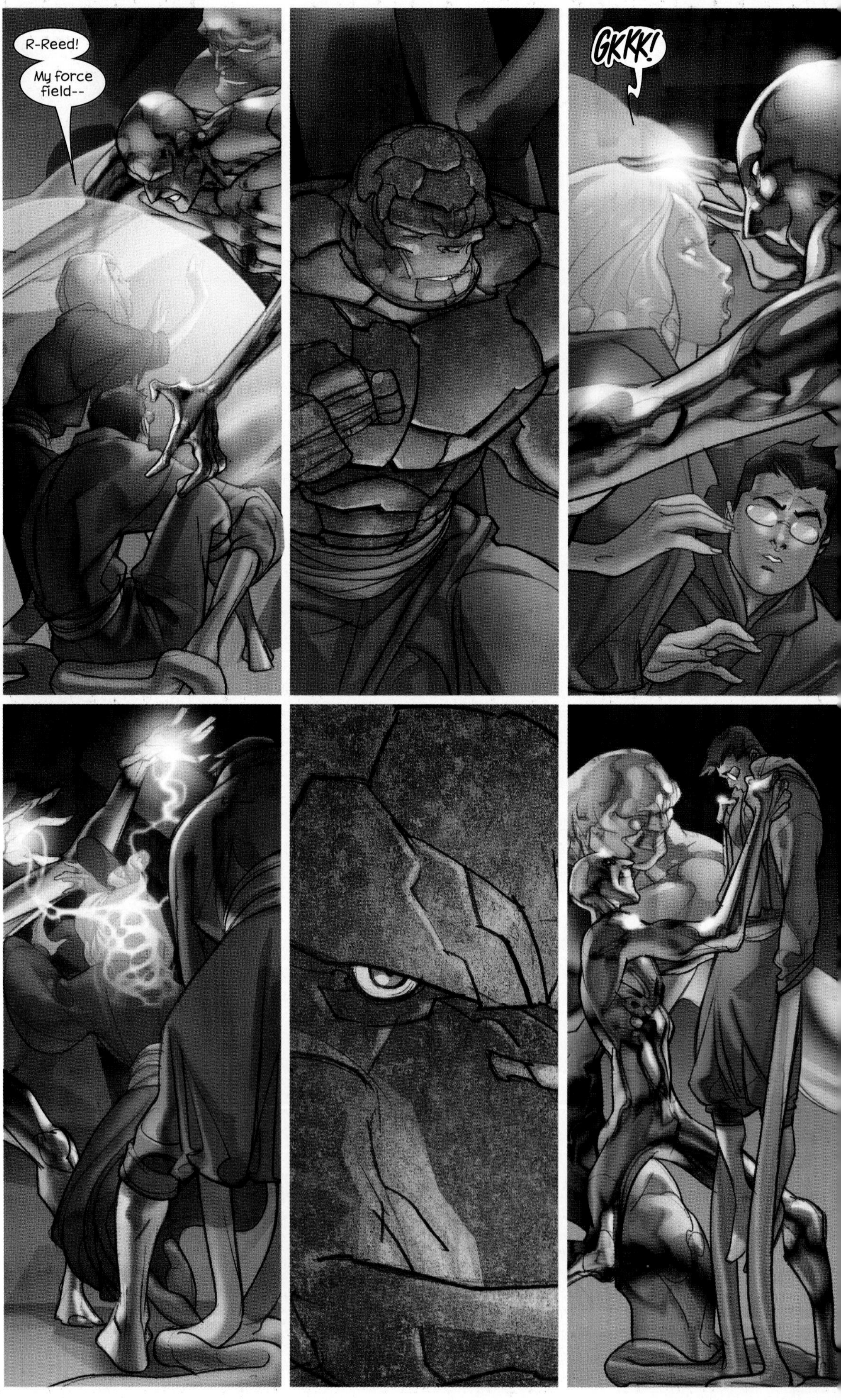
R-Reed!
My force field--
GKKK!

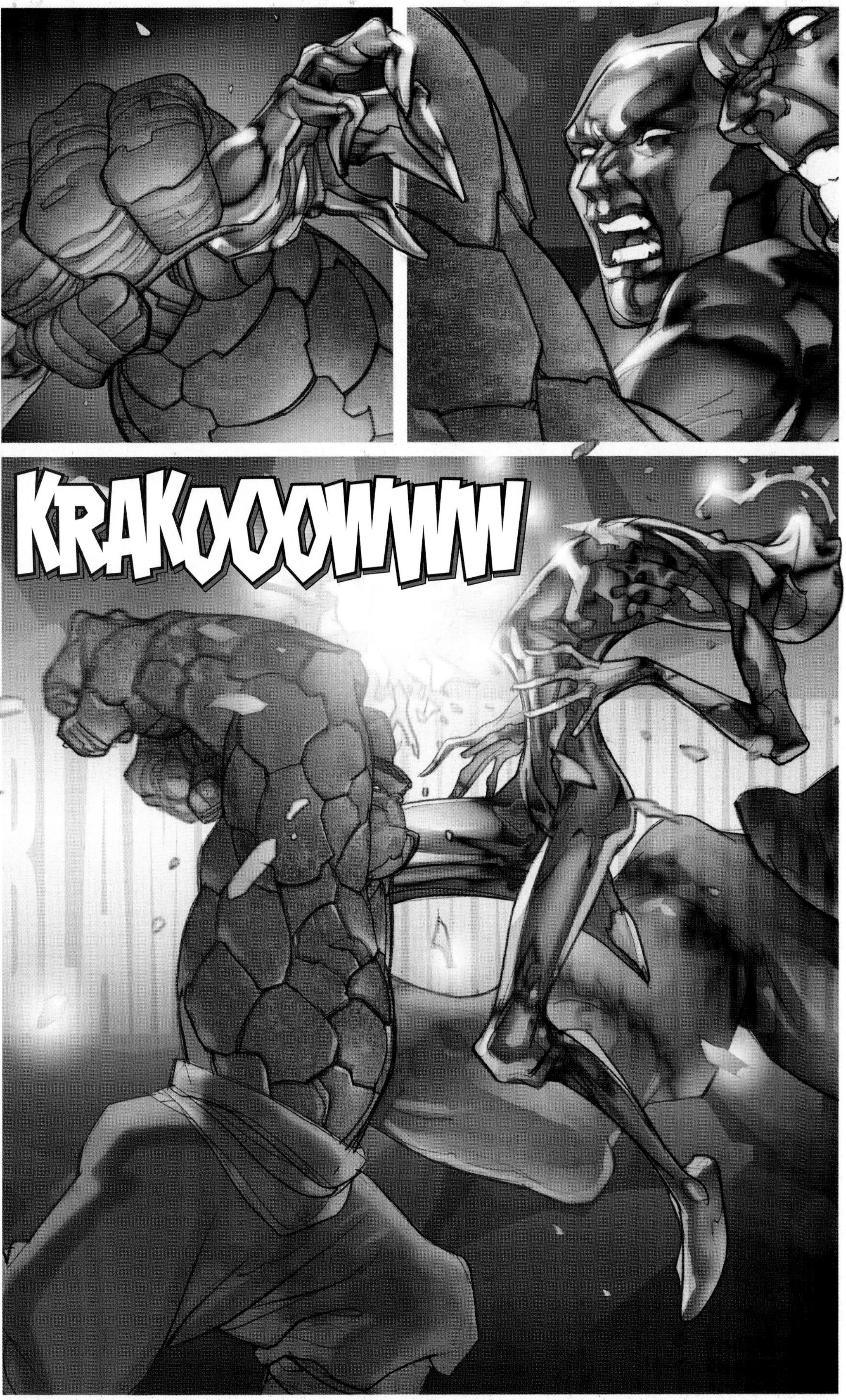
KRAKOOOWWW

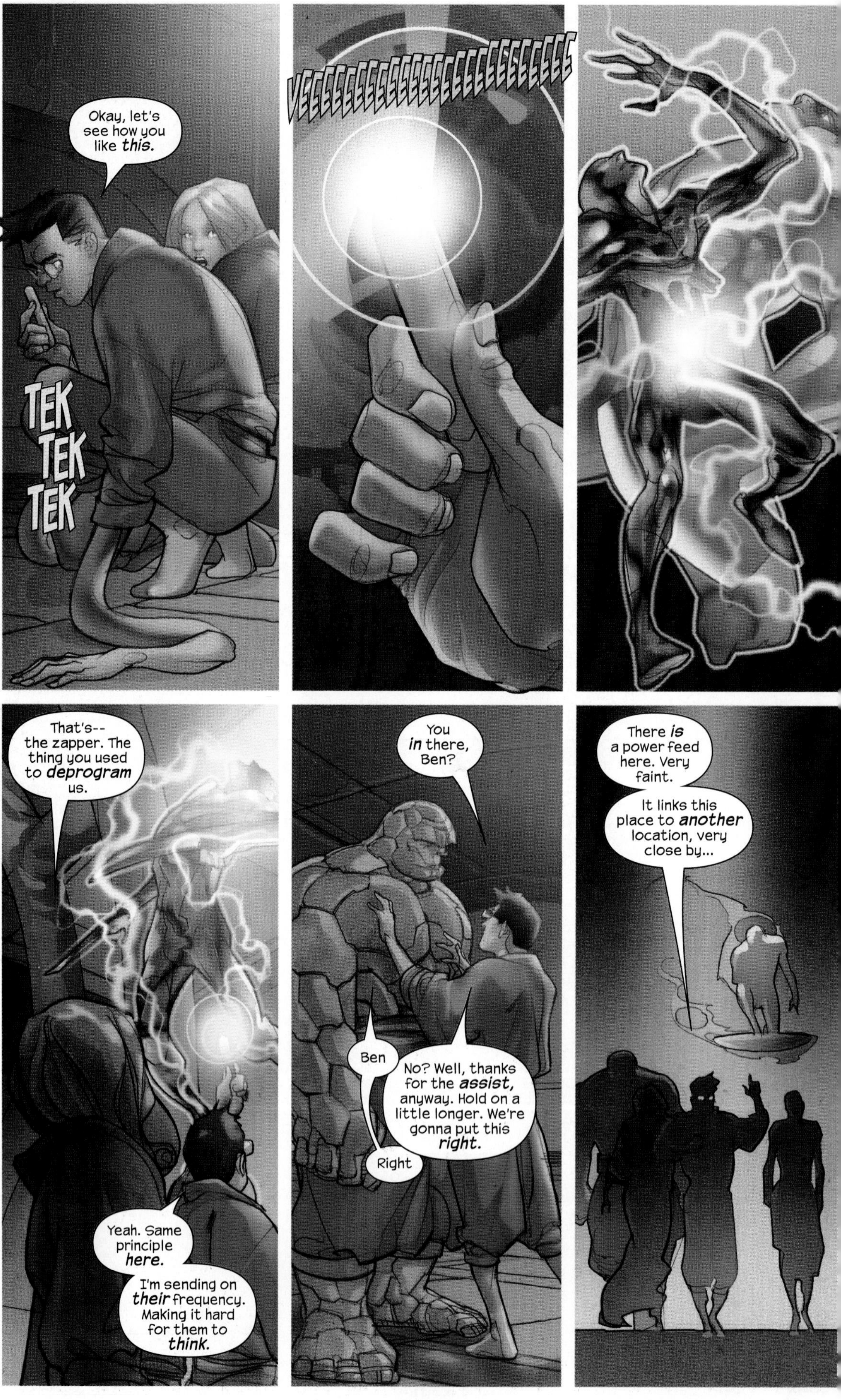
Okay, let's see how you like this.
TEK TEK TEK
VEEEEEEEEEEEEEEEEEEEEEEEEEEEE
That's-- the zapper. The thing you used to deprogram us.
Yeah. Same principle here.
I'm sending on their frequency. Making it hard for them to think.
You in there, Ben?
Ben
Right
No? Well, thanks for the assist, anyway. Hold on a little longer. We're gonna put this right.
There is a power feed here. Very faint.
It links this place to another location, very close by...

And then one seed in each hole you've dug. With a little water, and a tablet of the seed-food.

Will there be *flowers*?

Huge flowers, my poppet. Flowers that will bring butterflies and featherheads and pollen-sippers.

Majesty, the machines register an *anomaly*.

Then *summarize* it. Don't waste my time.

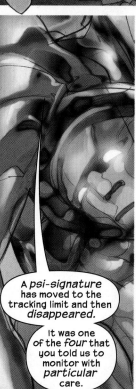

A *psi-signature* has moved to the tracking limit and then *disappeared*.

It was one of the *four* that you told us to monitor with *particular* care.

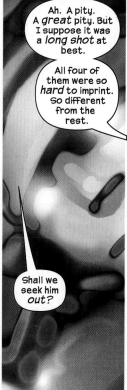

Ah. A *pity*. A *great* pity. But I suppose it was a *long shot* at best.

All four of them were so *hard* to imprint. So different from the rest.

Shall we seek him *out?*

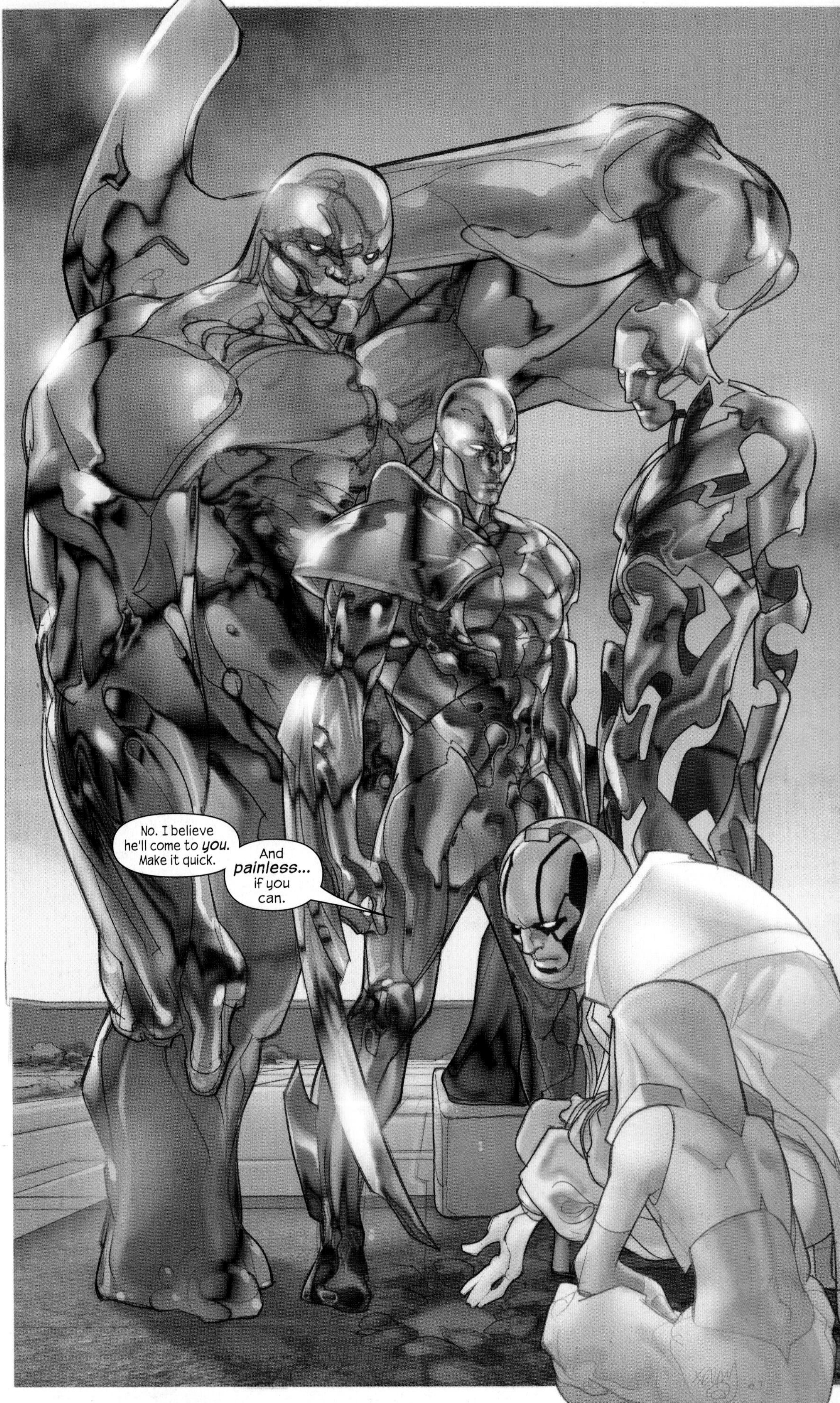
No. I believe he'll come to *you*. Make it quick.
And *painless...* if you can.

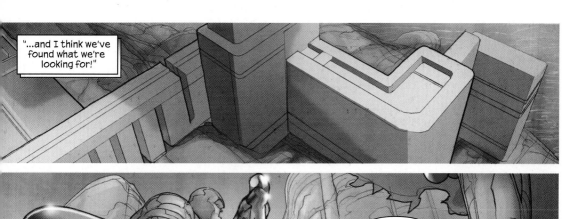

"...and I think we've found what we're looking for!"

Enid, go and tidy your *room.*

No. Don't *make* me.

I want to stay with *you.*

Did you honestly think you could *do* this?

Kidnap six billion people? *Destroy* Ben's mind? Steal my *sister?*

I think this is a battle you can't *win,* boy. Best not to start it.

He's the king! He can do whatever he wants!

See?

TCHOOOOM

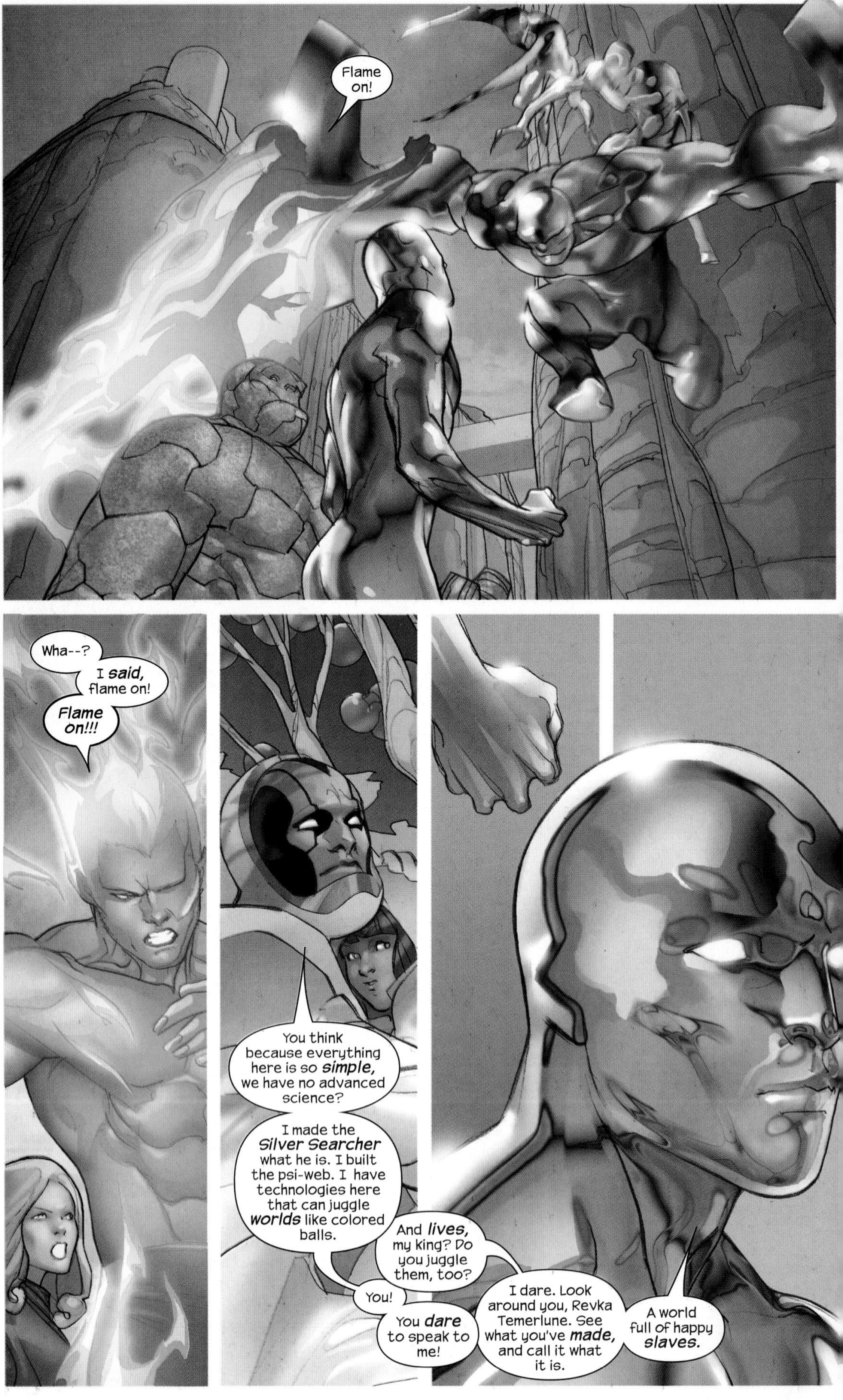
Flame on!
Wha--?
I said, flame on!
Flame on!!!
You think because everything here is so simple, we have no advanced science?
I made the Silver Searcher what he is. I built the psi-web. I have technologies here that can juggle worlds like colored balls.
And lives, my king? Do you juggle them, too?
You!
You dare to speak to me!
I dare. Look around you, Revka Temerlune. See what you've made, and call it what it is.
A world full of happy slaves.

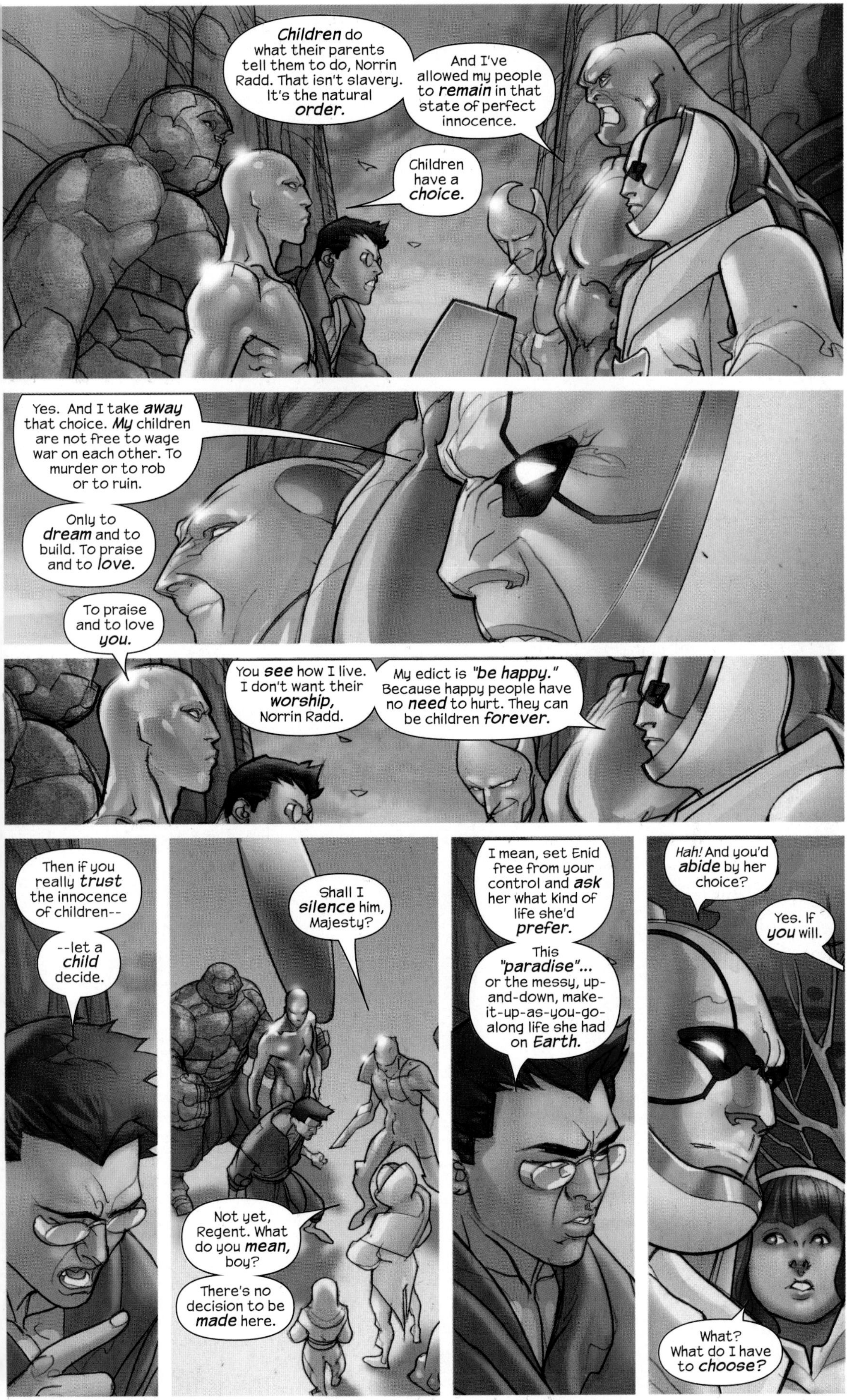
Children do what their parents tell them to do, Norrin Radd. That isn't slavery. It's the natural order.
And I've allowed my people to remain in that state of perfect innocence.
Children have a choice.
Yes. And I take away that choice. My children are not free to wage war on each other. To murder or to rob or to ruin.
Only to dream and to build. To praise and to love.
To praise and to love you.
You see how I live. I don't want their worship, Norrin Radd.
My edict is "be happy." Because happy people have no need to hurt. They can be children forever.
Then if you really trust the innocence of children--
--let a child decide.
Shall I silence him, Majesty?
Not yet, Regent. What do you mean, boy?
There's no decision to be made here.
I mean, set Enid free from your control and ask her what kind of life she'd prefer.
This "paradise"... or the messy, up-and-down, make-it-up-as-you-go-along life she had on Earth.
Hah! And you'd abide by her choice?
Yes. If you will.
What? What do I have to choose?

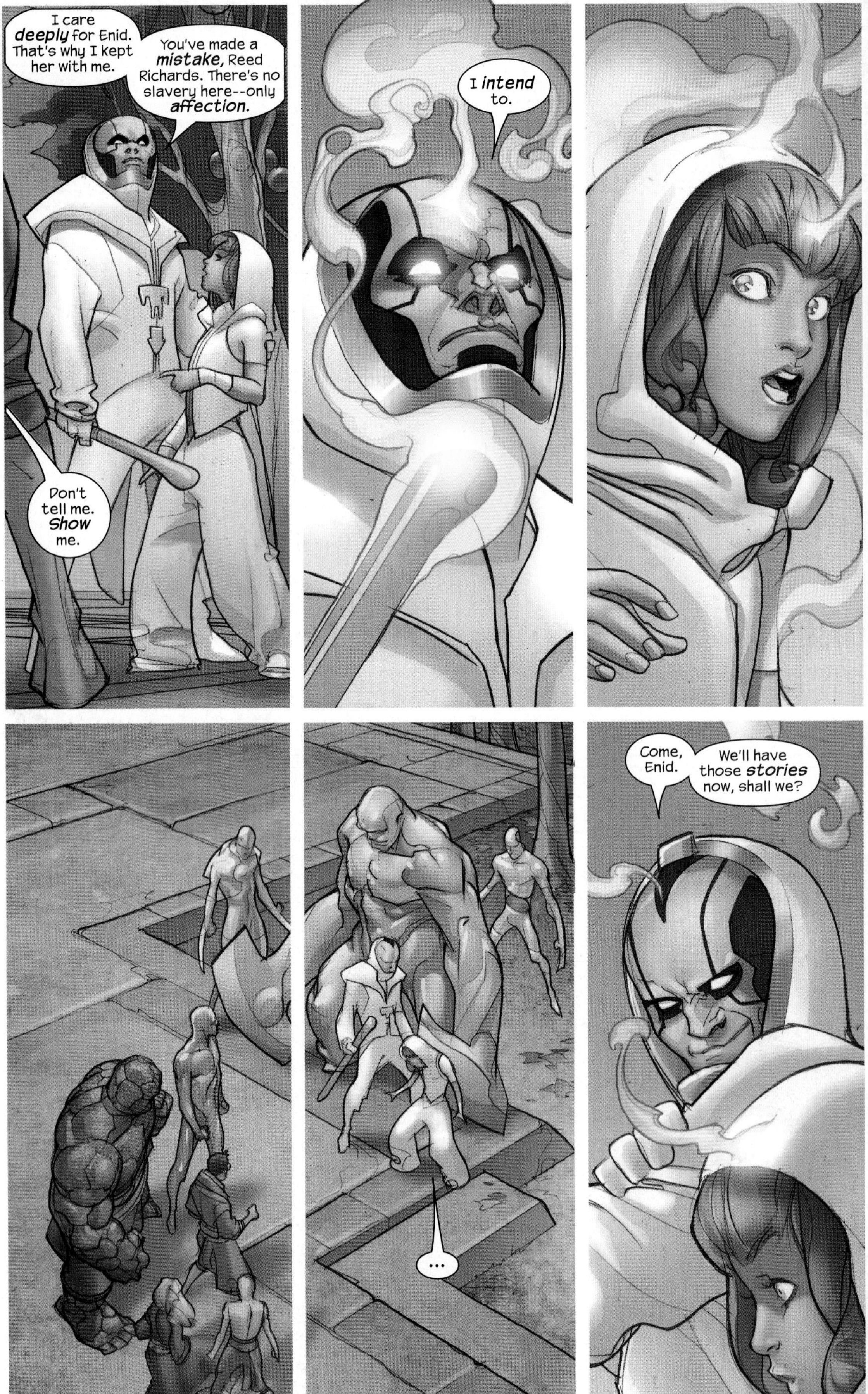
I care *deeply* for Enid. That's why I kept her with me.
You've made a *mistake,* Reed Richards. There's no slavery here--only *affection.*
Don't tell me. *Show* me.
I *intend* to.
...
Come, Enid.
We'll have those *stories* now, shall we?

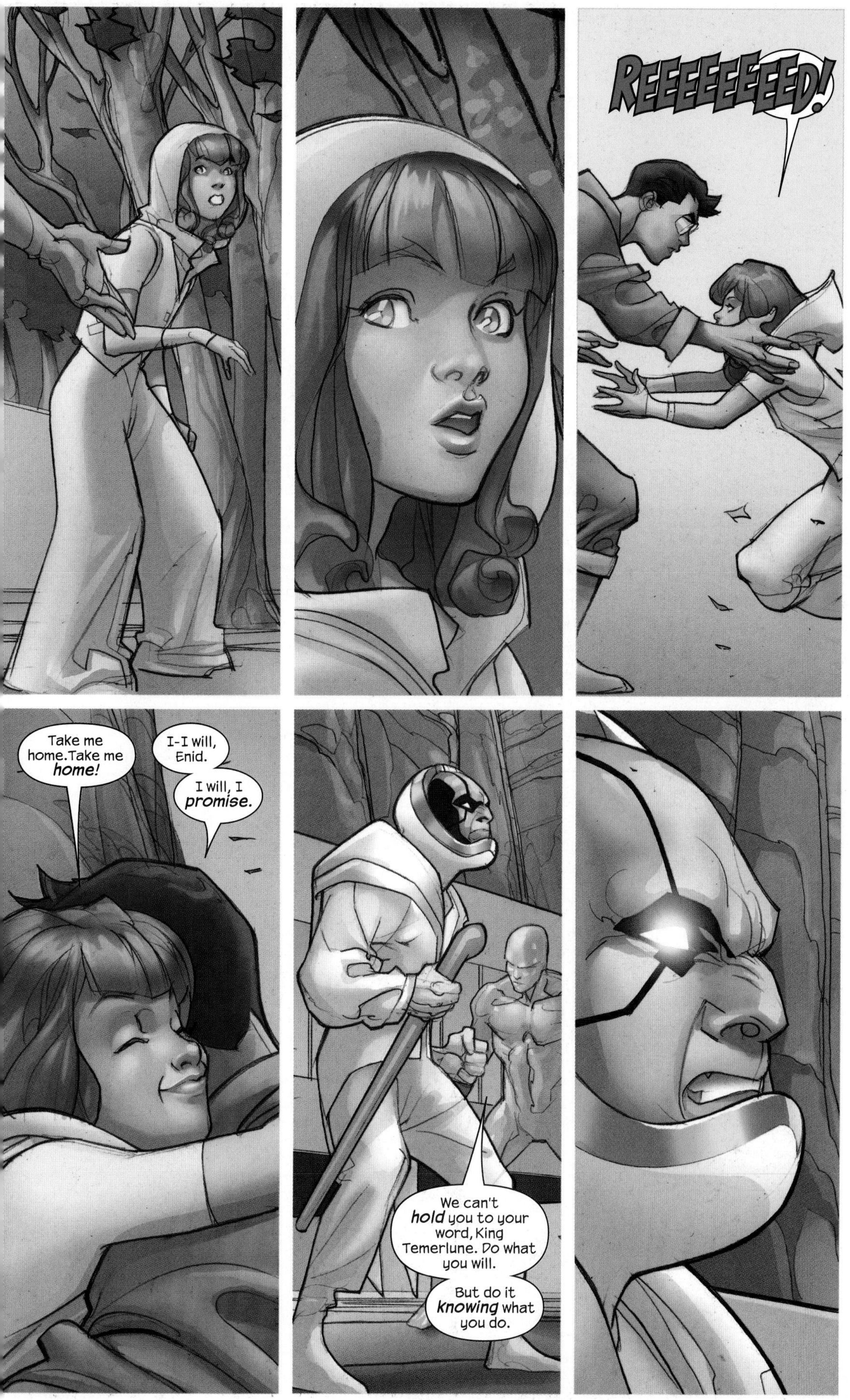
REEEEEEEED!
Take me home. Take me home!
I-I will, Enid.
I will, I promise.
We can't hold you to your word, King Temerlune. Do what you will.
But do it knowing what you do.

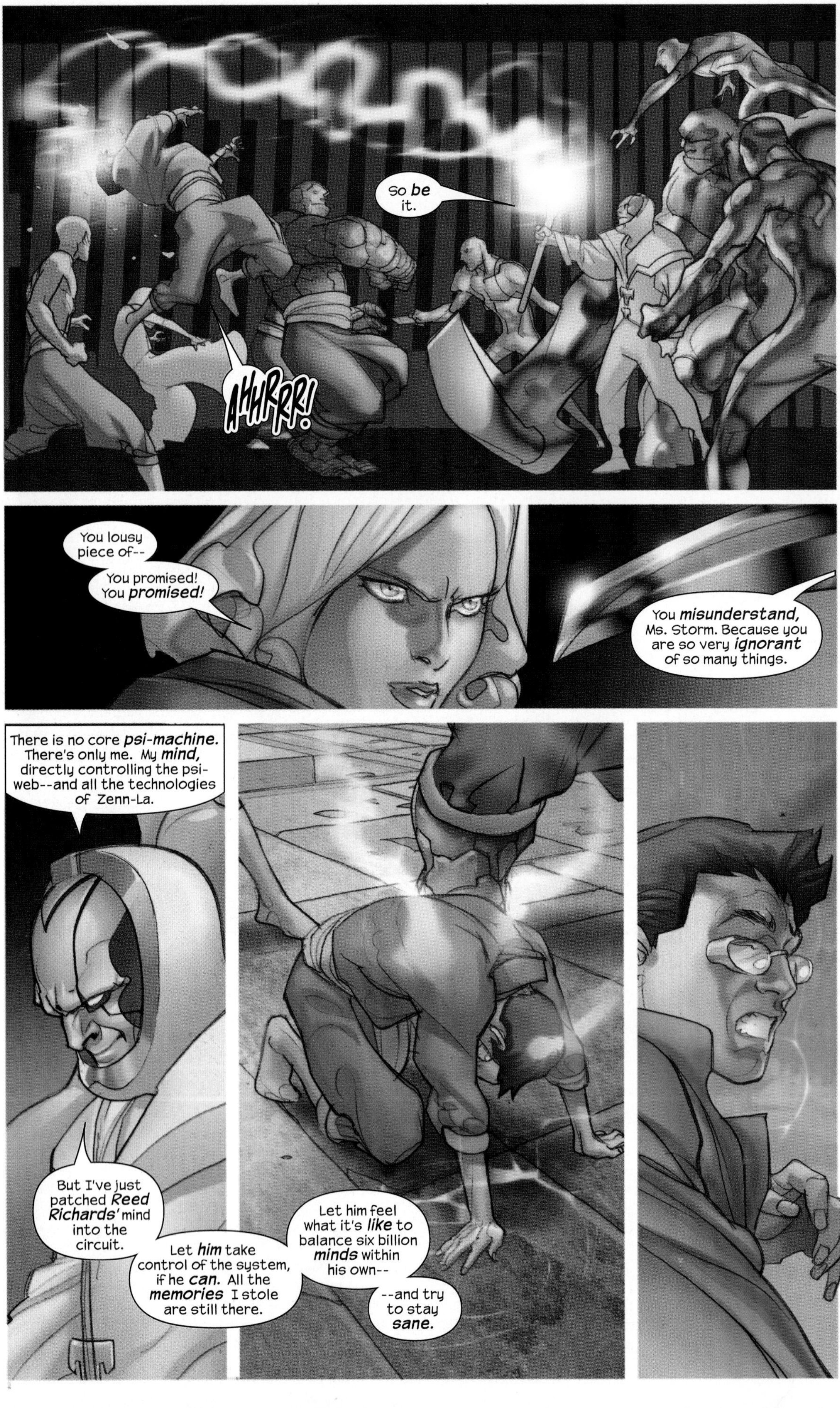
So be it.
AHHRRR!
You lousy piece of--
You promised! You promised!
You misunderstand, Ms. Storm. Because you are so very ignorant of so many things.
There is no core psi-machine. There's only me. My mind, directly controlling the psi-web--and all the technologies of Zenn-La.
But I've just patched Reed Richards' mind into the circuit.
Let him take control of the system, if he can. All the memories I stole are still there.
Let him feel what it's like to balance six billion minds within his own--
--and try to stay sane.

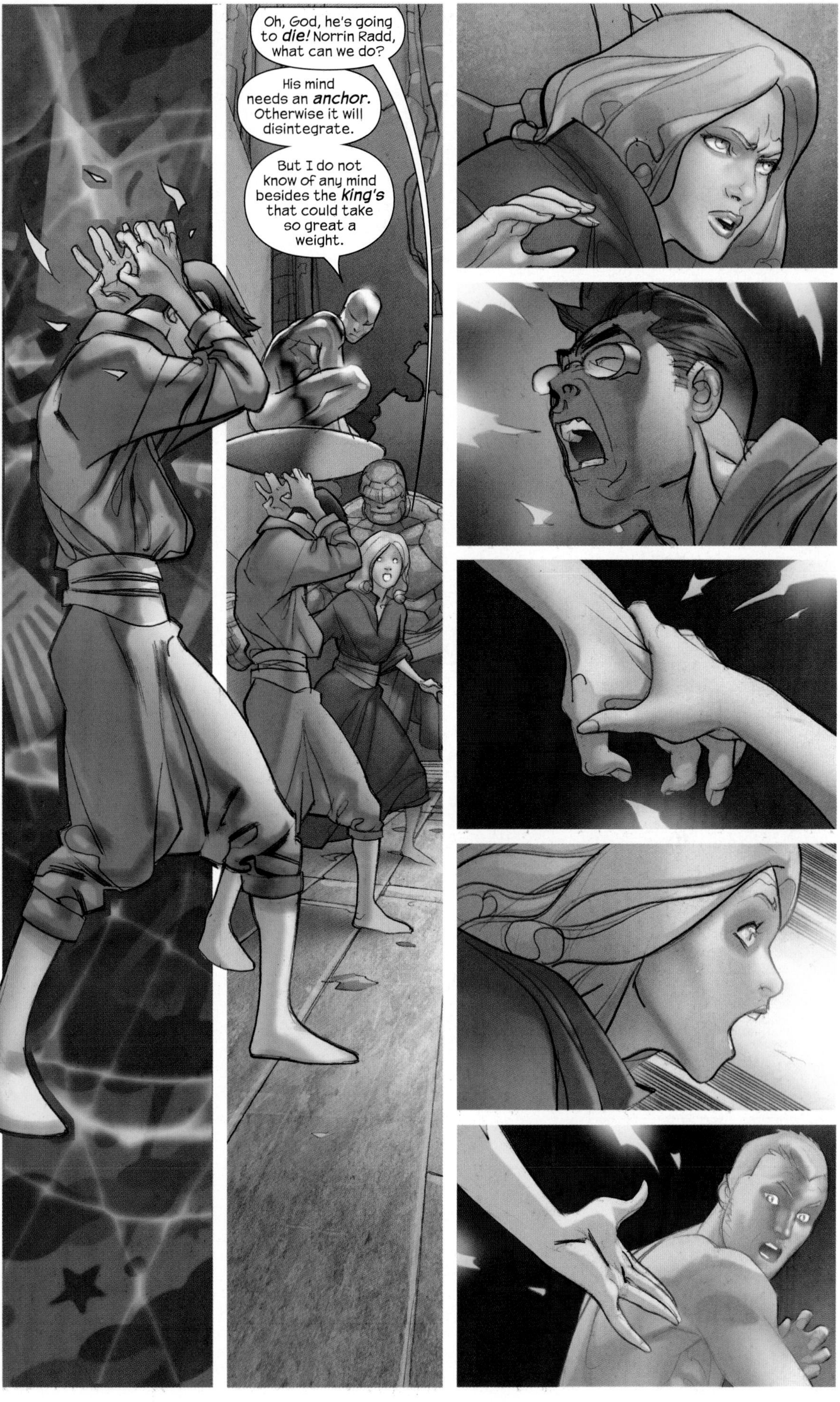
Oh, God, he's going to *die!* Norrin Radd, what can we do?
His mind needs an *anchor.* Otherwise it will disintegrate.
But I do not know of any mind besides the *king's* that could take so great a weight.

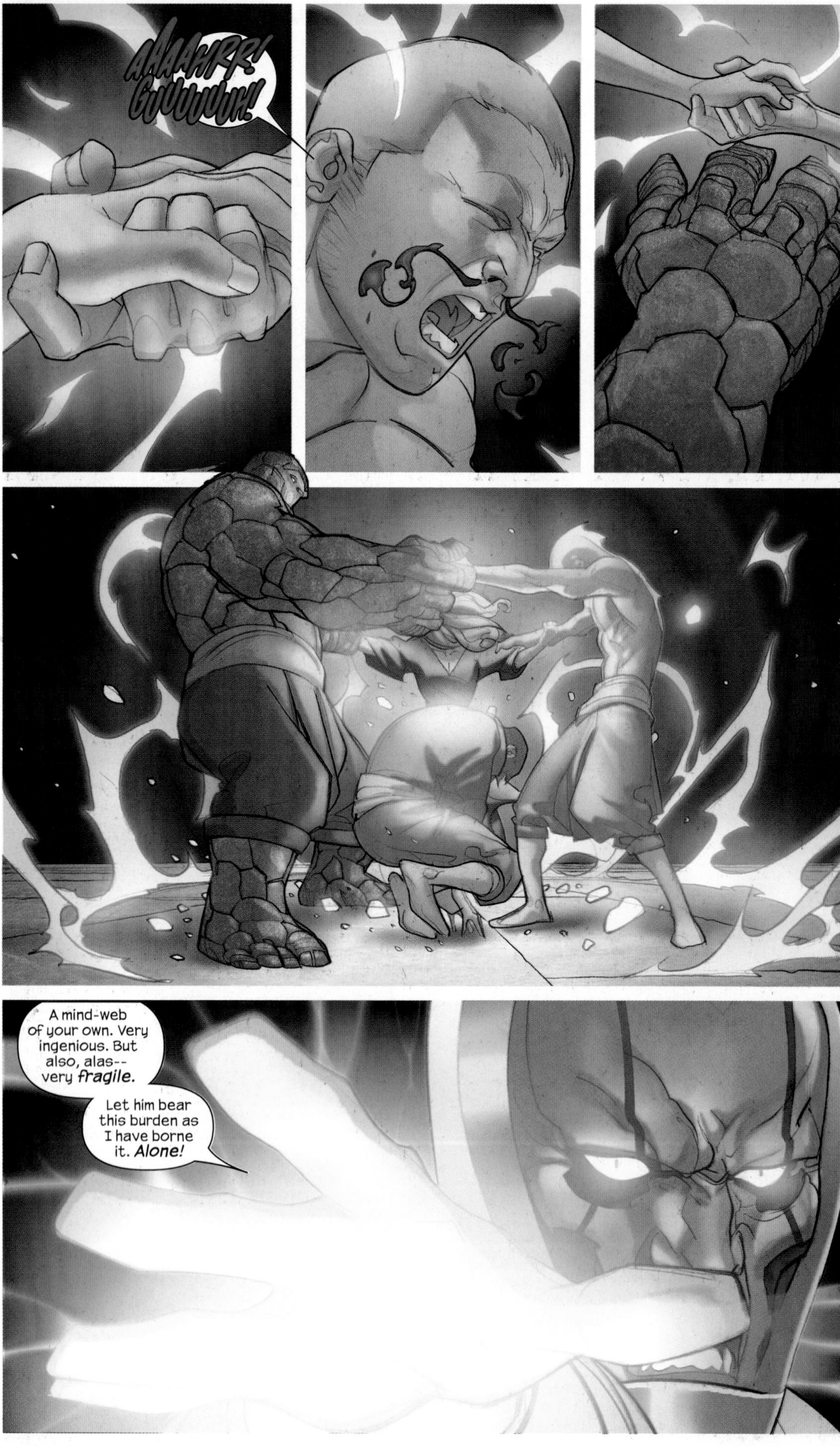
AAAAHRR! GUUUUUUH!
A mind-web of your own. Very ingenious. But also, alas-- very fragile.
Let him bear this burden as I have borne it. Alone!

Actually--

--we prefer to stick together.

NOOOOH!

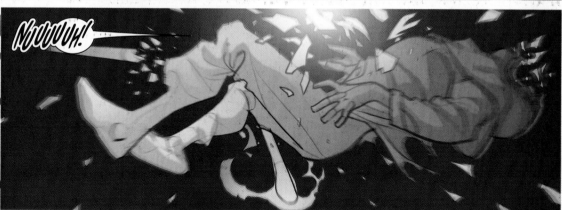

You struck the *king*, and you will die!

Stand down, Regent. If you try to use the *power cosmic* on me, there'll be nothing left of your *arm*.

I think I'm getting the *hang* of this now. *All* the technologies, he said.

Let's give it a *try*.

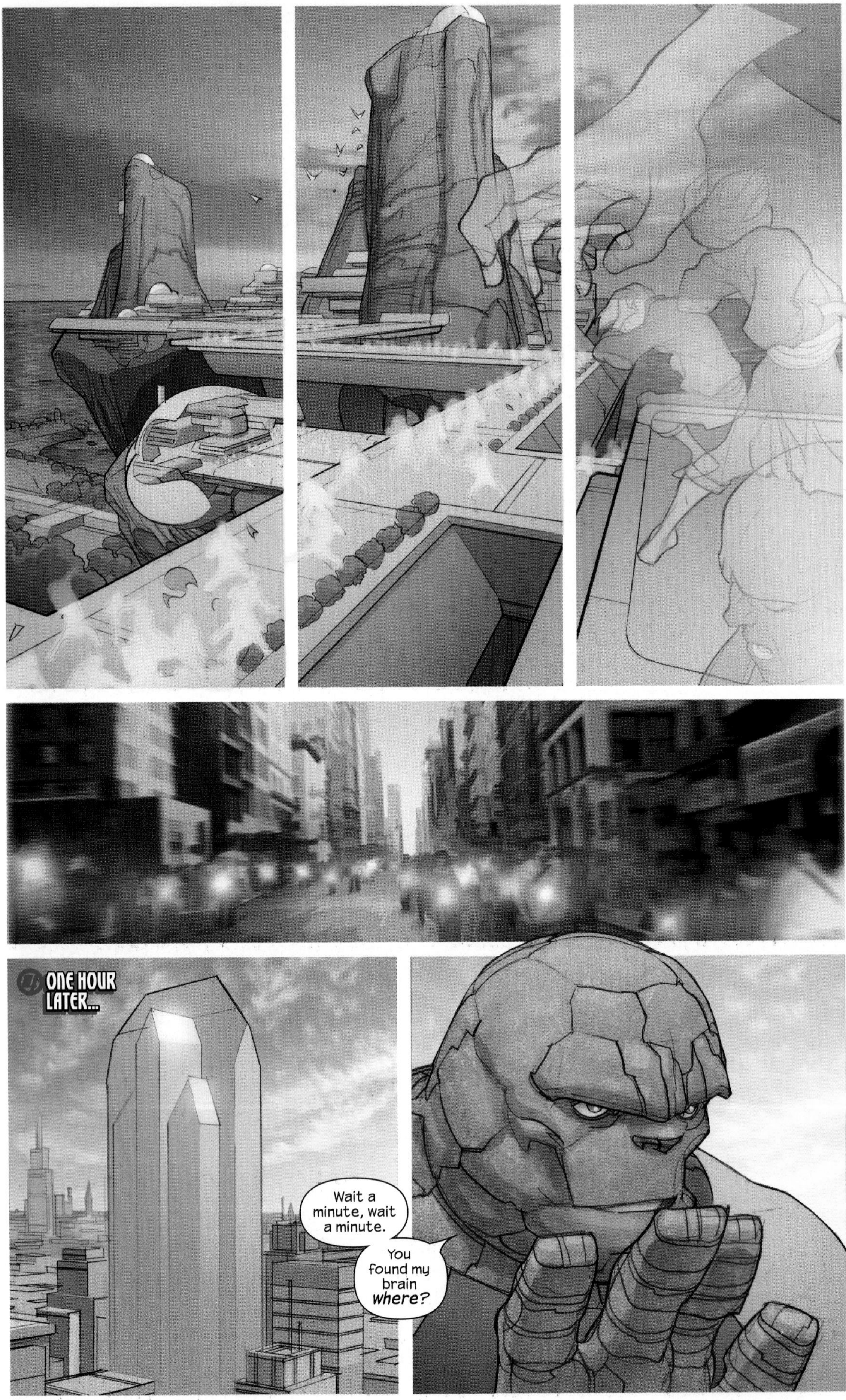
ONE HOUR LATER...
Wait a minute, wait a minute.
You found my brain where?

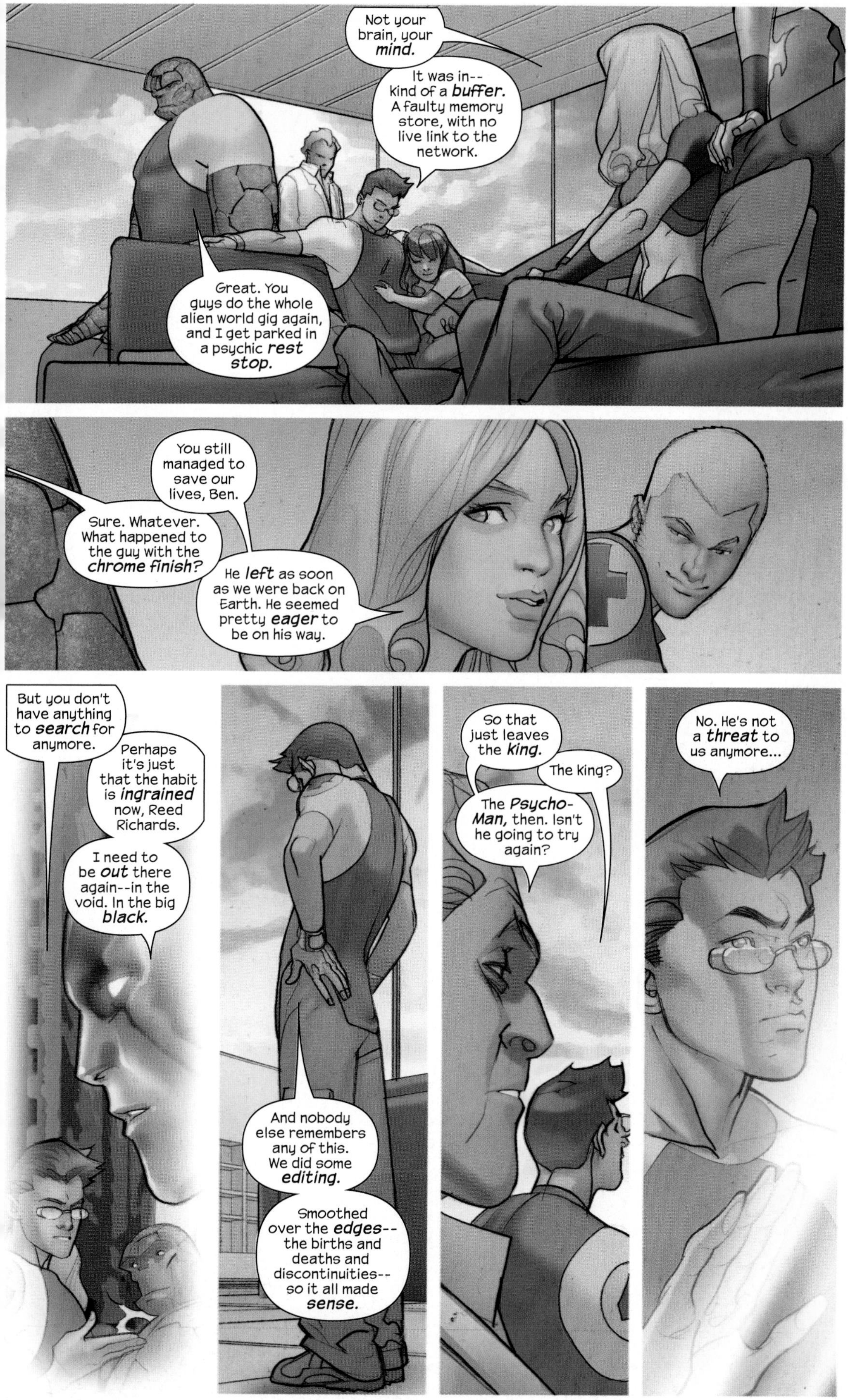
Not your brain, your mind.
It was in-- kind of a buffer. A faulty memory store, with no live link to the network.
Great. You guys do the whole alien world gig again, and I get parked in a psychic rest stop.
You still managed to save our lives, Ben.
Sure. Whatever. What happened to the guy with the chrome finish?
He left as soon as we were back on Earth. He seemed pretty eager to be on his way.
But you don't have anything to search for anymore.
Perhaps it's just that the habit is ingrained now, Reed Richards.
I need to be out there again--in the void. In the big black.
And nobody else remembers any of this. We did some editing.
Smoothed over the edges-- the births and deaths and discontinuities-- so it all made sense.
So that just leaves the king.
The king?
The Psycho-Man, then. Isn't he going to try again?
No. He's not a threat to us anymore...

"...In fact..."

"...he's very *happy* with the way things came out."

There! *Look!* I dug a big *hole.* In the ground.

For the *seeds.* Have we *got* any seeds?

If we plant seeds, there'll be *flowers.* Or tomatoes. Or maybe *mice.*

I will *find* some seeds, majesty.

And you're a *gold* man. A bright, shiny, gold man.

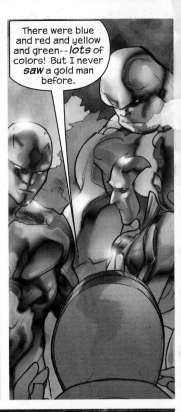

There were blue and red and yellow and green--*lots* of colors! But I never *saw* a gold man before.

"I think there might have been a *silver* one once..."

"...but I can't remember his *name.*"

NEXT: GHOSTS